Crosswords For Seniors

FOR DUMMIES®

by Timothy E. Parker,
with Joan Friedman

WILEY

Wiley Publishing, Inc.

Crosswords For Seniors For Dummies®

Published by
Wiley Publishing, Inc.
111 River St.
Hoboken, NJ 07030-5774
www.wiley.com

WILEY

Publisher's Acknowledgments

We're proud of this book; please send us your comments through our Dummies online registration form located at `http://dummies.custhelp.com`. For other comments, please contact our Customer Care Department within the U.S. at 877-762-2974, outside the U.S. at 317-572-3993, or fax 317-572-4002.

Some of the people who helped bring this book to market include the following:

Acquisitions, Editorial, and Media Development

Project Editor: Natalie Faye Harris

Acquisitions Editor: Lindsay Lefevere

Copy Editor: Christine Pingleton

Assistant Editor: Erin Calligan Mooney

Editorial Program Coordinator: Joe Niesen

Technical Editor: David W. Fisher (`http://puzzles.about.com/`)

Editorial Manager: Christine Meloy Beck

Editorial Assistants: Jennette ElNaggar, David Lutton

Cartoons: Rich Tennant (`www.the5thwave.com`)

Composition Services

Project Coordinator: Katie Crocker

Layout and Graphics: Brooke Graczyk, Erin Zeltner

Proofreader: Betty Kish

Publishing and Editorial for Consumer Dummies

    Diane Graves Steele, Vice President and Publisher, Consumer Dummies

    Kristin Ferguson-Wagstaffe, Product Development Director, Consumer Dummies

    Ensley Eikenburg, Associate Publisher, Travel

    Kelly Regan, Editorial Director, Travel

Publishing for Technology Dummies

    Andy Cummings, Vice President and Publisher, Dummies Technology/General User

Composition Services

    Debbie Stailey, Director of Composition Services

Table of Contents

Introduction

● ●

For my money, the best hobbies are inexpensive, portable, and beneficial to your health. And one of the best hobbies I can think of is solving crossword puzzles. (As a professional puzzle editor, I admit that I'm ever-so-slightly biased.)

You may be thinking that "inexpensive" and "portable" make sense, but what good can crosswords do for your health? Plenty! I'm not asking you to work crosswords during a yoga class or while you're on a treadmill (although if you can manage it, more power to you!). Crosswords have health benefits even if you're sitting on the couch. Your glutes and abs may not notice whether you've managed to fill in every blank on a crossword puzzle grid, but your synapses will. (Remember synapses? They're the junctions between the neurons in your brain. I talk about them in Chapter 2.)

The benefits of working puzzles occur within your brain. Essentially, working crosswords can do for your mental health what water aerobics do for your cardiovascular health. Whether you realized it or not, you picked up a book that can help your gray matter become fit and trim.

Oh, and by the way, crosswords are a lot of fun too. After all, what good is an inexpensive, portable, healthy hobby if you don't enjoy doing it?

About This Book

The heart of this book is crossword puzzles: page after page of entertaining, challenging crossword puzzles. If you're a puzzling pro and can't wait to dive in, you have my blessing to pick up your pencil (or pen) and go.

But if you've never worked a crossword puzzle before, take heart: I devote the first chapter of this book to explaining the basics of how crosswords are constructed and how they can be solved. I list the various types of clues you'll encounter, resources you may want to have on hand, and how to make solving crosswords a group activity if that's your thing.

If you're even the least bit curious about the health benefits of doing crosswords and other puzzles, spend a little quality time with Chapter 2. In its pages, I explore how you can work on improving your brain's health by getting lots of fun, stimulating mental exercise.

Brain health is a hot topic for a couple key reasons:

- **A growing senior population:** It's no surprise that we have a large — and expanding — senior population in the United States. As of this writing, more than 37 million Americans are 65 or older. The U.S. Census Bureau projects that by the year 2050, that number will grow to more than 86 million!

- **The prevalence of Alzheimer's:** We also have many cases of Alzheimer's disease in our midst. The Alzheimer's Association estimates that more than 5 million Americans are living with the disease now and that 10 million Baby Boomers will develop Alzheimer's during their lifetime.

If you're north of 60, chances are you know someone — or several someones — struggling with the harsh realities of mental deficiency. And chances are you're willing to work hard to avoid the same fate. A growing body of research indicates that there are concrete (and often very simple) steps you can take to give your brain the proper fuel for long-term fitness. Chapter 2 offers lots of ideas for how to start a mental fitness routine.

Conventions Used in This Book

I include a handful of Web site addresses in this book so you can explore additional resources if you'd like. The Web addresses appear in `monofont`, which makes them easier to locate if you want to go back and find them after you're done reading.

Keep in mind that when this book was printed, some Web addresses may have needed to break across two lines of text. If that happened, rest assured that we haven't put in any extra characters (such as hyphens) to indicate the break. So, when using one of these Web addresses, just type in exactly what you see in this book, pretending as though the line break doesn't exist.

Foolish Assumptions

I try not to make any assumptions about how much experience you have with working the types of puzzles that appear in this book. That's why Chapter 1 helps you get familiar with crosswords and how to solve them. That's also why I include puzzles of varying levels of difficulty in this book. I've grouped puzzles together into four categories: Easy, Tricky, Tough, and Treacherous. So whether you're a crossword novice or expert, you'll find puzzles to give you the challenge you need.

My only assumption is that you want to have fun and stimulate your brain at the same time. Oh, and that you bring two critical tools with you: pencils and patience!

How This Book Is Organized

The bulk of this book is devoted to what you came looking for: crossword puzzles (and their solutions). But I've tucked a few extra goodies around that exciting center.

Part 1: Crossword Strategies and Brain Benefits

My first task in this part is to get you familiar with crossword puzzles. If you're a crossword aficionado, you may just want to skim Chapter 1 to see whether you can pick up any new ideas for how to approach a puzzle. If you're new to crosswords, you'll likely benefit from a complete reading of Chapter 1 so you can understand how crossword grids are constructed, what types of clues you're likely to encounter, and how you may want to go about solving each one.

In Chapter 2, I explore some fascinating reasons for spending quality time with this book. I introduce you to what recent research says about the importance of mental exercise and the impact it can have on your cognitive abilities — including your memory — as you age.

Part II: Tackling the Puzzles

If you're looking for the meat of the book, you'll find it in Part II. This part contains 150 crosswords: easy puzzles, challenging puzzles, and maddening puzzles that may have you screaming. I've included puzzles with a variety of themes, so you're certain to find lots that pique your interest.

Part III: Checking the Solutions

One sure way to improve your puzzling skills is to push yourself to find solutions even when you're pretty sure your brain is maxed out. So use Part III as a way to pat yourself on the back after your hard work rather than as a crutch whenever you feel wobbly solving a puzzle.

Part IV: The Part of Tens

Every *For Dummies* book includes a Part of Tens, which features chapters that offer quick bites of information. The morsels I provide include ten of my best tips for solving even the trickiest puzzles and ten great Web resources that you may want to add to your "favorites" list.

Icons Used in This Book

In the Part I chapters, you'll notice two icons in the margins that help you navigate the text:

When you see this icon, know that the text next to it contains a helpful hint for solving crossword puzzles.

This icon points out information that you want to tuck into your mental filing cabinet — it's worth holding on to.

Where to Go from Here

Your entry point into this book depends on your relationship with crosswords. If you're a newbie, I recommend that you spend some time with Chapter 1 before putting pencil to paper.

If you're already a puzzling pro and picked up this book knowing exactly how to tackle the grid, go ahead and jump into the good stuff: the puzzles in Part II. But even if you're fairly experienced, consider starting with a puzzle labeled "Easy" — it always helps to get to know the puzzle editor's style before moving on to the tougher challenges.

My only rule is that you cannot jump directly to Part III! I don't want you eyeing the solutions before you've wined and dined at least one puzzle. But I assume that because you've taken the time to read this Introduction, you're a pretty patient person and you're not going to spoil your fun by looking at the answers first.

No matter what your crossword background is, I hope you'll stop by Chapter 2 at some time during your journey through this book. I find the topic of brain fitness fascinating, and I think you will too.

Part I

Crossword Strategies and Brain Benefits

In this part . . .

Chapter 1 introduces you to the basics of solving a crossword puzzle, including what you're seeing when you look at a crossword grid, resources you may want to have on hand, and tips to apply when you're truly stuck.

In Chapter 2, I explore the mental benefits of scheduling some quality crossword time into your day. I explain what current research says about the importance of exercising your brain, why crosswords fit the bill so perfectly, and what other activities you may want to add to your mental workout routine.

Chapter 1

Completing the Grid:
How to Solve a Crossword

Many of us started working crossword puzzles in elementary school, when our teachers had us fill in puzzles that reinforced our spelling, reading, science, or social studies lessons of the day. Chances are you've been familiar with the structure of crossword puzzles for a long time, and you've probably had at least some experience working them.

But that doesn't necessarily mean you're comfortable with them. In fact, you may feel downright nervous when you sit down to work a crossword these days. After all, what better way is there to test how much knowledge you've accumulated — and retained — over the years? And what better way to feel like a complete moron than to find yourself staring blankly at clue after clue?

Maybe you've long avoided crosswords precisely because they point out how much you don't know. And maybe you're now ready to overcome your fears. As I explain in Chapter 2, the benefits of working crosswords are potentially great. Plus, they're a lot of fun — after you get past the fear and frustration.

I offer lots of suggestions in this chapter for how to become a decent crossword puzzler. It doesn't matter what your IQ is or how many years of schooling you've had — you *can* enjoy crosswords, and I'm happy to show you how.

Becoming Familiar with Some Puzzle Components

I want to first explain a few basics about how crossword puzzles are constructed. Maybe you've never thought about it before, but puzzle constructors follow some pretty strict rules when they sit down to create new puzzles. I'm not just talking about the fact that some clues are labeled "Across" because their answers are written horizontally on the crossword grid, and some clues are labeled "Down" because their answers are entered vertically on the grid. The rules they follow are a bit more complicated than that, and knowing them provides information you can use to develop your own crossword-solving strategy. Here are a few key rules:

- **Each crossword puzzle grid is a perfect square and is perfectly symmetrical.** In other words, the pattern of black and white squares is the same if you look at the puzzle right-side-up and upside-down. These facts don't affect how you solve the puzzle, but they're part of what makes a crossword puzzle a thing of beauty.

- **On a crossword puzzle grid, you shouldn't encounter any *unchecked* squares** — white squares that are used in an Across entry but not in a Down entry, or vice versa. If unchecked squares were allowed, that would make your life harder — you'd have only one opportunity to figure out what belongs in that square. Instead, you always get two chances to fill a square: by solving the Across clue or the Down clue.

- **The phrasing of the clues largely determines the difficulty of the puzzle.** The answers themselves may be words you use every day, but the clues may or may not lead you directly to the answers. That's part of the beauty of making crosswords: The puzzle constructor can be straightforward or extremely creative and oblique, depending on how easy or difficult a puzzle needs to be. And that's part of the beauty of working crosswords: The more time you spend with a particular puzzle, the more familiar you'll become with how the puzzle constructor is phrasing the clues.

- **Each clue should be the same part of speech as its answer.** Puzzle constructors aren't perfect, and sometimes they mess up this rule, but in general you can rely on this being true. If the clue calls for a verb, the answer will be a verb.

- **No clue should contain a significant word that appears in its answer.** For example, "Chicago Sox" would be a lousy clue for the answer WHITESOX.

If you find yourself attracted to the symmetry of the crossword grid and wondering whether you have what it takes to construct puzzles, pick up a copy of *Crossword Puzzle Challenges For Dummies* by Patrick Berry (Wiley). In it, you'll find all kinds of information about how to craft a terrific crossword.

Considering the Theme

Many crossword puzzles — including those you find in Part II of this book — are developed around a central theme. What does that mean? It means that the puzzle constructor gives the crossword a title (other than just a number), and some, or possibly all, of the clues in the puzzle relate to that title — another tool to help you establish your puzzle-solving strategy. You just have to figure out what the title means!

Here are a few examples from this book:

- One of the Easy puzzles in Part II is titled "New Shoes," as in "Baby needs a new pair of shoes." Some of the clues and answers relate to gambling.

- You can find a Tough puzzle titled "Ringing in the Ears" in Part II that contains clues and answers relating to things that make noise.

- One of the Treacherous puzzles in Part II is titled "Off to the Shrink" and features psychiatric terms and phobias.

Identifying Specific Types of Hints and Clues

In any crossword puzzle, you're bound to find various types of clues. In the following sections, I explain some of the most common types you'll encounter and offer hints for solving them.

Filling in blanks

The fill-in-the-blank clue is often the easiest type to solve, which is why I mention it first. The clue usually takes the form of a familiar phrase or a title (of a book, movie, play, or TV show, for example). The puzzle constructor has left out one or more words from the phrase or title, and she uses an underline to indicate where those words are missing.

Here's an example: "*A Tale ___ Cities.*" Even if you haven't read Dickens for years, you may recall that the novel referenced here is *A Tale of Two Cities.* That means the answer to this clue is OFTWO, and that's what you'd write in the crossword grid.

Answering trivia

The trivia clue is often another fairly easy type of clue to answer. That's because if you don't know the answer to a trivia clue, you can probably find it if you're willing to use outside resources. For example, you may see a clue like "2008 best-director brothers" or "Ben Franklin birthplace." If you don't know that the COENS won the 2008 Oscar for their direction of *No Country for Old Men* or that Franklin was born in BOSTON, chances are you can find out by going online or to the right printed resources.

As I explain in the upcoming section "Gathering Your Resources," some people refuse to use outside resources because they think doing so is equivalent to cheating. I respectfully disagree. Using outside resources is part of the process of increasing your reservoir of knowledge. Ideally, the more puzzles you work, the more information you'll have stored in your brain, and the less frequently you'll need to turn to books or Web sites for help. But I see no shame in using these resources when you need them.

Punning around

This type of clue can be fairly challenging, depending on how the puzzle constructor phrases it. Unlike with a trivia clue, you probably won't get much help from outside resources to solve puns; you'll be left to your own creative thinking.

The pun clue is often (but not always) followed by a question mark to indicate that a play on words is at hand. Consider this example: The clue is "What cows dance to?" and the answer is MOOSIC. (Feel free to groan.)

Playing with descriptions

The puzzle constructor can get really creative here because there are endless ways to describe a single word or phrase. To get the answer ORANGE, for example, you might see a clue as simple as "Citrus fruit," which would require that you eliminate other possibilities (such as *lemon, grapefruit,* and *lime*) in order to arrive at the right answer. But the puzzle constructor could also pose a more oblique clue, such as "Rhyme eluder," which would require that you understand he's referring to a word that doesn't lend itself easily to rhymes.

Solving analogies

Maybe it has been a while since you took a standardized test, but this type of clue is something that educators love to include on them. Basically, the puzzle constructor offers three pieces of information, and you need to fill in the fourth. The way to do so is to determine the relationship between the first two pieces of information.

For example, you may see a clue such as "Poodle:Dog as Arabian:__." The way to read this clue to yourself is to say "Poodle is to Dog as Arabian is to Blank." When you figure out the relationship between "Poodle" and "Dog" (a poodle is a breed of dog), you can determine that your answer is HORSE.

Figuring out abbreviations

Answers can sometimes be abbreviations, and the clues should let you know that. An obvious way for the puzzle constructor to tip you off is for the clue to include "Abbr." For example, the answer to "U.S. central bank: Abbr." would be FED (instead of FEDERALRESERVE).

Another way that the puzzle constructor can indicate an abbreviation is required is by using an abbreviation within the clue itself. For example, in the sample puzzle shown later in this chapter, the clue for 37 Across is "Hosp. aides." The fact that you see "Hosp." instead of "Hospital" tells you that the answer will be an abbreviation (RNAS).

Speaking a foreign language

Just as the puzzle constructor has to let you know when an answer should be an abbreviation, he also must let you know if the answer should be in a foreign language. And as with abbreviations, he has a variety of ways to do so.

If the answer is supposed to be in French, you may see one of the following in the clue:

- ✔ **The tag "(Fr.)":** The answer to "Love (Fr.)" would be AMOUR, for example. This type of clue is rarely used nowadays.

- ✔ **Where the answer would likely be heard:** The answer to the clue "Love in Paris" would also be AMOUR.

- ✔ **Another word or phrase from the same language:** To arrive at AMOUR, you may see "Love, s'il vous plaît," for example.

Gathering Your Resources

Let's get real: Most of us can't work a crossword puzzle without a little outside help. Or a lot of it. Even fairly easy crossword puzzles are bound to contain a few clues that stump you. And when you build up the courage to work on the toughies, well . . . you may feel like you're doing battle. And no one should go into battle alone.

Thanks to the Web, the number of resources available to you while you're working a puzzle is pretty much infinite. But that doesn't mean I recommend entering the key words in every clue into a search engine to see where they lead you. Not only does that suck the fun out of puzzling, but it'll also probably lead you astray about 95 percent of the time.

Instead, I recommend that you spend some time gathering a handful of key resources that you're likely to use again and again. Whether you prefer online resources or the hard-copy versions, here are some I suggest you keep handy:

- ✔ A dictionary (particularly a crossword dictionary)
- ✔ A slang dictionary
- ✔ A thesaurus
- ✔ A quotation resource
- ✔ An atlas
- ✔ An almanac

In Chapter 6 at the end of this book, I list some specific Web sites that I consider worth using as resources.

If you have a friend who's particularly brainy or a fellow puzzler, feel free to consider that person part of your resource list as well. Puzzling can absolutely be a shared experience.

Some people consider it cheating to use any outside resource when working a puzzle. I respect that opinion but don't think it works for most of us. The fact is, nobody knows every word in the English language, every city in the world, every source of every quote that's ever been spoken. It doesn't matter how fit your synapses are, you're bound to need help sometimes. And if using an outside resource helps you learn something new, I'm all for it.

Sample Puzzle: "How Grueling!"

With the information from the preceding sections in mind, consider how you would begin to tackle the following puzzle:

Across

1. Type of lap dog once owned by Minnie Mouse
5. Road shoulder
9. K-9 attack command *Sic*
14. Place for an iris *FLOWER BED*
15. Mountains bordering China
16. As a friend, in French *Ami*
17. They go with studs
19. "Care for ___ of tea?" *A CUP*
20. Jumble of spilled letters?
21. "A votre ___!"
22. Scot's "not"
23. Member of a team that visits once per year
25. Historic Dead Sea fortress
29. Old phone user
30. *Saint ___ Fire*
31. Presley's costar in *Love Me Tender*
32. He can make you safe at home
35. 440-yard-long path
36. Huey and Howie
37. Hosp. aides
38. Battle of nations
39. One of the "Hi ho, hi ho" septet
40. Lead guitarist's output
41. It may be defended by a scholar

43. Flying off the shelves
44. Reply to a knock
46. Org. that gets you out of a rut?
47. Area of South Africa
48. "Perfect!"
54. "Not ___ in the world"
55. Klingons or Vulcans, for example *ALIEN's*
56. Most unsatisfactory
57. Lease length, often *1 yr.*
58. Expressions of puppy love?
59. Cosmologist Lauder
60. D.C. group
61. Honeymoon interrupter

Down

1. "___ sock in it!" *put A*
2. Witch's eye
3. Live up to your promises
4. A pop *SODA/COLA*
5. Cote cry *Coo*
6. Elmer's contented cow
7. Thoroughly involved
8. Femme fatale of The Muppets *Ms. Piggy*
9. Oceanic flavoring
10. Zonkers
11. Early morning favorite
12. Play act
13. Bishop's headdress

18. Domain
24. Explorer John and others
25. Calico's comment *MEow*
26. Thomas-Edison link *ANA*
27. A good breakfast for a genius? *Egg's*
28. "You've got mail" co.
29. Borge and Andersen, for example
31. Self-centered chatterboxes
33. Hammerhead kin
34. "Hey you!"
36. "Rikki Don't ___ That Number"
37. "Get ___ of it!"
39. Empty out
40. Make good use of class time
42. Suffering from phonasthenia
43. Some Consumer Reports employees
44. Wide-eyed with wonder *AWED*
45. Fiesta fare
46. Strain of flu
49. Peter Fonda's beekeeping role
50. Nest eggs, briefly *iras*
51. John Irving title protagonist
52. Medicare org. *AARP*
53. Microphone word

With your pencil in hand, read through the clues and see whether any seem obvious. I think most people find that fill-in-the-blank clues can be fairly easy, such as these found in our sample puzzle:

- 19 Across: "Care for _____ of tea?"
- 30 Across: *Saint _____ Fire*
- 54 Across: "Not _____ in the world"
- 1 Down: "_____ sock in it!"
- 37 Down: "Get _____ of it!"

If you can fill in even a half-dozen entries with certainty in this first stage, that's a great start.

Next, go back and troll the clues for less-obvious items that you can answer with at least some confidence — especially those that intersect with the entries you've got on the grid already. If you *think* you may have an answer but aren't certain, pencil the entry in lightly on the grid. If you get confirmation that one or more letters is correct (by solving clues that intersect with that entry), you've saved the time of having to return to that clue later.

Because our sample crossword has a theme, you may next want to consider how that theme plays out in the grid. If you've solved a few clues already, you'll notice that they don't all relate to the theme. But keeping in mind that some entries will be food-related (that's where the "gruel" comes from) may put you in the right frame of mind to solve some clues. For example, 20 Across ("Jumble of spilled letters?") may lead you to ALPHABITS more quickly if the theme is on your mind.

As a next step, consider which clues could be solved more easily if you consulted an outside resource. For example, you could probably solve 15 Across ("Mountains bordering China") and 25 Across ("Historic Dead Sea fortress") with the help of your favorite search engine. If you're willing to go that route, now would be a good time to fill in some additional entries by consulting your resources.

Identifying plural entries may be a good next step. For example, 17 Across ("They go with studs"), 31 Down ("Self-centered chatterboxes"), and 50 Down ("Nest eggs, briefly") seem likely to end in S. (And, in fact, they all do.) You can pencil in that letter on the grid until you solve the clues themselves. It may seem like small potatoes, but you never know when a single letter may help solve an intersecting clue!

Speaking of 50 Down ("Nest eggs, briefly"), it's a good example of the creative ways that puzzle constructors alert you that entries need to be abbreviations. You don't see "Abbr." here, but "briefly" is a hint that the answer will be abbreviated — in this case, IRAS.

If you've made it this far and still have lots of blank boxes staring you in the face, don't sweat it. Be proud of what you've accomplished already, take a break from this puzzle, and come back to it with fresh eyes later. Or, if friends or family members are nearby, share some clues and see whether they can help with one or two. You may be surprised by how solving just one clue can unlock other entries that had you stumped before.

And when you're truly ready to close the book on this sample puzzle, feel free to turn to the beginning of Part III for its solution.

Chapter 2

Staying Sharp: Giving Your Brain a Workout

onight on my local PBS station, the prime-time program is titled *Magnificent Mind at Any Age*. It's described as exploring "the many natural ways that we can not only keep our brains healthy as we age, but improve and enhance our brain power." Shows like this — along with countless newspaper and magazine articles, books, and Web sites — are increasingly focusing our attention on the subject of brain fitness.

Maybe you're a PBS fan and already know lots about this subject. Maybe you and your doctor have talked about how to prevent and even potentially reverse signs of brain aging. Or maybe these words are the first you've ever read about this exciting topic, in which case I feel privileged to introduce it to you! Either way, I hope this chapter opens your mind to new ideas about how to keep itself sharp throughout your golden years.

Stimulating Your Brain: It's Never Too Late

You may have been raised to believe that education is for kids and at a certain point, adults know everything they need to know to survive. And that may be true. But what you need to survive is much different than what you need to thrive, and I suspect most of us are more interested in thriving.

An ever-growing body of scientific research demonstrates that what our brains require in order to thrive — especially as our bodies get older — is lots of stimulation. I'm not talking about loud music or pungent smells here: I'm talking about the type of stimulation that encourages you to think new thoughts, get creative, and push your brain to work harder than ever before.

Work harder? Isn't that a bit unfair? After all, you get to a certain age and expect to reap some benefits from all the work you've done before. You know more now than you did when you were 16, right? Why isn't that good enough?

Your brain can't rest on its laurels any more than your body can rest on its past achievements. Maybe when you were 16 you could do 50 pushups without breaking a sweat, but that doesn't mean you've got arms of steel today. We all know that our bodies change — significantly — as we age. What you also need to know is that your brain changes in similar ways. And just as you recognize the need to exercise in order to fend off the worst effects of aging on your body, you must also recognize the value of exercising your brain.

Touring your brain

To follow the logic behind the brain fitness phenomenon, I'm going to take you on a quick tour of what's happening in your brain right now. I'll start with a couple key definitions:

- ✔ **Neurons:** *Neurons* are cells that control your central nervous system: your brain and spinal column, and the nerves connected to them.
- ✔ **Synapses:** *Synapses* are tiny gaps between the neurons in your brain.

When synapses are working correctly, they allow your neurons to communicate with each other, which keeps your nervous system functioning the way it should. Your nervous system must function properly in order for you to learn new things, retain information, and use your powers of logic and reason.

You have about 100 billion neurons in your brain. And you have literally trillions of synapses — possibly even a *quadrillion* (that's a 1 followed by 15 zeroes). With numbers like that, it may seem as if you have plenty to spare. However, as you age, your synapses deteriorate. And because your brain activity takes place courtesy of synapses, their deterioration equates to a decrease in your brain function, including memory.

So to have a healthy mind, you must keep your synapses in top condition. How do you do that? Keep reading!

Looking at recent research

In the late 1980s, a study published in the *Annals of Neurology* raised questions about why some people develop symptoms of Alzheimer's disease and others don't. Autopsies were conducted on 137 nursing home patients. As expected, the brains of those who had demonstrated symptoms of Alzheimer's were filled with *plaques* (brain deposits made up of dead cells and proteins) and *tangles* (nerve cells that had become tangled together) — characteristic physical signs associated with the disease.

Here's the unexpected part: The brains of ten patients who *didn't* show any symptoms of Alzheimer's contained the same levels of plaques and tangles. If the physical reasons for the disease were present in those people, why didn't they get the symptoms?

There was another twist: The ten patients in question had heavier brains and more neurons than they should have had given their age. What made these ten people different from their peers?

As a result of this study, a new theory emerged: the *cognitive reserve* theory. It essentially says that people who have a larger reserve of neurons and stronger cognitive abilities can tolerate some brain deterioration without showing symptoms. In other words, the more you use your brain, the greater your chances of avoiding symptoms of Alzheimer's. Strong stuff, huh?

Obviously, no one is offering guarantees here. I can't promise that anything I suggest in this book will add *X* number of years to your life, and that those years will be free of any symptoms of memory loss or other mental decline. But study after study in the past two decades has shown that mental activity can have a positive effect on your quality of life in the long run, and I can't argue with that.

How do you build a cognitive reserve? The same ways that you keep your synapses happy and healthy. Keep reading — I offer specific suggestions starting in the next section of this chapter.

The key to a strong cognitive reserve seems to be to start as early as you can. The younger you are when you begin actively pursuing brain fitness, the greater the reserve you can accumulate. But assuming you're already past "early," don't panic — just make the commitment to start now. Some studies have shown that even people well into their 70s can improve their cognitive health by making lifestyle changes and increasing their mental stimulation.

Creating a New Health Routine

The way I see it, there are two broad categories of activities you can do to take care of your gray matter:

- The things you're already supposed to be doing to improve your physical health
- Things that specifically rev up your brain by giving it more stimulation than it's used to

I discuss each category in turn.

Following your doctor's advice

Here's a lightning-quick tour through some activities you're supposed to do to benefit your physical health — which also have pleasant side effects for your brain:

- **Reduce stress.** You probably already know that stress affects blood pressure, heart function, and much more. But did you know that stress causes synapses to malfunction?

  Long-term stress can cause a *neurotransmitter* (a chemical that carries messages between nerve cells) called glutamate to build up in your synapses. If enough of it accumulates, it can become toxic and interfere with your memory and your ability to learn.

- **Get aerobic exercise.** Aerobic exercise can strengthen your heart and help you manage and resist stress. A bonus: Studies suggest that it also stimulates the creation of new neurons and strengthens the connections between them.

- **Eat a diet rich in antioxidant foods.** If your physical health alone hasn't inspired you to stock up on blueberries and spinach, do so for your mental health. Foods rich in antioxidants may help counteract effects of free radicals in your brain. (*Free radicals* are molecules that contain oxygen and attack cells throughout your body. They have been linked to cancer and heart disease, as well as brain deterioration.)

- **Control high blood pressure and diabetes.** A study published in the journal *Neurology* in 2001 showed that the mental abilities of participants with high blood pressure or diabetes declined more rapidly than those of other participants. High blood pressure is a risk factor for a condition called *vascular dementia,* in which a series of tiny strokes can affect memory and other cognitive abilities.

Early diagnosis and tight control of these conditions may help prevent some of the ill effects on your cognitive health.

Revving up your synapses

So you're already trying to reduce your stress, exercise, eat right, and get serious health conditions under control. What else could you possibly have time for?

Please believe me when I say that stimulating your brain doesn't have to be a complicated process. And it certainly isn't a one-size-fits-all proposition. In a nutshell, here are the goals:

✔ To encourage your brain to work in new ways by engaging in new activities or doing your routine activities in new ways

✔ To achieve the first goal on an ongoing basis, which means continually shaking up your routines

An infinite number of roads can lead to these goals. Here are just a handful of ideas to get you thinking:

✔ **Add new workouts to your exercise routine:** Not only will your muscles be challenged, but if you're trying something new to you, your mind will have to be engaged as well. Consider doing something truly challenging, such as taking a dance class or joining a sports team for seniors.

✔ **Volunteer for an organization that truly interests you:** Make sure you're coming from a place of genuine interest — not obligation. Choose an organization whose mission you find fascinating, and let the staff know that you're eager to learn new things.

✔ **Read something new:** One of the best ways to boost your brain power is to read more — and to read more carefully. Consider types of books and magazines that you've never picked up before. If the only books on your shelf are mystery novels but you think historical biographies might pique your interest, visit the library and give one a try.

✔ **Take a class:** Some colleges and universities offer special programs that allow seniors to take courses at discounted tuition rates. Also, check with community centers, churches, and other nonprofit organizations that may offer classes. Again, new is best: If you've been knitting for 40 years, an introductory knitting class may offer social opportunities (which are always good for mental stimulation) but not much in the way of a challenge.

✔ **Get together with friends:** Staying social is key to keeping your brain in gear. But don't get stuck in routines: If you find yourself hearing the same conversations every time you see certain people, figure out how to shake things up.

Come armed with questions to ask about current events, politics, movies, books . . . anything that may get all of you thinking and interacting in new ways.

✔ **Tackle some puzzles:** In the next section, I talk about how crosswords can play a part in your mental fitness routine. But don't limit yourself to crosswords. Sudoku, logic puzzles, riddles, word searches . . . any type of puzzle that really engages you is going to get your mind working.

Whatever activities you choose to do to keep your brain stimulated, you need to enjoy them enough to do them regularly. You can't get your body fit by working out three hours in a row and then ignoring your health altogether for two weeks (because you're so sore from the marathon workout that you can't move!). You benefit much more from working out consistently for shorter amounts of time — for example, every day for 30 minutes, or four days a week for 45 minutes each time.

The same is true of mental exercise. Your goal should be to make time for mental stimulation at least several days a week, if not every day. If you can't devote time to working a crossword puzzle or taking a class every day, no problem. But don't let a month go by between mental workouts.

Realizing Why Crosswords Fit the Bill

Working a crossword puzzle is all about stimulating your mind and testing your memory. Any given clue is going to prompt you to pore through your mental filing cabinet searching for names, places, events, foreign words, and other items that you knew once upon a time but perhaps haven't thought about in years.

Working crosswords on a regular basis can give your memory a boost for a couple reasons:

✔ **The more puzzles you work, the more you'll want to rely on your own knowledge base for answers (as opposed to using outside resources).** It's simply more satisfying to pull the answer from your own brain than to pull it from an atlas or a Web search engine.

✔ **You'll discover that puzzle constructors have certain words that they like to work into puzzles on a regular basis.** The more of these words you commit to memory, the easier working crosswords becomes.

Demanding discipline

Most crossword puzzles require at least an hour to solve. Some require two hours or more. When you tackle a crossword, you're taking on a pretty serious mental commitment, and succeeding requires discipline.

It's normal to feel frustrated when you get stuck halfway through the puzzle and can't seem to fill in any more entries. But if you're going to complete a crossword grid, you have to develop the discipline to back up, reread clues, consider what resources you may want to consult, and chip away at the empty spaces.

Touring the world from your kitchen table

In Chapter 1, I explain that while some people bristle at the idea of using outside resources to help solve crossword clues, I think doing so is fine. Better than fine, in fact. If you get stuck on a clue, what are your options? You can give up and flip to the solution (*not* my preference), ask someone else for help (a great idea), or check for the answer in a book or on a Web site.

If your goal is to give your brain lots of new fodder, researching challenging answers seems like a great way to accomplish it. With a dictionary, a thesaurus, a book of quotations, and lots of other resources on hand, you have a world of knowledge at your fingertips. And with the crossword clues prompting you, you have lots of motivation to seek out that knowledge.

Revisiting your curiosity

Curiosity is one of the things we love about kids (except when you're on a long car trip with a 3-year-old grandchild in the *why* phase). When a child encounters something completely new, he asks questions about it and genuinely wants to find out more. He wants to understand it and figure out how it relates to the stuff he already knows.

Carrying adult responsibilities (and schedules) often squeezes the life out of curiosity. But working crosswords can inspire you to be more curious. You may find that one little clue with a surprising solution leaves you wanting to know more about why that answer is correct. Feel free to put your puzzle on hold and find out more, right then and there. Your brain will benefit from it.

Finding Out More about Brain Fitness: Key Resources

This chapter barely scratches the surface when it comes to brain fitness, and I encourage you to find out more (especially if you're truly curious about it, because what better way to stimulate your brain than to read about stimulating your brain?). Following is just a handful of resources to consider:

✔ **Alzheimer's Association:** From the home page (www.alz.org), you can find a wealth of information on the disease. If you click on the "We Can Help" tab and go to "Brain Health," you'll find helpful links, including one to a crossword puzzle site!

✔ **American Association of Retired People (AARP):** The Web site, www.aarp.org/health/brain, features links to articles on the latest brain research and tips for keeping your brain healthy.

✔ **Brain Fitness Channel:** At http://bfc.positscience.com, you can test your current level of brain fitness, read news stories about brain research, study how the brain functions, take part in online forums that focus on specific subjects that may interest you, and more.

✔ **Prevention:** The magazine's Web site (www.prevention.com) features a Brain Fitness section that you access through the "Health" tab on the home page. You'll find lots of articles that link physical and mental fitness, and you can join the Prevention online community to share stories or ask for feedback from other people with similar interests and concerns.

✔ **SharpBrains:** The home page of www.sharpbrains.com provides links to more information than any one brain may be able to absorb. Whether you want to read about brain-training software, nutrition, memory, stress management, or just about anything else brain-related, you have a good chance of finding what you're looking for here.

Part II
Tackling the Puzzles

The 5th Wave   By Rich Tennant

"FOUR-LETTER WORD FOR RESCUE! FOUR-LETTER WORD FOR RESCUE!"

In this part . . .

Got your pencil ready? Good. Ready for a mental workout? Terrific. In this part, you can choose whatever level of puzzle challenge you feel up to, from Easy to Treacherous. And you can tackle as many puzzles as you'd like, all at the same time. (Doing so can ease the frustration of getting stuck on one puzzle for too long.) So settle into a comfortable chair, pick a page, and show that grid who's boss!

Chapter 3

Tackling the Puzzles

*P*lease be aware that not all crosswords are created equal. Puzzle constructors aim to please, and that means that they create puzzles with a wide variety of difficulty levels to satisfy the needs of a wide variety of puzzle lovers.

The puzzles in this book are labeled by difficulty level. Levels are Easy, Tricky, Tough, and Treacherous, with "Easy" being (of course) the easiest puzzles, and "Treacherous" being the most difficult puzzles.

If you're new to working crosswords, don't jump to the puzzles labeled "Treacherous" in this book. Chances are you'll only get frustrated, and your puzzling career will come to a premature end. It's sort of like trying to run a 10K race when you've never strapped on running shoes before in your life. Be honest with yourself about the difficulty level you can handle. Better to start easy and build your skills slowly than to burn out in a quick burst of frustration.

If you're going to work the puzzles in your daily newspaper, find out whether the difficulty level is different on different days. For example, *USA TODAY* runs its easiest crosswords on Mondays, and the difficulty level ramps up each day through Friday. (The Universal Sunday puzzle is intended to mirror the difficulty level of a Thursday puzzle.)

When you finish solving all of these puzzles, please see Part III for the answers. Good luck!

Puzzle 1: A Pinpoint Solution
Easy

Across

1. "Dancing Queen" quartet
5. Chicago terminus
10. Determines a sum
14. Agile deer
15. Body parts that have lifelines
16. Roman numerals for Henry
17. Was right on time
20. *You ___ Your Life*
21. Eagle by the sea
22. Eat away at the beach?
23. Sound from the meadow
24. They're found beside temples
26. Shrubs with lavender blooms
29. Lawnmower part
30. Sign at a broadcasting station
31. Make judgments
32. Doctor of sci-fi
35. 19th-century England
39. Nice hot time?
40. Garner
41. ___ prosequi (charges will be dropped)
42. Awakens
44. Burns with water
45. Soft, light, and fluffy
48. Galactic bit
49. Regarding birds
50. Cripple
51. ___ Palmas
54. Starting location
58. Peter Fonda title role
59. Sing Swiss-style
60. *Peyton Place* first name
61. Stack part
62. One cubic meter
63. Lacking in liveliness

Down

1. "Ahab the ___" (Ray Stevens song)
2. Cause yawning
3. Former Miss America host Parks
4. "___ was saying . . ."
5. Met productions
6. Common contraction
7. Balm ingredient, perhaps
8. L.B.J.'s successor
9. Low or high end?
10. Not favoring
11. Mischievous pranks
12. Tube invented in 1904
13. Internet destinations
18. Zipper substitute
19. Beer foam
23. Can of worms, maybe
24. Geriatric orbiter of '98
25. Item with a gooseneck
26. Puppy follower?
27. "What's ___ for me?"
28. "Chantilly ___" (The Big Bopper's biggest hit)
29. "Lions and tigers and ___, oh my!"
31. Frank account?
32. Humorist Rogers
33. Business phone button
34. English I readings
36. Horse-and-buggy handful
37. Put down stakes?
38. Niagara Falls sound
42. Ear bone
43. Morrison or Tennille
44. Archie Bunker command
45. Cuisine featuring dirty rice
46. Rudimentary seed
47. What X may mean
48. Less hazardous
50. How something is done
51. One not to be believed
52. First name in a Tolstoy novel
53. Seize with a toothpick
55. Sen. Clinton once represented it
56. Came by
57. Word with hat or school

1 A	2 B	3 B	4 A	■	5 O	6	7 A	8 R	9	■	10 A	11 D	12 D	13 S
14 R	O	E	S	■	15 P	A	L	M	S	■	16 V	i	i	i
17 A	R	R	i	18 V	E	D	O	N		19				T
20 B	E	T	■	21 E	R	D	E	■		22 E	R	O	D	E
■	■	■	23	L	A		■	24	25					S
26 L	27 i	28 L	A	C	S	■	29 B	L	A	D	E	■		
30 O	N	A	i	R	■	31 D	E	E	m	■	32 W	33 H	34 O
35	i	C	O	■	36	A		37	38 R	i			
39	T	E	■		40	R		■	41 N	O	L	L	E
■	■	■	42	43		S	■	44 S	C	A	L	E	S
45	46	47		O	■		48 S		R	■			
49			N	■	50 M	A	M	E	■	51 L	52 A	53 S
54			i	55 G	56 F			■	57 i	T		
58		■	59 Y	O	D	E	L	■	60 A	A		
61		■	62 S	T	E	R	E	■	63 D	R	A	B

Beginning

Puzzle 2: Turn-Ons
Easy

Across

1. Bat the breeze
5. Steakhouse order, perhaps
10. "Here comes trouble!"
14. "If I Were a ___ Man"
15. DNA structure
16. Space-race goal
17. ___ snuff (adequate)
18. "___ we all!"
19. Pierce player on *M*A*S*H*
20. Early yarn machine
23. Fiji's neighbor
24. Wee colonist
25. Talk, talk, talk
28. Start of a cheer
32. Greg's sitcom wife
34. Half-wit
38. Cafe au ___
39. He goes in circles
42. Tennis star Mandlikova
43. Porridge-type foods
44. With fervor
47. Bad to the bone
48. Herbal brew
49. Driver of a four-horse chariot, in myth
51. Jed Clampett portrayer Buddy
56. Certain halftime performers
61. The world, to Mr. Magoo
63. Pope John Paul II's first name
64. Strip the skin off
65. Vidal's Breckenridge
66. Play hard to get
67. "Beauty ___ the eye . . ."
68. What some willows do?
69. "Walk Away ___" (Four Tops)
70. Baby duster

Down

1. The mashed potatoes on shepherd's pie
2. *Fantasia* ballerina
3. Be a cast member of
4. Beachwear that leaves little to the imagination
5. Cambodian's neighbor
6. Swiss capital
7. Mr. Cassini
8. Old Japanese mercenary
9. Stretch outward
10. Arabian monarchy
11. Famed chalice
12. East of Eden
13. Stop ___ dime
21. Bellybutton
22. Nonacademic degree
26. Out of order
27. Financial shellacking
29. Roll call reply in French class
30. Italian wine
31. Aquarium microorganisms
33. Thomas ___ Edison
34. "___ a dream" (Martin Luther King)
35. Kind of golf
36. One of the Brady Bunch
37. 1999 Ron Howard film
39. "Huh?"
40. Beatles label
41. Make available to new tenants
45. Island necklace
46. *The New* ___ (humor magazine)
50. Bondservant
52. Suit
53. Dance or sauce
54. Correspondence created on keyboards
55. Former boy-band
57. Fur stole
58. Ayatollah's land
59. Lymph, for one
60. Feeling of delight
61. Pricey wheels
62. Caustic substance

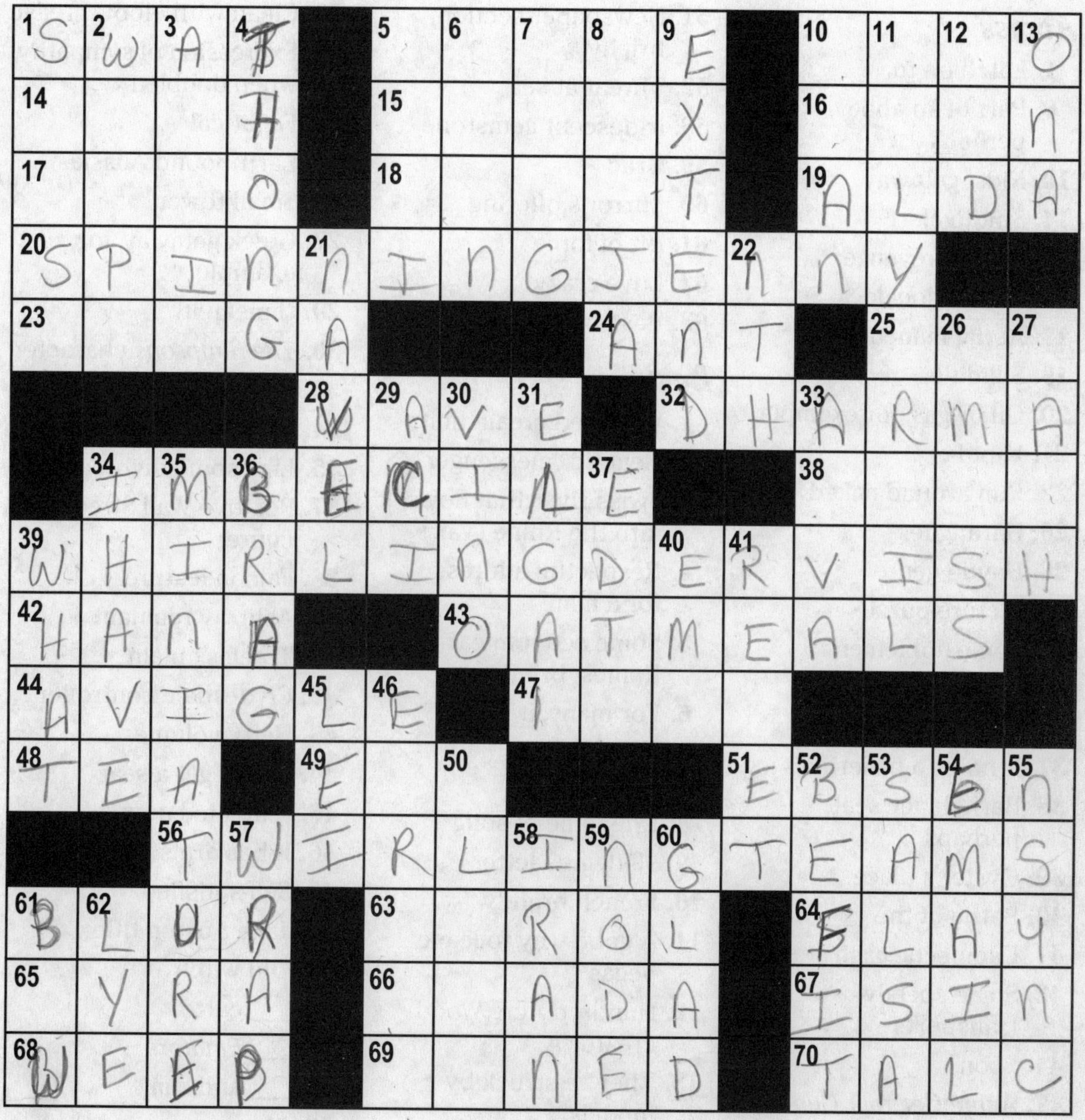

Puzzle 3: Shoot!
Easy

Across

1. Latch on to
6. Part of an abbey, perhaps
10. Kids' getaway
14. Studio alert
15. Santa's revenge
16. Canton locale
17. Aerial maneuver
19. Solidifies
20. Oil or gas, for example
21. Vapid
22. Run around naked
26. Harangues
28. Haydn genre
31. Picture puzzle
32. Some noblemen
33. Emeril's word
36. *The Haj* author
37. It holds a ballerina's leg
38. Barn-dance seat, perhaps
39. Oyster's place
40. Battle of the ___
41. Campeche cash
42. Some speedy transports
44. Soon
47. *Annie Get Your Gun* subject
48. Quietly understood
49. Circle or final start
51. Newspaper section, briefly
52. Threat at sea
58. Iridescent gemstone
59. Grad
60. Mirror's offering
61. Bit of force
62. Love crazy
63. Bass-baritone Simon

Down

1. Whipped cream unit
2. Genetic "messenger"
3. Swiss river that flows into the Rhine (Var.)
4. Respectful address for a man
5. Some economical homes, briefly
6. For many, it may be a lot
7. Combine
8. Erie mule of song
9. 90-degree letter
10. French brandy
11. A good way to leave Vegas
12. Hundred Acre Wood creator A.A.
13. They're struck by models
18. New Testament book
21. It controls a pupil's size
22. Clean with elbow grease
23. Expression of sympathy, when doubled
24. Fanatical
25. Earthbound Aussies
26. Small tower
27. Greek getaway, for example
29. "I mean it!"
30. *The Simpsons* character
33. Pesto base
34. Isolated
35. Like some divorces
37. Positive Wall Street figure
38. Falcon feature
40. Ashtray remnant
41. Treeless plain
42. Clydesdale controller
43. Hefty volume
44. Didn't get a seat
45. "Satisfied now?"
46. It has arms and waves
49. Self-satisfied
50. Jane Austen title
52. Old witch
53. ___ carte
54. ___ *Pinafore*
55. ___ and run
56. Mature
57. ___ Plaines

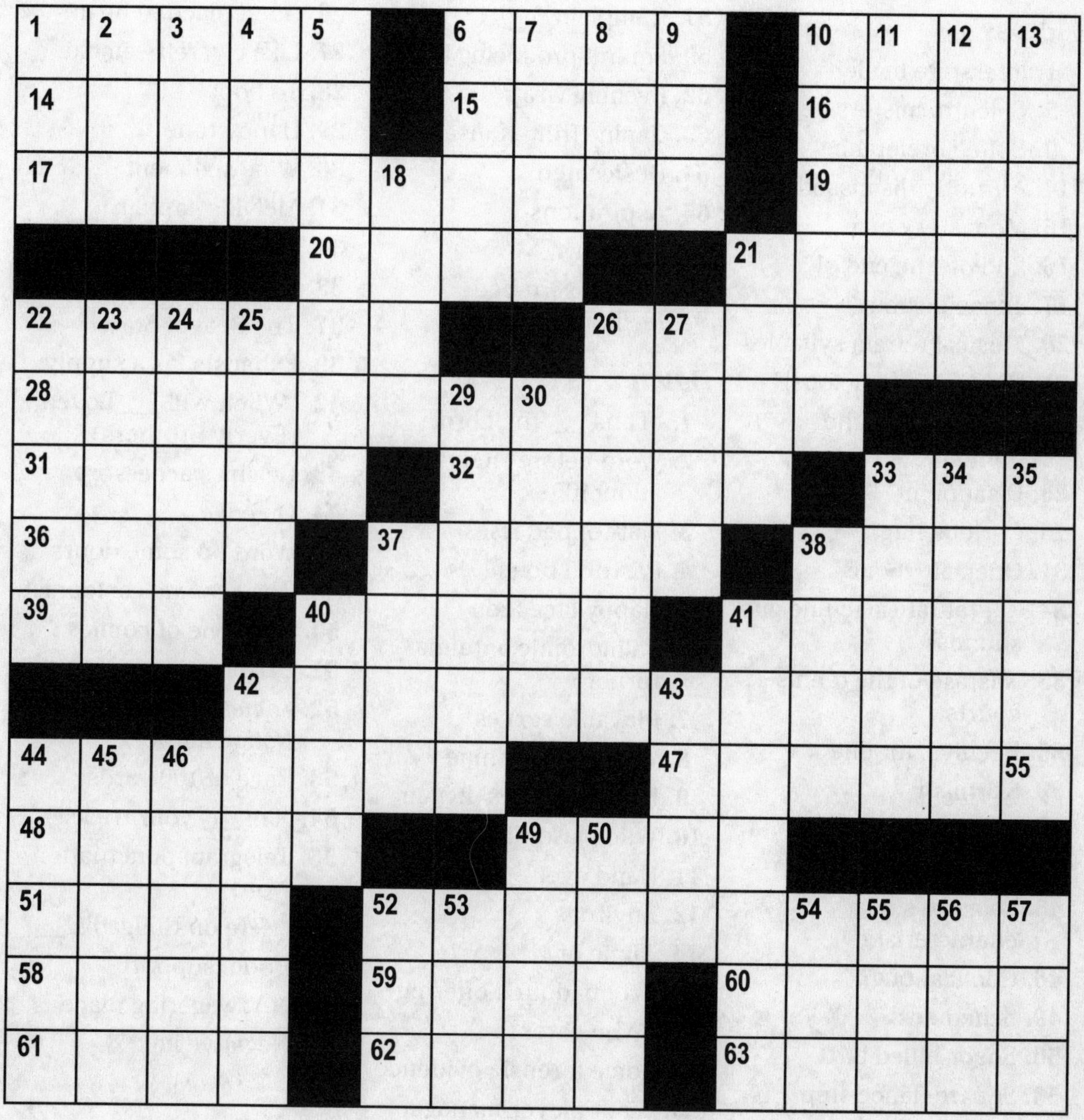

Puzzle 4: Stop Bugging Me!
Easy

Across

1. Interstate hauler
5. Calcutta misters
9. Coffee preference
14. Abruptly dismissed
15. Monastery man
16. End of "the end of"
17. Tenacious bug?
20. Musical refrain syllables
21. "Goodness gracious!"
22. "Elvis ___ left the building"
23. Disappoint
26. Curious bug?
31. Open-air rooms
34. ___-tat-tat (machine gun sounds)
35. Nastase of the tennis courts
36. Beehive, for one
38. Skirmish
40. Backdrop for Heidi
41. Jazzman's lick
45. Leopard's coat characteristic
46. Comical bug?
49. Schedules
50. Razor-billed bird
53. Square-dance step or call
57. Complain
59. Squirm-producing bugs?
62. Evening wrap
63. Canine from Kansas
64. Desiccated
65. Aspirations
66. ___ Mawr
67. Breakfast-in-bed facilitator

Down

1. "Thus ___ the Lord"
2. Word before "Read all about it!"
3. Flat-topped rises
4. Pastoral poem
5. Happy face icon
6. Palindromic antenna turner
7. Playable serves
8. Where stars shine
9. Frasier Cranes' live-in
10. Wife of Geraint
11. Hand over
12. Environs
13. Jamie of *M*A*S*H*
18. Troubadour's offering
19. "Who cares?"
24. Some forensic evidence
25. Giant player-manager Mel, 1942–47
26. Good place to be in?
27. Like cigarette smoke
28. To boot
29. Happy tune
30. Wine sediment
31. Melville captain
32. Imaginary narrative
33. Ready for the pickin'
37. The Beaver State
39. Exhausts, as a supply
42. "When Will ___ Loved" (Everly Brothers)
43. Geisha's accessory
44. On edge
47. Word on some doors
48. *The Far Side* cartoonist
50. "Li'l" one of comics
51. Extreme
52. *Sometimes a Great Notion* author
53. Race of 100 yards
54. "I'm ___ your tricks!"
55. Telegram punctuation word
56. "Here on Gilligan's ___"
58. Boom support
60. N.Y. wagering place
61. Negative link

Puzzle 5: From the Crow's Nest
Easy

Across

1. Evil Norse giant
5. Humphrey's nickname
10. Nautical hazard
14. "... ___ to tell a lie"
15. Item in a cheek pouch, sometimes
16. Alternative to pizzicato
17. Escapees from a mythical box
18. "... with ___ of thousands!"
19. Fraught with danger
20. New World explorer
22. Calculator that doesn't need batteries
24. Super duper?
25. Show scorn, in a way
26. Humidor item, perhaps
29. Galsworthy's *The Forsyte* ___
30. Chop down
33. Rocky Rockies ridge
34. St. ___ Cathedral, London
35. Chronology component, perhaps
36. Mudder's father
37. Social class
38. People rush to get in here
39. It goes over the road
40. Old-time transportation
41. Nene and brant

42. That, in El Salvador
43. Like a squid's squirt
44. Beginning of a tape
45. Mrs. F. Scott Fitzgerald
47. Title for Helmut Kohl
48. Stun with brilliance
50. Portuguese navigator
54. Barbra's *Funny Girl* guy
55. Born yesterday
57. Relaxation
58. "Stormy Weather" singer Horne
59. Air raid alert
60. Downhill aids
61. Eve's grandson
62. Make scholarly revisions, for example
63. Word with catbird or bleacher

Down

1. Not of the clergy
2. Scandinavian capital
3. *To ___ a Mockingbird*
4. Set apart
5. Sheepish farewell?
6. Transpire
7. Wear the disguise of
8. They handle a lot of returns
9. Knot up
10. *M*A*S*H* company clerk
11. Greenland explorer

12. Eggshell color
13. Far from friends
21. First word of "The Battle Hymn of the Republic"
23. Feathery neckware
25. Prepare mushrooms, in a way
26. Urgency
27. Opera solos
28. Certain Italian navigator
29. Smart-mouthed
31. Use a pencil end
32. Firefighter's need
34. Nanook's coat
37. Abridge
38. Unafraid
40. Nob or Bunker, for example
41. *Pretty Woman* star
44. Paul Bunyan, for example
46. Pound and Cornell
47. Place to seek sanctuary
48. 1996 presidential candidate Bob
49. Congregational response
50. Wet, spongy earth
51. One place to get fresh water
52. It touches the Pacific Rim
53. Digs of twigs
56. Intent

1	2	3	4		5	6	7	8	9		10	11	12	13
14					15						16			
17					18						19			
20				21					22	23				
			24					25						
26	27	28					29					30	31	32
33						34					35			
36				37						38				
39				40					41					
42				43				44						
		45	46				47							
48	49					50					51	52	53	
54				55	56					57				
58				59						60				
61				62						63				

Puzzle 6: Hut, Two, Three, Four
Easy

Across

1. Type of carved pole
6. Juvenile salamanders
10. March through mud
14. Giraffe cousin
15. Handlebar feature
16. Public art show, for example
17. "An apple a day . . ." is one
18. Stare open-mouthed
19. Baloney producer
20. It opens with a click
23. Place for sweaters
26. Fa follower
27. ___ *on a Grecian Urn*
28. Countdown of top tunes
31. Bridge locales
36. Curved arch
37. African plains grazer
38. Clog
39. Horse with a graysprinkled coat
40. Heart chambers
42. Sorvino of *Mighty Aphrodite*
43. Florentine, for example
45. Rhea relative
46. Mice, to owls
47. Mrs. Peel's partner
48. Cost increase
50. "Who ___ to judge?"
52. Cowboy Ritter
53. Wee bit
54. Best Actor of 1931 and 1946
60. Miner's strike
61. School talent show staple
62. Studio stand
66. Kelp, for example
67. Model Macpherson
68. Stockholm native
69. Sharp-witted
70. Cincinnati sluggers
71. Emulate Sonja Henie

Down

1. Aunt Polly's nephew, in a Twain classic
2. Volga tributary
3. Uncle Sam collects it
4. *Gone with the Wind,* for one
5. Bloody Mary alternative
6. Ratatouille requirement
7. Haus wife
8. Move with stealth
9. The going rate?
10. Word with "taught" or "effacing"
11. 62, in old Rome
12. Stone with color flashes
13. Pierce with a tusk, for example
21. Railroad tycoon J.P.
22. Monthly payment, for many
23. Summer attire
24. Engorge oneself
25. "Relax, soldiers!"
29. Coins for Sherlock Holmes
30. German engraver Albrecht
32. Pizazz
33. The ___ of St. Louis
34. "What a great discovery!"
35. Incapable of littering
38. Chinaware piece
41. Copies
44. Jewish month before Nisan
48. Deli dill
49. Overindulgence
51. Tight-fisted type
54. Strong criticism
55. Auditioner's quest
56. Upper hand
57. Faculty boss
58. Gentle
59. Atlanta basketball pro
63. Kind of lion or horse
64. Summer hrs. in N.Y.C.
65. *Enter the Dragon* star

Puzzle 7: Get It Together
Easy

Across

1. Superior at work
5. ___ of Two Cities
10. Directed
14. A little of this, a little of that
15. Board, as a train
16. Together, in music
17. A clothes-knit union?
18. Les ___-Unis (the United States, in France)
19. Created
20. Family financial figure
23. Some checkers men
24. "So, there you are!"
25. Eye covering
28. Entice
30. Span. lady
33. It goes with "wash"
34. Petitions
36. Reuters competitor
39. Baby beds
40. Ancient theaters
41. No seats sign, briefly
42. Physicist Fitch and actor Kilmer
43. *Gorillas in the Mist* author Dian
45. Legal matter
46. Lectern platform
47. Flier with two Us in its logo
54. Baby-sitter's nightmare
55. Nita of silent films
56. Worst possible market share
57. Freedom from hardship
58. Blood leaves one
59. Gentle firelight, for example
60. "Oh, me!"
61. ___ living (bring home the bacon)
62. Disrespectful back talk

Down

1. Anjou alternative
2. A shortening, in more ways than one
3. *Anna and the King of* ___
4. Some hats
5. Meeting outline
6. Heads of France
7. Just ___ (not much)
8. *An Iceland Fisherman* author Pierre
9. Caught in a trap
10. Polynesian island group
11. Wax-wrapped cheese
12. Sans clothes
13. Kicker's need
21. Cash or cloth additive
22. Nestling's noise
25. Cotton-tipped sticks
26. Migrants' advocate Chavez
27. Attachment to a rodeo saddle, often
28. Some Baltic natives
29. Functions
30. Garage relatives
31. Visit for a second time
32. Analyze, as an ore sample
34. Yellow, edible Indian fruit
35. Channel events
37. Musk-secreting mammal
38. Somehow
43. A Little Rascal
44. Squeak-stopping application
45. Word after "last" or before "of passage"
46. Slew
47. Range separating Europe and Asia
48. Org. with many missions
49. Computer input
50. Banned fruit tree chemical
51. Vincent Lopez hit of 1922
52. *The Dukes of Hazzard* deputy
53. Hems but doesn't haw?
54. *Maude* star Arthur

1	2	3	4	■	5	6	7	8	9	■	10	11	12	13
14				■	15					■	16			
17				■	18					■	19			
20			21						22			■	■
■	■	23				■	24				■	■	■
25	26	27			■	28	29			■	30	31	32
33			■	■	34				35				
36			37	38									
39						■	40						
41			■	42			■	43	44				
■	■	45			■	46			■	■	■	■	■
■	47	48			49	50				51	52	53	
54			■	55			■	56					
57			■	58				59					
60			■	61				62					

Puzzle 8: It's In the Mail
Easy

Across

1. Jesse Owens event
5. Site of thousands of flowers, perhaps
10. Biosphere sci.
14. *Black Stallion* boy
15. Fats Domino's "Whole __ Loving"
16. Kemo ___ (The Lone Ranger)
17. *Ghostbusters* star
19. Country club instructors
20. Depict deceptively
21. One of the major leagues, briefly
22. Horace collection
23. Gives a pep talk to
25. Piece of an orchestra?
27. Broadway latecomer's sign
28. Terribly upset
31. Enticing word on a sign
34. You, in the Bible
37. Demand at a breakup
38. Rock hound's find
39. Routine thing
41. One who cries foul, briefly
42. Hurler's delivery
44. Aerobic instructor's word
45. Lively, perhaps for one's age

46. Enmities
48. Bit for a stable diet?
50. Overseas money
51. Some tan sources
56. Where you might turn up a lot of dirt
58. Gershwin and Levin
60. Streetside pickup
61. It could be in your throat
62. Deserving attention
64. Like some history
65. Photographer's problem
66. Short list shortener
67. Glass unit
68. ___ *and Sensibility*
69. Moist in the morning

Down

1. Temple figure
2. 1979 Sigourney Weaver thriller
3. Biological units
4. Celestial phenomenon
5. Winter malady
6. Greene of *Bonanza*
7. Spanish others
8. Rat tail?
9. Twelfth U.S. president
10. Get married
11. One with an ace up his sleeve?
12. Double-reed orchestra instrument

13. With a discount of
18. Golda's surname
24. Portnoy's creator Philip
26. Core of a canine, for example
28. Salad veggie, perhaps
29. Who or when conclusion
30. Stand up to
31. Frosh, next year
32. Cantatrice's offering
33. Star seen late at night?
35. British pianist Myra
36. Good mo. for candy companies
39. Sonny's song partner
40. Drifters' classic ___ *the Roof*
43. Buckle
45. Appeared in the lead
47. Happenings
49. Chorus voice
51. Beelzebub
52. Product requirements
53. Not glossy, as a photo
54. "Fiddle-faddle!"
55. In a demure way
56. Decided failure
57. Surrounding glow
59. It's credited
63. Pint-size

Puzzle 9: Now's the Time
Easy

Across

1. Catch forty winks
5. Charger's acquisition
9. Bony fish
14. Cut from the same cloth
15. Friendly intro?
16. "Egads!"
17. Be offended by
18. College sports gp.
19. Act the lurker
20. Of lesser importance
22. Big teeth
23. Christmas carol
24. Leave it, editorially
26. Prohibit
29. Authentic
31. Breakfast order
35. Nebraska city
37. Old Soviet news agency
39. Three ___ Island
40. Puerto ___
41. Jerk's creations?
42. Opera solo
43. Stocking shade
44. Not kosher
45. Flying pests
46. Bogart film *High* ___
48. *Nautilus* captain
50. *Dick and Jane* verb
51. Actress Lollobrigida

53. Swarm
55. Chew out
58. Castles in the air
63. Like some Vatican bulls
64. Japanese people
65. "Dagnabbit"
66. Be the life of the party
67. March fifteenth, to Caesar
68. Crowning point
69. In disarray
70. Pro ___ (proportionate)
71. Moistened clay

Down

1. Glen Canyon and Grand Coulee
2. *Grapes of Wrath* character
3. Coating metal
4. "___ a high note"
5. Hogan role
6. Moving staircase
7. One of a storied threesome
8. Cafeteria items
9. Bettor's aid
10. Revolutionary War figure
11. Barely achieves, with "out"

12. A drop in the bucket, perhaps
13. "Bad!" sounds
21. Mrs. Nick Charles
25. Play horseshoes
26. Drills a hole
27. Latin friends
28. Mother-of-pearl
30. Heavily burdened
32. Turkish money units
33. Social crème de la crème
34. Add body to hair
36. Primitive timepiece
38. Trapeze artist's security
41. Comic Laurel
45. Word with movie or party
47. *Black Hawk Down* director Scott
49. Snake-haired woman of myth
52. Noted fighter of oil fires
54. Olympic quest
55. Canned meat brand
56. "And it ___ to pass . . ."
57. Major musical composition
59. Verdi opera
60. With the bow, in music
61. *I Remember* ___
62. Cherry part

Puzzle 10: Hair Today, Gone Tomorrow
Easy

Across

1. Turkish honorific
5. Colossal, moviewise
9. Woven fabric
13. Motel unit
14. Volcano shape
15. Serve broth, or a broth server
16. Short-cropped hairstyle
18. Victims of the Iroquois
19. River bottom
20. Lean (on)
21. Wavy hairstyle
22. Like some vaccines
24. Where a famous stone was discovered
25. Shoulder-length hairstyle
28. Neck and neck
29. Primal impulse
30. Hammer-operator, for example
32. Ballet step
35. Onion relatives
37. Event from 1914 to 1918, briefly
38. Compete in a bee
40. ___: A Dog
41. Birchbark watercraft
44. Savvy about
45. Trunk of a tree
46. Type of crew-cut haircut
48. Thought a lot of
51. Something ___ (extraordinary thing)
52. Rogaine alternative
53. Network signal
55. Greek letter
58. Prefix for "net" or "state"
59. Upswept hairstyle
61. Borough near Manchester
62. Hawking's *A Brief History of ___*
63. Christiania, nowadays
64. Williams and Turner
65. Wing-shaped
66. First name in slapstick

Down

1. Fine mount
2. Y2K runner-up
3. Showed off
4. "Who ___ to judge?"
5. Troops arranged in a line
6. Combine, as resources
7. Like an octopus' defense
8. Bee chaser?
9. Beatty of *Reds*
10. King's proclamation
11. Admiral's charge
12. Unit of flux
15. Some new car drivers
17. Seafood delicacy
21. Pawn to Queen's Bishop 3, for example
23. Stink to high heaven
24. Load off the mind
25. Skeet shooter's shout
26. Region
27. Displayed boredom
31. *Sands of ___ Jima*
32. Whitsunday
33. Singing voice
34. Hog filler
36. They pass the plate?
39. Kitchen equipment
42. Away from the wind
43. Woody Allen film
45. Two-footed ones
47. Burghoff's costar
48. Not perfectly upright
49. Gift recipient
50. Stifled
53. Aluminum sheet
54. Mrs. Peel on *The Avengers*
56. Maui dance
57. Its work is decreasing?
59. Sch. group sans kids
60. Spanish couple?

1	2	3	4	■	5	6	7	8	■	■	9	10	11	12
13				■	14				■	15				
16				17					■	18				
19			■	20				■	21					
■	■	22	23			■		24				■	■	■
25	26				■	27	■	28				■	■	■
29				■	30		31				■	32	33	34
35			36	■	37				■	38	39			
40			■	41	42			43	■	44				
■	■	■	45				■	46	47					
48	49	50				■	51					■	■	■
52					■	53	54			■	55	56	57	
58				■	59				■	60				
61				■	62			■	63					
64			■	65			■	66						

Puzzle 11: To the Rear
Easy

Across

1. Bolivia's capital
6. Genesis victim
10. They're for hacks
14. Rounded molding
15. Brand of toy blocks
16. Solo delivered at the Met
17. Emulating a private
20. Uncommon dice rolls
21. Type of meat or pepper
22. Works dough
23. At that time
25. The thing there
26. Biblical Promised Land
29. Bowl over
30. Did the butterfly
34. Bitter
35. Blazing
37. Mother of 6-Across
38. Getting nowhere
41. Nameless woman
42. Drops of sadness
43. Trunk with a chest
44. Old name at the pumps
46. You can dig it
47. Census unit
48. Monocle part
50. Come in behind the others

51. Borg and Edberg, for example
54. Aurora's counterpart
55. Capital on a fjord
59. In last place
62. Do high-tech surgery
63. Sandpaper surface
64. *Otello* composer
65. Makes a choice
66. Launching org.
67. Licorice-flavored seed

Down

1. Artist's studio
2. State with assurance
3. Ball-and-mallet game
4. Premier players
5. Disorderly situation
6. Sci-fi character
7. Reach for your toes
8. Fabergé creation
9. Photographer's request
10. Military trainees
11. General vicinity
12. Boston Celtic legend, Larry
13. Backtalk
18. Meadowlark's warbling cousin
19. Stuff studied in genetics
24. Tough thing to kick

25. Mary Kate and Ashley, for example
26. Secret storage spot
27. Aspirin targets
28. Closes in on
29. Prefix for "mentioned"
31. Deteriorates from use
32. Dispatch boat
33. Item in a patch
35. Seaweed extracts
36. Colorado park
39. Broadway attention-getter
40. Ripped into, as a bag of chips
45. They're golden
47. Swanky
49. Slim, slimy swimmer
50. "Whole ___ Shakin' Goin' On"
51. Town of Normandy
52. "That's a ___!" (director's shout)
53. Geographic area
54. Sponsorship
56. Wrap for a rani
57. Digital displays
58. Depression-era migrant
60. Gun owners' grp.
61. One of the Gabors

Puzzle 12: Money, Honey
Easy

Across

1. "Come to ___"
5. Horse's hock
10. Downhill aids
14. Diving duck
15. Pertaining to the moon
16. Astronomer Sagan
17. Shrewd investment
20. A three-year-old is one
21. Bridge table seat
22. Way to go
23. Rate of progress
24. Speak with spotty knowledge
26. Warship assemblage
29. Loses leaves or hair
30. Mean partner
31. Word with "tag" or "booth"
32. Public transport
35. Value appraisal
39. Engage in espionage
40. Creeping plants
41. Citrus hybrid
42. Haughty gaze
43. Fragrant resin
45. Stays on
48. Mammoth tooth
49. Certain graduate exams
50. It may stop a runaway
51. "That's yucky!"

54. Like a sound investment
58. Slight advantage
59. Indian princess
60. First gardener
61. Bassoon accessory
62. Fed the kitty
63. Word with "ghost" or "boom"

Down

1. "Ahem!"
2. A loaded gun is full of it
3. About 60 percent of the world's wetlands
4. Belt-maker's tool
5. Llama kin
6. Tend with tenderness
7. Wrinkle one's brow
8. Fond du ___ (Wisconsin city)
9. Poetic "before"
10. Moves hastily
11. Out of commission
12. Fit to be tied
13. More cunning
18. Promising clue, to a detective
19. Wall Street type
23. Twinge of distress
24. Chases away
25. Mouth-watering reading material

26. Priestly vestments
27. Harvest grain
28. It comes before happy returns
29. Less vocal
31. Is a busybody
32. Computer software glitches
33. Pacific Ten sch.
34. Milk label word, perhaps
36. Polish off
37. Heating apparatus
38. Kind of mail
42. Like some margarita glasses
43. Held up?
44. Stat equivalent
45. Crew member
46. Wear away
47. Homer Simpson's wife
48. Number of scores in sixty
50. Got going
51. Useful word processing feature
52. Emulate a beaver
53. Song of praise
55. Historical period
56. It may move you
57. Make "all gone"

Puzzle 13: Back Me Up
Easy

Across

1. Mil. branch since 1947
5. Wolfgang Puck, for example
9. Partner of Brahma and Vishnu
14. Bucks intro
15. Blast furnace sound
16. Exhibit supporter
17. English carriage
18. Something to grow on
19. American novelist Cather
20. Be last
23. They're supportive
24. Kind of duck
25. Cautiously
28. Unusually intelligent
30. Muscat's milieu
34. Swindler's name, perhaps
35. Basketmaker's willow
37. Narcissist's problem
38. Emulate a sheep
41. Weather vane letters
42. Explosives ingredient
43. Encumbrances
44. Cincinnati baseball club
46. Syndicate head
47. William Kidd, for one
48. Hand wringer's feeling
50. Direction from Eden?
51. Pull an upset
58. Without a connection
59. Musical McEntire
60. Watch part
62. Ointment
63. "I second that!"
64. Not very clear
65. UFO passenger
66. Indicates yes, in a way
67. Your family is part of one

Down

1. "Kill the ___!" (ball park cry)
2. 1999 war combatant
3. *Fort Apache* actor, 1948
4. Hereditary
5. Rock-strewn and steep
6. First word in magic
7. Dodge City lawman
8. Fingerboard ridge
9. Made a dress
10. Pageboy, for example
11. Any of the Antilles
12. The Sail (southern constellation)
13. Wing-shaped
21. Ozzie or Harriet
22. It has its reservations
25. Symbol of thinness
26. Unaccompanied
27. Agitated
28. Anemic looking
29. Marina feature
31. She was jilted by Jason
32. Secret one
33. Scandinavian language
35. Preminger or Graham
36. Dog topper
39. Having greater extent from one side to the other
40. Like some alibis
45. Turn abruptly
47. Praiseful songs
49. "Come here ___?"
50. Receded
51. What Castro calls home?
52. Milky-white gem
53. West African republic
54. Mediterranean port
55. Office note
56. Get closer to
57. Knock for a loop
61. Salinger's grain

Puzzle 14: Fool Me Once
Easy

Across

1. Altar areas
6. Lake in Africa
10. Headliner
14. Courage
15. Man of the Haus?
16. Perry Mason creator Gardner
17. Monkey business
19. Tender entree
20. Hosp. area for critical cases
21. Put on notice
22. Sunny and bright, as a personality
24. Beat it
26. Oblique
28. Told a fish story
30. Sea creature that may be smoked
31. Wrestling official
34. Bowler's nightmare
37. ___ St. Vincent Millay
39. Occupy the throne
40. Bit of baloney
43. Pay to join the hand
44. Someone usually brings it up
45. Famous Colorado peak
46. Encouraging word
47. It can be fresh or hot

48. Visibility reducer
50. Right to enter
53. Chronological records
57. Beatty of *Bonnie & Clyde*
59. Some sturdy trees
61. Monotonous routine
62. Golden Fleece ship
63. Horseplay
66. What equestrians hold
67. Mater starter
68. Honey badger
69. Show restlessness, in a way
70. Goatish glance
71. Greta Garbo was one

Down

1. Agricultural pest
2. Take the silver
3. Break of day
4. Catholic theologian who opposed Luther
5. Design meaningful contrails
6. Blacken, as meat
7. Redhead's secret?
8. Covenant holder
9. Work for George Jefferson
10. Common dice roll
11. Bole

12. Controversial pesticide
13. Bank (on)
18. Finely chopped liver
23. Roach of Hollywood
25. One of *The Honeymooners*
27. Madrid Misters
29. Puts off until later
32. Ultimatum ender
33. Fixed charges
34. Prepare for a bout
35. ___ colada
36. Sluggish
38. Modern-day evidence
39. Royal rule
41. Type of rug
42. Backers with the bucks
47. Top of a suit
49. Shark variety
51. Witchlike woman
52. River past Amiens
54. Sharp narrow mountain ridge
55. Enticed
56. What the rich live in?
57. Get bent out of shape
58. Field or field of expertise
60. A distant point
64. Grand-Opry connector
65. Order partner

1	2	3	4	5	■	6	7	8	9	■	10	11	12	13
14					■	15				■	16			
17					18					■	19			
20			■	21				■	22	23				
24			25			■	26	27				■	■	■
■	■	■	28			29	■	30			■	31	32	33
34	35	36			■	37	38			■	39			
40				41					■	42				
43			■	44				■	45					
46			■	47			■	48	49			■	■	■
■	■	50	51				52	■	53			54	55	56
57	58				■	59	60			■	61			
62			■	63	64				■	65				
66			■	67				■	68					
69			■	70				■	71					

Puzzle 15: Nice House!
Easy

Across

1. "Abraham, Martin, and John" singer
5. Switch partner
9. Family men
14. Part of a magician's phrase
15. It could be part of a plot
16. Woolly-haired cud chewer
17. Scouts' supervisor
19. Its first is for fools
20. Certain playing marble
21. Roald Dahl book
23. What libraries do
24. Nevada's second largest city
25. Knights-in-training
28. Word with "ill," "well," or "mild"
32. "Tut-tut!"
33. Purplish colors
35. Fish with a long snout
36. Bestowed titles
37. Sisters' three
38. Until all hours
39. Swell place?
40. Sleep inducers, once
41. "Rag Mop" brothers
42. Arrange with some effort
44. They take the cake
45. Heading for morph
46. Also known as H.H. Munro
48. Hard to interpret
51. Place for Earl Grey and light snacks
55. Natural talent
56. Between-classes area
58. Quiz answer, perhaps
59. Construction wood
60. Lamb's *Essays of* ___
61. Knight's mount
62. Goes on and on and . . .
63. Claim innocence

Down

1. Some family members
2. "Likely story!"
3. Alencon is its capital
4. How some shall remain
5. Drive home, as a run
6. Yearned
7. Fury
8. Prison stretch
9. Typewriter rollers
10. Skiing style
11. Charades or Pictionary, say
12. Centrally located
13. Hacienda room
18. Shouts at a bullfight
22. *Gunsmoke* star
25. Like yesterday's news
26. Completely unfamiliar
27. Neighborhood event
28. One deep in thought
29. State point-blank
30. Polished-off
31. Kind of rehearsal
33. Sort of shower
34. Tennis legend Arthur
38. Expended profusely
40. Hung in there
43. Cut into
44. Word of assent
46. Was awful
47. Culex's cousin
48. Switch positions
49. Utter loudly
50. Glimpse from afar
52. Hearty partner
53. Lena of *Havana*
54. Kind of bill
57. Familia member

Puzzle 16: Fire!
Easy

Across

1. Hot, melted cheese dish
6. ___ of the tongue
10. Pantheon members
14. ___ of expertise
15. Deteriorated
16. Fencing sword
17. U.S. ambassador's employer
20. Came apart at the seams
21. Arabian Sea gulf
22. Thickness
23. Hay unit
25. Relations
26. Internal combustion device
33. Standoffish
34. Souvenirs from 53-Down
35. Bond creator Fleming
37. "___ of Love" (Bacharach song)
38. Looks ___ everything
40. "Lamp ___ My Feet"
41. Sternward
42. The "dismal science," for short
43. ___ Joe (Twain character)
44. McQueen film classic
48. Grow older
49. River leading to the Caspian
50. Line dance

53. It grows on trees
55. Words of horror
59. Union in Chicago, for example
62. It turns a bachelor into a woman
63. "Add ___ to the fire"
64. Pang
65. "___ light through yonder window . . ."
66. It can precede the last word of 17-, 26-, 44- and 59-Across
67. They may be found hanging in malls

Down

1. Like some inaccurate watches
2. "___ take arms against . . ." (*Hamlet*)
3. Within shouting distance
4. You can plan on it
5. ___ NO HOOKS
6. Garbo's homeland
7. Easy stride
8. Persia, since 1935
9. ___ capita
10. Sign of the twins
11. Essay page, for short
12. Nick's kin?
13. Dickens' Pecksniff
18. Painter of limp watches
19. Sprigs

24. Houseguest from Melmac
25. Purl counterpart
26. Swinging event
27. Among the clouds
28. Starter for "fast" or "sayer"
29. "Maria ___" (Dorsey hit, 1941)
30. Poetic time of day
31. Type of warrior
32. Really enjoy
36. What one little piggy had
38. 43,560 square feet
39. Certain egg mass
40. Disrobe
42. Actress Samantha
43. Rose-rose connector
45. Bald baby bird?
46. Skirmish
47. Once, once
50. All hands on deck?
51. Curse or vow
52. Actress Talbot or Naldi
53. A Hawaiian island
54. Polish border river
56. Give employment to
57. When many go to lunch
58. Unnamed people or things
60. Out of tune
61. Ma Bell

Puzzle 17: Mr. Fix-it
Easy

Across

1. Worldly rather than spiritual
5. Bringing up the rear
9. Pound prospect
14. "Money ___ object"
15. Length × width
16. Cast mightily
17. Quit working
19. Instrument at the ballpark
20. Removes by ballot
21. Elbow counterpart
23. Suffix with "lemon" or "lime"
24. Nautical hazard
26. Come to the rescue
30. Cola mixers
32. "If ___ say so myself"
34. Green Gables girl
35. Fly in the ointment
37. TV time that begins in the evening
39. Mommy deerest?
40. Not available for use
43. Canton in Switzerland
44. Trumped-up
45. They'll question you
46. Invite letters
48. Short winter illness
49. Take wing

50. Do a slow burn
52. Prerequisite for gain?
54. Greek letter
57. Woofer output
59. Refrigerator drawer
61. Argo pilot
64. Went to pieces
66. Tale of the Trojan War
67. City in Yemen
68. The vain put them on
69. Well-bred Londoners
70. Velvety growth
71. Lazy Susan, for example

Down

1. Astrological sign
2. Start of a comparison involving a beet
3. Not running
4. Blast-furnace fuel
5. Soup dippers
6. "___ by any other name . . ."
7. Hem, but not haw
8. It may be full of gas
9. Closet staples
10. Mother of mercy
11. Certain piano piece
12. Sinatra's Gardner
13. It's tender to the Japanese

18. Drum cover?
22. Wynonna's mom
25. Braces
27. Needing parts
28. Condescending type
29. They're between 12 and 20
31. Sci-fi vehicle
33. Phone call cost, in Bogart films
35. Goes bad, as milk
36. Nightingale or Barton, for example
37. Survey
38. Baltic republic
41. Coffeehouses
42. One of the seven water sources
47. Kennedy's was 109
49. Warning devices
51. Clock parts
53. Highest points
55. ___ firma
56. ___-craftsy
58. Hoodwink
60. Minor quarrel
61. Rustic dance
62. Hearty pub order
63. Pride, lust, or envy
65. Fuss

1	2	3	4	■	5	6	7	8	■	9	10	11	12	13
14				■	15				■	16				
17				18					■	19				
20						■	21	22			■	■	■	■
23			■	24			25	■	26			27	28	29
■	■	30	31			■	32	33		■	34			
35	36				■	37			■	38	■	39		
40				41					■	■	42			
43			■	44				■	45					
46			47	■	48			■	49			■	■	■
50				51		■	52	53			■	54	55	56
■	■	■	57			58	■	59			60			
61	62	63			■	64	65							
66					■	67				■	68			
69					■	70				■	71			

Puzzle 18: Top Performance
Easy

Across

1. A good one is usually square
5. The end, in Revelation
10. Snatch
14. Auto part
15. Punic Wars soldier
16. Dude ranch prop
17. Renders suspect
19. Protected, nautically
20. Brothers who popularized "Mom always liked you best!"
21. Fruity-smelling chemical compounds
23. Australia's largest lake
24. Homesteader's stake
25. Farm measures
27. Comes into one's own
30. Which cheek to turn?
31. Word with "booby" or "sand"
32. Sandra or Ruby
33. Occasion at Minsky's
34. Cleaners' concern
35. Small price to pay
36. Plumber's connection
37. The Hatfields and the McCoys, for example
38. Teen hangouts
39. Having a finger in every pie
41. Oater prop
42. Appears
43. Columnist Barrett
44. Common airline carry-on
46. Meathead, to Archie
50. Mr. Gardner's first name
51. Way out West, once
53. Glum drop?
54. More than merely ready
55. Jasmine or morning glory, for example
56. Verbalizes
57. Isn't supporting
58. Resurgently

Down

1. Raincoats, in Liverpool
2. Academic challenge
3. "And another thing . . ."
4. Received a varsity award
5. They may be marching
6. Van Dyke co-star
7. Layers of green eggs
8. Some consider it a gift
9. Deer playmate, in song
10. Without charge
11. They're often emulated
12. Copycat
13. Partner of birds
18. Less vocal
22. Talk trash to
24. Smackers
25. Whale of ___
26. Simple task, for example
27. Fetch
28. Edison's park
29. The sun does it every day
30. Neighbor of Provo
31. Mission start?
34. Sneaks a peek
35. Amorously inclined male
37. Asp victim, for short
38. Word with depressive
40. Puts a damper on
41. Extreme introverts
43. Received, at NASA
44. Answer to "Shall we?"
45. Kind of rug
46. *Roots,* for example
47. (Has) reclined
48. Teenage problem that breaks out
49. Exclamation of exertion
52. Tit for ___

1	2	3	4	■	5	6	7	8	9	■	10	11	12	13
14				■	15					■	16			
17				18						■	19			
20							■	21	22					
■	■		23				■	24				■	■	■
■	25	26				■	27					28	29	
30					■	31				■	32			
33			■	34					■	35				
36			■	37				■	38					
39			40				■	41					■	■
■	■	42				■	43				■	■	■	■
44	45				■	46				47	48	49		
50			■	51	52				■					
53			■	54				■	55					
56			■	57				■	58					

Puzzle 19: Bye!
Easy

Across

1. Unexpected development
6. Kind of tense?
10. Felt sorry about
14. *The Good ___* (Pearl Buck)
15. Grades 1-12, for short
16. Golden rule preposition
17. Knightly wear
18. Appear imminent
19. Evening, in some ads
20. Classic sitcom
23. Lobe's location
24. Actress Deborah
25. 1900, on a cornerstone
28. South of the border order
31. Ran amok en masse
35. Flower of one's eye?
37. Sticky-tongued critter
39. Ex-New York governor, Mario
40. Careless disregard
43. Causing chill bumps
44. Lilliputian
45. Collection of facts
46. Loofah, for example
48. Peon
50. "May I help you?"

51. Coastal flooding factor
53. Western treaty grp.
55. "To boldly go," for example
63. Branch of math
64. Conflicted
65. Submarine equipment
66. Per
67. Designer Cassini
68. Those opposed
69. Denial from Yeltsin
70. Figure of interest
71. Sierra ___

Down

1. Short-necked duck
2. Silver ending?
3. *My Friend ___*
4. Kitchen appliance
5. Bit of saber-rattling
6. Clobber with snowballs
7. "Thanks ___ !"
8. Rattled
9. Woodsman's cry
10. Evasive treatment
11. Inst. of higher learning
12. Novel ending?
13. Procrastinator's opposite
21. Incensed

22. Writer Jong
25. Bogs down
26. Move in typical rush-hour traffic
27. Prefix for "phone" or "miniskirt"
29. Part of any profit calculation
30. Mirage subject
32. Before midnight
33. Overact
34. Ladies of Spain
36. Close-fitting, as an outfit
38. Citizen of Denmark
41. On the up and up
42. "Don Juan" poet
47. Newspaper executive
49. Saudi Arabian king
52. Gay over Hiroshima
54. Biblical weapon
55. British weapon
56. Evangelist's suggestion
57. Wingless suckers
58. Guitar part
59. *Come Back, Little Sheba* playwright
60. "Out of the frying pan, ___ . . ."
61. Stuck on oneself
62. Irish language

Puzzle 20: New Shoes
Easy

Across
1. Hole in a Vegas machine
5. Teeny finish
11. Watch the baby
14. Vagrant
15. Maryland state bird
16. Sting action
17. He's no pro
18. Stunk up the place
19. Marching syllable
20. One shoe
23. Wallach of *The Two Jakes*
24. Hero in *The Matrix*
25. Canine coating
28. Ecclesiastical assembly
30. Surveillance org.
33. Tarzan's weapon
34. "My country ___ of thee . . ."
36. Percent addition
38. Common knowledge
39. One shoe
42. Three-toed bird
44. Sherpa's beast of burden
45. Lamb's mama
46. Change, as bylaws
48. Baking meas.
50. Wealthy John Jacob
54. Cement mixture
56. Keeper's charge
58. Stand buy
59. One shoe
63. Bearded beast
65. Fountain sound
66. Suffix with "gab" or "slug"
67. Summer mo.
68. Ogle
69. Electrical safeguard
70. Game-deciding stat
71. Walks onstage
72. Engage in repartee

Down
1. Some eyewear
2. In need of companionship
3. Gain possession of
4. Work hard
5. Water or air attachment
6. Eugene's place
7. Like Browning's piper
8. Nudge
9. Professeur's charge
10. Loss indicator, on paper
11. Plotting
12. Gambler's last resort
13. Blasting material
21. Home of the sacred cow
22. Poodles and pit bulls, for example
26. Gee antecedent
27. Sign in the zodiac
29. European strait
31. Jockey's attire
32. Foreman fighter
35. Optimist's limit
37. Vane direction
39. Rathskeller vessels
40. Have something
41. "All ___ for Christmas is my two . . ."
42. Battering device
43. Medical service grp.
47. Be suspended
49. Structural support
51. Begin, as a hobby
52. *Potemkin* mutiny locale
53. One paying a flat fee?
55. Where Joan of Arc died
57. Moscovite's negatives
60. ___-a-porter (ready to wear)
61. Shrek, for one
62. Switch positions
63. Deficit
64. Bolt's adjunct

Puzzle 21: Lit Up
Easy

Across

1. "Once ___ time . . ."
6. Featherbrain
10. Use a bubble pipe
14. French philosopher Georges
15. Anagram of vile
16. Another anagram of vile
17. Doberman's warning
18. Absolute must
19. Gazetteer datum
20. What a firefly does
23. Shade tree
24. Fire, so to speak
25. Move out
29. Overdo the TLC
31. Play piece
34. Revered image
35. Plumbing problem
37. Charmed animal?
39. Polishes the pumps
42. E-mail predecessor
43. Fast time?
44. Remote button
45. Balaam's transport
46. Word in a song performed at midnight
48. TV screen grid
50. Roadie's load
51. Perched
52. Feels puffed up
60. Cornfield measure
61. Malarial fever
62. Mixologist on *The Love Boat*
64. Companion of thick
65. Kimono cousin
66. Part of UHF
67. Warty-skinned critter
68. "Phooey!"
69. Implied

Down

1. Destroyer letters
2. Ping-___
3. ___ Roberts University
4. Seneca's student
5. Completely off-base
6. Levi's material
7. Where one's goose is cooked?
8. Atkins offering
9. Outdated
10. Main part of a knife
11. It equaled 100 kurus
12. Partner of "done with"
13. Like light-colored coffee
21. Bob's vehicles?
22. Biz bigwigs
25. Panoramic view
26. Charley horses
27. Spring features
28. Frank with a famous diary
29. Went to a fancy restaurant
30. Candid
31. Give or take
32. Minoan's island
33. Stun gun
36. 50 pennies
38. Resistance units
40. Finals
41. Bikini part
47. Northbound, on maps
49. Courtyard
50. Change a bill
51. Ream component
52. Cotton stuffing
53. Sound effect
54. High point at the Met
55. Humpbacked helper
56. Brass member
57. Avalon, for one
58. Facts and figures
59. Bring in
63. Kind of burglar

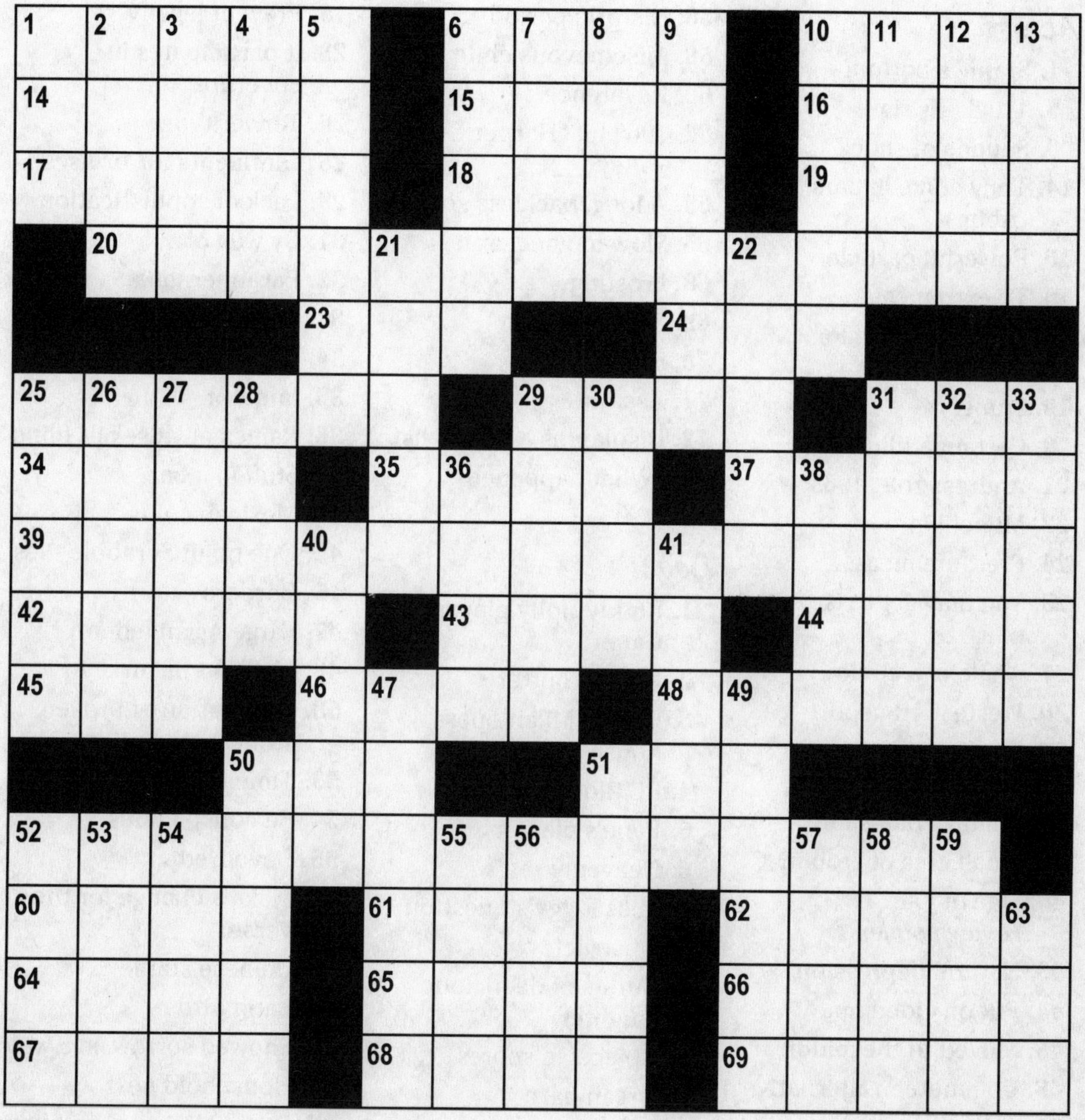

Puzzle 22: Getting Around
Easy

Across

1. Statue's bottom
5. Trucker's rig
9. Sounds of shock
14. They come in bars (Abbr.)
15. Powerful particle
16. To extremes
17. *The Enterprise,* for example
19. Stupefy
20. Certain addition
21. Andress role, 1965
22. Munchkin
24. Pressure meas.
25. You may get a rise out of it
27. Angle of a circle
30. Western transport
35. Like some famous fables
38. Military blockade
39. Small area of ground
40. One of *The Honeymooners*
43. Natural depression
44. Put on cloud nine
46. Moved to the middle
48. Commuter's alternative
51. Selfish person
52. Symbols of silliness
56. Historic period
59. Mischievous child
60. Reverence
62. 1968 hit "Harper Valley ___"
63. A long, backless sofa
65. Slow-moving craft
68. Frosting
69. At the summit
70. Farm section
71. Assays
72. Display, as a dean's list
73. "What happened next . . ."

Down

1. Buddy Holly player Gary
2. Kind of butter
3. La ___, Milan opera house
4. PC tilde topper
5. Pane's place
6. Heavenly
7. Miss Piggy's question
8. Obstruct
9. Bursts of deep, loud laughter
10. Apiece, in scores
11. Organ part
12. Those with know-how
13. Bombay dress
18. Prevent legally
23. It participates in coverups
26. Terrier type
28. Ointments for bruises
29. Lack of sophistication
31. By way of
32. Paraphernalia
33. Girl-watch or boy-watch
34. Can't live without
35. Imitator
36. Raines of '40s–'50s films
37. Stuff in a bar?
41. Mexican coins
42. One-point Scrabble tiles
45. Borders
47. Large Asian feline
49. Male cat or turkey
50. Foundation of broken stones
53. Time to remember
54. Be conspicuous
55. Devoured
56. Make a change for the verse?
57. Chinese staple
58. Latin bird
61. Showed sorrow, in a way
64. Household pest
66. Prime Minister Hirobumi
67. Cave creature

Puzzle 23: Kingdoms
Easy

Across

1. Male cheerleader's move
5. Ball's partner
10. Syndicate bigwig
14. "Texaco ___ Theater"
15. "Who goes ___?"
16. First guy
17. King of sports
20. Autocrat
21. Drive back
22. Fat farm feature
24. Summer, in France
25. Try not to be pinned down?
27. Quiets down
29. Unmixed, to a mixologist
30. Gained a lap
31. Sandusky's lake
32. Stopped marching
34. King of cable
39. Burden bearers
40. Factory whistle time, perhaps
42. Certain bunt, on a scorecard
45. Kind of market or circus
46. Scandal subject, in the music business
48. Went after
50. Attila, for one
51. Relay segment
52. Plenty sore
53. Year-end temps
55. King of horror
60. Geometry class calculation
61. Way to go
62. Word repeated after "Que"
63. Long and lean
64. This snake counts?
65. Site of temptation

Down

1. Acid, to a hippie
2. "What was ___ think?"
3. Disney film of 1940
4. City betrayed by a horse?
5. Plate appearances
6. River through Lyons
7. Barber's call
8. Jackie's second spouse
9. Path to enlightenment
10. Bistros
11. Turns a book into a film, for example
12. *Dallas* role
13. Breakfast or brunch order
18. For the taking
19. Gingerbread house visitor
22. Any ship at sea
23. Knitting stitch
25. Whip marks
26. Tat-tat preceder
28. Trumpeter Alpert
29. 1993 treaty acronym
32. Watered the lawn
33. Fashion initials
35. Stop at the pump
36. Ivy League school
37. Backyard building
38. Meadow rodent
41. Old horse
42. Tap type
43. Northern sky sight
44. Chicken-hearted
46. Fourth-down specialist
47. Poker-pot starter
49. "Turf," not "surf"
50. It makes waste
53. Breeding horse
54. Basilica end
56. Gershwin or Levin
57. Ground layer
58. Before, to Browning
59. Palindromic Bobbsey

Puzzle 24: Connected
Easy

Across

1. Mite
5. Type of car in San Francisco
10. Salt measure
14. Bonito shark
15. Galactic visitor
16. Raines of *Phantom Lady*
17. Neutral hue
18. Charlton Heston epic
19. Handy to
20. No-goodnik
22. Pilfer
24. They can bear cafeteria food
26. You can't row, row, row your boat without one
27. Checkers, compared to chess
30. How some boxers fight
35. Crookedly
36. Zodiac dozen
37. Coffeehouse container
38. Cookie selling org., originally
39. Held title to
40. ___ for tat
41. Back muscle, to a bodybuilder
42. Sidewinder, for one
43. Man with many parts
45. How some like to see things
47. Quick on the uptake
48. Humble dwelling
49. Less common
51. Uno, for one
54. After a while
58. Holder of combs, perfumes, and so on
59. Gerald Ford's birthplace
62. Heavenly glow
63. Give some lip to
64. Pat or Richard
65. Word with "line" or "post"
66. The other team
67. Wield, as influence
68. Princely Italian family

Down

1. Brothers who sang "Rag Mop"
2. Crunchy Tex-Mex munchie
3. Stew vegetable
4. Dudley Do-Right, for example
5. Julius or Sid
6. Metal mixture
7. Pen or lighter
8. Sweet-smelling necklace
9. Contiguous
10. *Taxi Driver* star
11. On the safe side, at sea
12. Montenegro native
13. Fabled fast starter
21. Accepted a gunslinger's challenge
23. Pillboxes and porkpies
25. Word in a Bugs Bunny catchphrase
27. Bird of prey
28. Ore examination
29. Make tracks on ice
31. Molding type
32. "___ Frutti" (Little Richard tune)
33. Celestial hunter
34. Journal item
36. Dance romantically
39. Kind of confrontation
42. Causing puckering
43. Vicinity
44. Horror film feature, sometimes
46. Belief in one God
47. Legendary Bear of Alabama
50. Find loathsome
51. Bird's-___ soup
52. Beehive State
53. Erato, for one
55. Twosomes
56. Impish one
57. Harvard rival
60. Be sociable
61. Give the heave-ho

¹	²	³	⁴	■	⁵	⁶	⁷	⁸	⁹	■	¹⁰	¹¹	¹²	¹³

Puzzle 25: Visiting the Zoo
Easy

Across

1. Gossipy gal
6. Lift in Aspen
10. Wild way to run?
14. Purfle
15. Dashiell's colleague
16. Prom-goer's pursuit
17. Network test show
18. Word with "act" or "gear"
19. Hardly ruddy
20. Snitcher
23. Peg of the links?
24. For each
25. Fast North American snakes
27. Start for "day" or "wife"
30. Forster's had a view
33. Peter the Great, for example
34. Sal the mule's canal
36. Lustrous gem
38. Aluminum manufacturer
41. Fall guy
44. Shenanigan
45. House of Lords title
46. Jidda native
47. Swedish chain
49. Gestured greeting
51. Like some wines
52. Picked out
54. "Murder, ___"
56. She may feel cooped up
57. Easy target
64. Asian caregiver
66. Tie at anchor
67. Insurance ploy
68. One in a million
69. Oppositionist
70. Berry's Johnny B.
71. Cameo stone
72. Pinky and Spike
73. Toaster, often

Down

1. Talks noisily
2. Cut out the boring scenes
3. "___ contendere" (no contest plea)
4. Group of Girl Scouts, for example
5. Deer's tine
6. Dustin's *Tootsie* costar
7. Cell at sea
8. Succulent perennial
9. Witty reply
10. 1961 Susan Hayward film
11. Plastic supplier?
12. Wise leader
13. *The Jolson Story* actress
21. Smoking gun
22. Describing the nose passages
26. Lily variety
27. Flat tableland with steep edges
28. It's south of Georgia
29. Definitive book?
31. Mayberry resident
32. Colorful parrot
35. Satie and Estrada
37. Italian coin no longer minted
39. Mr. Sharif
40. "Dear" adviser
42. Slurpees competitors
43. Famous chipmunk
48. Member of a certain kingdom
50. Mesh gears
52. Gyrating guitarist
53. Defender of Castle Greyskull
55. Computer drive insert
58. Tuning fork's output
59. Shopping bag
60. Subject for Monet
61. Sports org. based in Colorado
62. Secret language
63. Dummy's perch
65. Evil spell

1	2	3	4	5		6	7	8	9		10	11	12	13
14						15					16			
17						18					19			
20					21					22		23		
			24						25		26			
27	28	29		30		31	32		33					
34			35		36			37		38			39	40
41				42					43					
44					45					46				
		47			48		49			50		51		
52	53								54		55			
56				57		58	59	60				61	62	63
64			65		66					67				
68					69					70				
71				72					73				

Puzzle 26: What Did You Say?
Easy

Across

1. Weakens, as support
5. Thin cracker
10. Pack gently
14. Hoodwink
15. Bakery lure
16. Above
17. Approach the gate
18. Businesses
19. Spanish surrealist
20. Madison and Lincoln, for example
23. Reason for a shot in the arm?
25. Boat's stopover
26. Beneficiary
27. Brisk
29. Senior celebration
31. Speedy delivery
35. Blubber
38. Stink big-time
39. Some oilmen
40. Fashion magazine
41. Be human, so they say
42. 18th Amendment outgrowths
44. Officer Malloy of *Adam 12*
45. Ditto!
46. One place to roll in
49. Forefather
52. FDR's successor
53. Baloney!
57. Campus sports org.
58. Cropped up
59. Important stretches of time
62. "Now hear ___"
63. South Korea's capital
64. Apportion
65. New Year's word
66. Great expectations
67. Inkling

Down

1. Young newt
2. Constrictor, for example
3. Church meal, perhaps
4. Buttonhole, for example
5. Floats through the air
6. Israel's Sharon
7. Military might
8. Samms of *Dynasty*
9. Grating sound
10. Hand-beaten drum
11. Birdlike
12. Haggard songwriter?
13. The written word
21. Hand lender
22. Matinee is one kind
23. "___ Jacques"
24. Less strict
28. Annoy
29. Monopoly place
30. Shine's partner
32. Mo. for sapphires
33. Barrie bad guy
34. She played Rosemary
35. Emulated a snake
36. Spreads on breads
37. Ply with drink
40. Legal conclusion?
42. Tiresias, for one
43. Pre-meal word, perhaps
44. Gratify
46. Cousin providers
47. Like some trigger fingers
48. Laundry problem
49. Eavesdropper
50. Magazine installment
51. Staggers
54. *A Beautiful Mind* subject
55. Cookie treat
56. Big rig
60. Partook of
61. Kind of horse

Puzzle 27: Two of a Kind
Easy

Across

1. German family member
5. Bossa ___
9. *Avalon* author
14. Doctor's advice
15. Steel girder
16. "Rawhide" singer
17. Put one's chips on the table?
18. To a smaller extent
19. Think alike
20. Wedded pair
23. Net receipt?
24. Physics particles
25. Sports network
28. She played Laurie Partridge
29. Be beholden to
31. ___ Paulo, Brazil
33. Tic-tac-toe winner
34. Cowgirl Dale
36. Protective covering
38. Quiet business associate
42. Part of a play
43. Evidence of cooking
44. Herd word
45. Afternoon affair
48. Type of liner
49. It's pressed for cash
52. First name in mysteries
54. Jazzy Fitzgerald
56. Turf starter
58. Certain look-alike
61. Garden gastropod
63. On the apex
64. Key partner
65. Camping digs
66. Hardly genteel
67. Sal the mule's canal
68. Out
69. Earned a citation
70. "I guess so"

Down

1. Like mirrors and windows
2. Appellative change
3. How the innocent may be led
4. Development areas?
5. World's longest river
6. Yielding to supervision
7. ___ da Gama
8. Illegal firings?
9. Stick starter
10. Two below par
11. Tedious
12. Penultimate word in a countdown
13. Part of an extended name
21. "What a great gift!"
22. Patriotic shout
26. Flimsy, as an excuse
27. Neither counterpart
30. Pallid
32. Kind of cookie
34. Wallach, for one
35. Treadmill site
37. Genetic messenger letters
38. Mark left by a healed wound
39. Pisa residents
40. Three-digit number
41. Singer Orbison
42. Lincoln's nickname
46. Velvet ender
47. Religious platforms
49. On the job
50. Nixon's daughter
51. Business beginner
53. Corrects copy
55. Illuminated
57. Pope of the fifth century
59. Apart from this
60. Did a Little bit?
61. NASCAR advertiser
62. Class-conscious org.?

1	2	3	4		5	6	7	8		9	10	11	12	13
14					15					16				
17					18					19				
20				21				22						
23						24				25		26	27	
28				29	30			31		32		33		
			34				35			36	37			
	38	39						40	41					
42							43							
44				45	46	47		48				49	50	51
52			53		54		55			56	57			
	58		59					60						
61	62				63					64				
65					66					67				
68					69					70				

Puzzle 28: Physically Fit
Easy

Across

1. Hula-Hoops, lava lamps, and so on
5. Colored portion of the eye
9. Confound
14. "Hard ___!" (helmsman's cry)
15. Vegas lighting
16. At no time
17. Cerebellum section
18. Certain short skirt
19. Sports setting, sometimes
20. In great shape
23. Immature newt
24. The go-to guys on staffs
25. Choir members
29. Beer-drinker's overhang
30. Married Italian woman
31. Spick-and-span
34. Narrow strip of wood
36. Cork source
37. In excellent condition
41. Brain wave record
42. It's good when they meet
43. Church recesses
44. Bitter, as in taste
47. Part of a Morse code letter
48. What tennis balls are packaged in, typically
49. Support in wrongdoing
51. Calendar abbr.
54. In fine fettle
57. Bow application
60. Electricity conductor
61. Inspiration for an author
62. Amid
63. Aroma if pleasant, smell if bad?
64. Exclamation of sorrow
65. Ridges of wind-blown sand
66. Oculist's piece
67. Ancient musical instrument

Down

1. Trumped-up
2. Emotionally detached
3. Broadway opening
4. Scene homophone
5. Still in one piece
6. Recycle
7. Very small amounts
8. Cold-shoulder
9. Similar to another thing
10. Arthurian magician
11. Cousin of St. or Blvd.
12. Buddhist sect
13. Bullpen stat
21. Intimidate
22. Andrew Lloyd Webber musical
26. Beer from Golden, Colorado
27. Obliterate
28. "Land ___ alive!"
29. "Sleepy Time ___" (1925 song)
30. Insolence
31. Flimflam
32. Freeloader
33. Enthusiastic
34. Put in harmony
35. *A Shropshire ___*
38. It should set off alarms
39. Country on the island of Hispaniola
40. Choose
45. Process, as sugar
46. Homo sapiens, for example
47. Yields
49. Stage whisper, perhaps
50. Title of nobility
51. Strangely
52. Understandable
53. Display poor sportsmanship
55. MP's prey
56. I–XII locale
57. X-ray unit
58. Cassowary kin
59. Wally, to Ward

1	2	3	4		5	6	7	8		9	10	11	12	13
14					15					16				
17					18					19				
20				21					22					
23				24					25			26	27	28
			29					30						
31	32	33				34	35					36		
37					38					39	40			
41					42					43				
44			45	46					47					
48							49	50				51	52	53
			54			55					56			
57	58	59				60					61			
62						63					64			
65						66					67			

Puzzle 29: Opposites Attract
Easy

Across

1. Expressed disdain, in a way
6. Computer info
10. It may cause one to scratch one's head
14. Relative of the giraffe
15. Prayer finale
16. Draft animal
17. Leading
19. Domain of a king and queen
20. *Get Smart* enemy spy org.
21. Vex
22. Maniacs
24. Christiana, today
26. Endangered giant
27. Some long-time Manhattanites?
31. Prepare to propose
32. Where you can be all you can be?
33. Some change it regularly
35. Thumbs-up votes
36. Apothecary measures
38. Dance that tells a story
39. One feted in June
40. Automatic start?
41. Small digit
42. Laura Bush?

46. Use it to stand tall
47. Alley cry
48. Literary spoof
50. Tampa Bay NFLer
51. 1871 Verdi opera
55. Gang's territory
56. Cookout leftover?
59. Central Asian sea
60. Hooligan
61. Telemarketer's necessity
62. R&B singer Marvin
63. Hook's underling
64. Fishy or fishing stories

Down

1. Left the ground (with "off")
2. Northern seabird
3. "Green Hornet" driver
4. Sitcom segments
5. "Gunga ___"
6. Scopes' defender
7. One way to run
8. Alexander Hamilton bill
9. Some small colonies
10. Obstruct
11. Reverse course
12. Lummox
13. They're tailor-made
18. Register as a candidate

23. One of Pac-Man's pursuers
25. NBC show for three decades, briefly
26. Skin opening
27. Ryan or Tatum
28. Guide down the wrong path
29. Mr. Arafat
30. Soft and smooth
31. *The Spanish Tragedy* dramatist
34. "Now I ___ me down to sleep"
36. Blocks
37. Leave out
38. Longfellow's Native American hero
40. Cook's instruction
41. Al Fatah's org.
43. Repress
44. Mark from dirty fingers
45. Type of support
48. Large male deer
49. Saintly quality
50. Sad color?
52. Worshiped celeb
53. Completed
54. Word on a toy package
57. Electrician's measure
58. Decide

Puzzle 30: Careful!
Easy

Across

1. Off-the-cuff comment
6. Fearless and daring
10. Electrical framework
14. Fess Parker role
15. Polo explored it
16. Gave a hard time to
17. Dead end
19. Shakespeare's stream
20. Still, to poets
21. Small combo
22. Beautiful
24. Italian greeting
25. Address for a king
26. Impediment
32. Task for a child
33. Sounds coming from inside a bowl
34. Forty-niner's tool
35. Decorative vases
36. Approached with stealth
38. Locks in a barn?
39. Hillbilly band instrument
40. Downfall
41. Word in some temperature readings
42. Place for hurdles
46. Fit of shivering
47. Encourage heartily

48. Self-evident truth
51. Etc. relative
52. Faux ___ (blunder)
55. Word with "dance" or "union"
56. Traffic-jam cause
59. River through Pisa
60. Beach bird
61. Ranchero's rope
62. Verb with "down" or "out"
63. Target of a swift kick
64. Nautical spar

Down

1. Ex of Cugie
2. 1996 presidential-race loser
3. Choice meat cut
4. Room offerer
5. "Nighty-night" time
6. King of Scotland, 1292–96
7. Scandinavian capital
8. Tell it like it isn't
9. Vampire's undoing
10. Driveway stones
11. Travel randomly
12. Joss house figure
13. Declare untrue
18. Damascus resident

23. The sun, moon, and planets, for example
24. Mutts
25. Rice Krispies sound
26. Hedge unit
27. Ice cube grabbers
28. "Goodnight ___"
29. Gemstones from Australia
30. Craft for Pocahontas
31. Was familiar with
32. Stephen King novel
36. Salad ingredient
37. Ruffle feathers
38. A ___ bagatelle
40. From ___ to riches
41. "Taps" players
43. One who hems but doesn't haw
44. Single-masted sailing vessel
45. Tough exam
48. Dissolve, as ice
49. Pink, to a chef
50. It parallels a radius
51. Sicilian rumbler
52. Anjou or bosc
53. Play opener
54. Card game for three
57. Piece of mine?
58. Tuck partner

Puzzle 31: A Little Seasoning
Easy

Across

1. Isaac Hayes classic
6. Some files
11. Did not stand for it?
14. "I ___ Symphony," (Supremes hit)
15. Keep from happening
16. Alleged mentalist Geller
17. Post-thaw restlessness
19. Election-year ammo, maybe
20. Word with "boot" or "pole"
21. Wool coat wearer
22. Executive's deg.
23. Lovey-dovey
27. Short end of the stick
29. Lord of the ring, once
30. Twice-monthly tide
32. Bring up, as kids
33. Way over there
34. Sticks together, in a way
36. Phonograph records
39. Aware of
41. Maze word
43. Red's meaning, at times
44. Holders of many frames
46. Spud
48. Lord's Prayer opener
49. Descartes the mathematician

51. Founder of *Time* and *Life*
52. Bean counter, for short
53. Apt to break
56. Janitor's aid
58. Surfing site
59. Part of TGIF
60. Hawaiian garland
61. Wall St. deal
62. World Series
68. Feather mate
69. Arctic shelter
70. Dubya's wife
71. Street often near Oak
72. Out of humor
73. Chilling forecast

Down

1. Calls for quiet
2. Cool, in the '50s
3. Bernese flower
4. Search, as a perp
5. Doing horribly
6. Spitfire org.
7. "Hail!" to Horace
8. Discontinue, as relations
9. Period prior to 1941, in the United States
10. Scattered about
11. Certain theater productions

12. Caribbean paradise
13. Pertaining to neap and ebb
18. MacKenzie of *Your Hit Parade*
23. "Key to the City" presenter
24. Having no company
25. Something school kids hope for in December?
26. Stamping ground
28. Place for roasting
31. "He loves me" piece
35. Deceptive scheme
37. Two-door vehicle
38. Fine drops of water
40. Table tub
42. Carmaker's woe
45. Kick the bucket
47. Closes again, as an envelope
50. Infuriate
53. Come together
54. Sherpa's home
55. Some pickles, familiarly
57. Hemp fiber
63. Studio site
64. Affectedly modest
65. Seek redress
66. It makes one hot
67. One familiar with litter

	1	2	3	4	5		6	7	8	9	10		11	12	13
14							15						16		
17					18								19		
				20					21				22		
23	24	25					26		27			28			
29				30			31			32					
33				34				35		36				37	38
39			40		41				42		43				
44				45		46				47		48			
		49			50		51					52			
53	54					55		56			57				
58				59					60						
61				62			63	64				65	66	67	
68				69					70						
71				72					73						

Puzzle 32: Table Setting
Easy

Across

1. Whimpers
6. Take it easy
10. "Deck the Halls" syllables
14. "Farewell, François"
15. Soft spread
16. NYSE rival
17. Irish export
18. Certain championship event
20. "___ A Beautiful Morning"
21. Economize
23. Spooky
24. Oft-kicked item
25. Perpetual
27. Mirror, of yore
31. Making eyes at
32. Falsify, as prices
33. Put to the test
36. Crinkled cotton fabric
37. It shoots the breeze
38. In a foul mood
40. It may be tapped
41. Jackie's second
42. Golf great Arnold
43. Site for a state slogan, perhaps
46. Books that may display where and tear?

49. Maui music makers
50. Hackneyed
51. Crossed one's fingers
53. GPs
56. Yellow flower
58. Net letter
60. Need liniment
61. Ives of song
62. Work on a pumpkin, perhaps
63. Pebble Beach pegs
64. ___-bitsy
65. Manipulate dough

Down

1. African republic
2. Abridge, maybe
3. First number in season records
4. Remick or Strasberg
5. Hawaii draw
6. Type of proposition
7. Styptic material
8. Dirigible balloon
9. Classified ad letters
10. Mailing supply
11. Love in Milan
12. Author Sinclair
13. Rods on rigs
19. Warren Beatty flick
22. Word with crab or cobra

24. Hop, ___, and jump
26. Faultfinder
27. It may be picked
28. Storybook monster
29. Cassini of fashion
30. Type of alcohol
33. Plebe's sch.
34. Annotation in proofreading
35. Bronte governess
37. Like some flowers
38. Stereo accessory
39. Building additions
41. Crackerjack
42. Lap dog, for short
43. Some coffeehouse orders
44. "That makes sense"
45. Furnish
46. Trip to the plate
47. Break in hostilities
48. Supple
52. Possessive pronoun
53. She ain't what she used to be
54. Opera star
55. Cold weather transport
57. Box score stat
59. "A ___ Called Horse"

Puzzle 33: Brushing Up
Easy

Across

1. Church fixture
6. Chianti, for example
10. ASAP, to an MD
14. Lead-and-tin alloy
15. Tied
16. Place for a honey bunch?
17. Endangered tropical region
19. *The African Queen* screenwriter James
20. Participants in a debate
21. Interferes (with)
23. Regions
25. Penitent one
26. Strolls leisurely
29. Set of clothes
31. Misfortune
34. Modern Greece's legislative assembly
35. Billie Holiday's "You Can't Be Mine (And Someone ___ Too)"
36. Suffix with rigor
37. Word with "cheeks" or "outlook"
38. Culpability
39. Pipkins
40. Kind of can
41. *Saturday Night Fever* setting
42. Podge attachment

43. Funnyman Brooks
44. "Dedicated to the ___ Love"
45. School assignment
46. Israeli leader Barak
48. Ages and ages
50. Ensnared
53. Okay, informally
57. Louie De Palma's office setting
58. 1942 Sabu flick
60. Air conditioner units
61. Viva voce
62. "When ___ You" (Irving Berlin)
63. Have a session
64. Former nickname for Brigitte Bardot
65. 100,000 in a newton

Down

1. Big name in razors
2. *Maude* producer Norman
3. Advanced math
4. Once a year
5. Ring authority
6. Vice ___
7. "___ Got You Under My Skin"
8. Bird's-___ soup
9. Precise
10. Mold

11. He's responsible for long drives
12. State
13. Eighteen on a course
18. Taconite and tinstone
22. State of confusion or disorder
24. Pt. of the British West Indies
26. Sarai's mate
27. Large ruminant
28. Second-rate
30. Christiania, today
32. Income's antithesis
33. Ruhr industrial center
35. The life of Riley
38. College graduate's goal, perhaps
39. Perhaps
41. Ill-humored
42. Actor Paul of *Casablanca*
45. Recline
47. 1952 Eniwetok event
49. American symbol
50. Subject of SALT
51. Hoopster Archibald
52. Simple partner?
54. Hired thug
55. Running attire?
56. Some adv. purchases
59. Capture, as a fugitive

Puzzle 34: Off to the Races
Easy

Across

1. Dangerous reptile
4. Mail org.
8. Acknowledges with one's fedora
13. Nada, zip
14. Bowler's 7-10, for example
15. Florida citrus center
16. Barely achieve (with "out")
17. George's brother
19. Bric-a-brac stand
21. Takes umbrage
22. Formerly
23. Radio station sign
24. Place to haggle
28. Important time, historywise
31. Off-Broadway theater award
32. Instant greenery
33. Missing-person locator
35. Fatty compound
37. Highly reliable evidence
39. Range
40. Handsome young man
42. Stowe's little heroine
44. Zeno's birthplace
45. Stimpy's cartoon buddy
46. Classroom diversion
49. They may be locked or blown

50. Brewed drink
51. Attire
54. Not deep at all
58. Certain researcher
60. Pub potion
61. *The Canterbury Tales* pilgrim
62. Second or sixth president
63. One getting the red carpet treatment
64. Canadian physician Sir William
65. Turner and Cole
66. Picnic problem

Down

1. "There's ___ day dawning . . ."
2. Punjabi believer
3. "Guilty," for example
4. Displaces
5. Blinds crosspiece
6. Snowball in *Animal Farm*
7. Breastbones
8. Some FBI files
9. Fall color
10. Kowtow
11. Dart
12. Without
14. Scorch
18. Do a double-take, for example

20. Absorb
23. Been there, done that
24. Grinding tooth
25. Tolerate
26. Wisconsin college town and college
27. Peas' place
28. Eleve's place
29. Drive back
30. "He's ___ nowhere man" (Beatles)
34. Compound used in perfume manufacture
36. Chaos
38. Clark's *Mogambo* costar
41. Hag
43. National songs
47. Temporarily at the museum
48. Beloved ones
49. Split
51. Dr. J wore one
52. Slapstick-movie missiles
53. Rind
54. Game with 32 cards
55. Magma exposed
56. Actress Lena
57. Turned on the waterworks
59. Nutritional advisory, abbr.

Puzzle 35: Heard Through the Beanstalk?
Easy

Across

1. Disney dog
6. Party type
10. Peaked
14. "I was out of town," for example
15. Head of France
16. Russian "John"
17. 200 milligrams
18. Suspicious of
19. Wither
20. Secretly watch
21. Hollywood investment
24. Epsom product
25. 747 kitchen
26. Ms. Lansbury
29. Be revolting?
30. Collector's ultimatum
33. Dallas inst.
36. Alda or Arkin
37. Be under the weather
38. Famous septet
39. Soak
40. Impersonal mail
44. Treats hides
45. More cruel
46. Attack
49. Oriental
51. Gridiron goof
53. "A bird," "a plane," or "Superman" preceder
56. Sweet sandwich
57. Bedouin
58. ___ *Is Enough* (TV show)
60. Bring up
61. Urn
62. Be crazy about
63. Slips up
64. Pitcher
65. Roman meeting place

Down

1. Anatomical pouches
2. Show fan support
3. Stadium without a dome?
4. Deg. for Wall St.
5. Trap
6. Ermine
7. Big tops
8. Aleutian isle
9. Virgil work
10. Nonsense
11. Do the trick
12. Big dipper?
13. One on a Nixon list
22. Gung-ho spirit
23. Relaxation
24. Penn in pictures
26. At some distance
27. Battle of the ___, 1798
28. Punkie
29. Lunar valley
31. Skiff propellers
32. "Tiny" Dickens character
33. Observed
34. Stable mom
35. Cold War concern
38. Getz on the sax
40. Pass alternative
41. Vacationing
42. Ludwig or Jannings
43. Shredded and bagged item
44. Small drums
46. In advance
47. More certain
48. Apply lipstick poorly
49. Humiliate
50. It has a duel purpose
52. Performer who fills the club
53. Inventor Sikorsky
54. Drive-___ (fast food convenience)
55. Blossom support
59. Words that leave you in a bind?

Puzzle 36: Eyes Right
Easy

Across

1. Ear parts
6. Sort of skirt
10. Taj Mahal locale
14. Accumulated
15. Andy's friend
16. Party cheese
17. Author Loos
18. Hideaway
19. Result of downsizing
20. Look at seductively
23. Narc org.
24. ___ and terminer
25. Name appendages, sometimes
28. Hit sign?
30. Goes to school for the right reasons
35. *Hud* star Patricia
37. "No way!"
40. Essential oil from flowers
42. She's busy in Apr.
43. Humpty Dumpty's sound
44. Nicholson in *Chinatown,* for example
47. Fodder structure
48. Certain Beethoven work
49. *Law & Order:* ___
51. Corn holder, perhaps
52. He's tickled
55. Spanish year
57. She's cherished
64. Blue dye
65. Silents star Naldi
66. Back-forty measure
67. Second of a series
68. ___ bon
69. Historical novels
70. Noted lake
71. Placed in the mail
72. Irregularly notched

Down

1. Use a trawl, for example
2. Indian princess
3. Pt. of UNLV
4. Stifled
5. Outpourings
6. Form check box, perhaps
7. Insect stage
8. Decorative mat
9. Begin, for example
10. Part of a ready trio
11. Western novelist Zane
12. You may do it with the sun
13. Political monogram of '52 and '56
21. Mata ___
22. Lees
25. Goes over the edge
26. Type of rocket
27. Sheet material, perhaps
29. Nursery rhyme starter
31. Some vipers
32. Venerated object
33. African antelope
34. Not vacillating about
36. Hawaiian bubbly?
38. Primatologist's subject
39. Proves worthwhile
41. Honey badger
45. Mimicry and musicianship, for example
46. Writer Hunter
50. Discomfort
53. Rippled-surface fabric
54. More than occasionally
56. Prize for 35-Across
57. Again
58. Pocket bread
59. A or B, for example
60. Kiln
61. Thus
62. Some voters
63. Latin I lesson word
64. Many are crunched

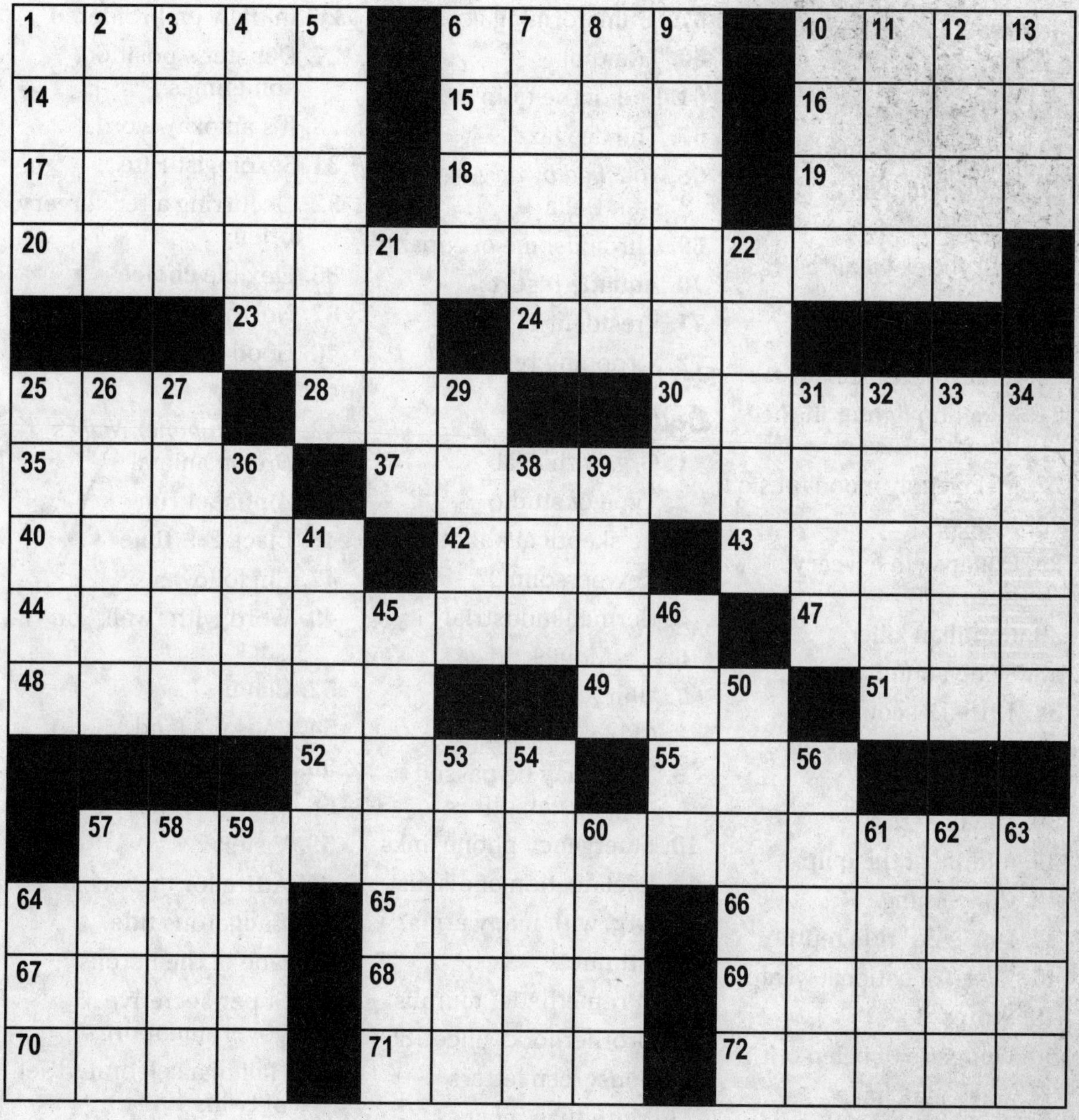

Puzzle 37: Opposite Attraction
Easy

Across

1. One true thing
5. Proclamation
10. Inconclusive, as a jury
14. Donkey delivery
15. Medicinal plant
16. Storybook villain
17. Start of a quip by Mamie Van Doren
20. It may become bald
21. Infection fighter in the blood
22. Melancholy mood music
25. Meager
29. Collapse in a weary heap
30. Reptilian killer
33. Sleep soundly?
34. 1918–19 scourge
35. Meals on wheels server?
38. Son of Seth
39. Middle of the quip
42. Concerning
44. Dr. Seuss' title reptile
45. Meas. of national wealth
48. Stores
50. Opposite of paleo
51. They may have Hawaiian roots
53. Naturally illuminated
55. Shah ousted by Khomeini
57. Brainstorming goal
60. Tranquil
61. End of the quip
67. Thirties jazz
68. *Touched by an Angel* star, Della
69. Chromosome occupant
70. Aquatic resorts
71. President of Syria
72. Stropping result

Down

1. Org. with a lab
2. Type of studio
3. Be skeptical about
4. Key personnel?
5. German industrial city
6. ___ Moines, Iowa
7. "Put a sock ___!"
8. Cable network
9. They may be passed around campfires
10. Emergency phone links
11. Exclamation of disgust
12. Org. with many arms?
13. Attain
18. "Prometheus" muralist
19. Brotherhood since 1868
22. Sunscreen letters
23. More than most
24. Where everything's coming up roses, maybe?
26. Initially embroidered
27. Debater's position, sometimes
28. It's an okay word
31. Sexologist Hite
32. Occurring after surgery, briefly
36. Flexible choice
37. Norton, to Kramden
40. Good-for-nothings
41. Deadly
42. *A Midsummer Night's Dream* animal
43. Alphabet run
46. Black Fri. time
47. Chi follower
49. Word with "walk" or "kick"
52. Claim
54. Caesar's land
56. Role-played
58. Many moons
59. Visits
61. Attire for the wee hrs.
62. Dangerous tide
63. One of the Perons
64. Super-secretive government org.
65. Half of a celebrated set of twins
66. Formerly known as

1 2 3 4 5 6 7 8 9 10 11 12 13
14 15 16
17 18 19
20 21
22 23 24 25 26 27 28
29 30 31 32 33
34 35 36 37 38
39 40 41
42 43 44 45 46 47
48 49 50 51 52
53 54 55 56
57 58 59 60
61 62 63 64 65 66
67 68 69
70 71 72

Puzzle 38: On the Surface
Easy

Across

1. Duel invitation
5. Tramp's love
9. ___ Benedict
13. American Indian corn bread
14. Basic French verb
15. Large-eyed primate
17. Official records
18. Cookbook direction
19. People and verbs have them
20. It may be used to test for phosphorus
23. Two-star performance?
24. One billion years, in astronomy
25. Much of Cuba
27. Visual aid, perhaps
31. All in
32. Meadow
33. *National Velvet* author Bagnold
35. Had trouble pronouncing "s"
38. Homer's issue?
40. Schoolyard game
42. Leave helpless with laughter
43. Emanating from stars
46. Whipping site at sea
49. Hail from the past
50. Altar promise
52. Read, as a bar code
54. Showed curiosity
57. Commemorative poem
58. Smear with grease or mud, for example
59. One who works his own land
64. Deformed circles
66. Make a blunder
67. 15th Amendment topic
68. West Coast pro
69. What the "poor dog" got
70. Cupid's counterpart
71. Smaller amount
72. Burned rubber
73. Making its way there

Down

1. Where jets don't fly
2. Meshuga
3. With the enemy, perhaps
4. Went ding-dong
5. Arab League member
6. Energy source
7. Tap problems
8. Deliver a mouthful
9. Hackberry, for example
10. "My word!"
11. First floor proposal
12. The hit on a 45, usually
16. Grounded fleet
21. Sensitive to the touch
22. Sermon subject, sometimes
26. Noted Onassis, to friends
27. Island east of Corsica
28. Supportive voices
29. Catastrophic event
30. Kind of boss or bull
34. Equine mother
36. Roof part
37. Not natural, as hair
39. Bothers
41. Word with "tank" or "range"
44. *Wheel of Fortune* purchase
45. Baltimore or Fauntleroy, for example
47. Displayed disdain
48. "I did it!"
51. Wields the scepter
53. Impulse transmitters
54. Person or object of devotion
55. Type of blockade
56. Hang down
60. Sound quality
61. Second helping, for example
62. Type of collar
63. Take a load off
65. Many dads, briefly

Puzzle 39: What's On?
Easy

Across

1. Quits wavering
5. Certain Pindaric poem
8. Cipriano, Americo, or Fidel
14. Snow remover
15. ___ Paese (cheese)
16. It goes overboard
17. Wan and not tan
18. "Flapper" follower
19. One with fixed eyes
20. TV sitcom from '75 to '84
23. Religious repast
24. It's not gross
25. Lawyers' grp.
28. Tokyo, before 1868
29. Touch-and-go game
31. Disciple of Paul
35. More threatening
37. They put you in your place
38. TV sitcom from '77 to '84
41. Lao-tzu follower
42. Steer clear
43. Blew a gasket
45. Flub
46. DNA synthesizer
49. Replies of refusal
50. "The ramparts" lead-in
52. Words with "two" or "hole"
54. TV sitcom from '77 to '81
59. Minor but aggravating problem
61. AAA's opposite?
62. Stratagem
63. Making less sense
64. Hotel addition?
65. Between ports, for example
66. "Anti" attachment
67. Lennon's bride
68. Suburban sale venue

Down

1. Avoid agreement
2. Shaved wood
3. Holy city?
4. Bjorn Borg, for example
5. Follow orders
6. Disturbs mentally
7. Make one's day and more
8. Playbill listing
9. "Social" leader
10. Source of illegitimate income
11. Promise punishment, for example
12. Sole source
13. Bruins' legendary Bobby
21. Most bohemian
22. Downed a sub
26. Cover to conceal
27. Beast of burden
30. Range ridge
32. Unconfirmed info
33. Remedy taken in pairs
34. Certain herring
35. Plumbing problem
36. Letters on some TVs and VCRs
38. Tropical tuber
39. Minded the mansion, for example
40. Supervised
41. "Lords a-leaping" number
44. Point to be made?
46. Author Alcott
47. One who's casting about?
48. Use a guillotine
51. Letters from childhood
53. "You're kidding!"
55. "Money ___ everything"
56. Type of club
57. Munchen man of the house
58. First name in architecture
59. That guy
60. Santa ___

Puzzle 40: Waist Management
Easy

Across

1. Ruth on the field
5. Splash clumsily
10. Cypress, for one
14. Got 100 on, as a test
15. Overly self-confident
16. Certain something
17. Wild guess
18. More than disliked
19. Tip, nautically
20. Schedule limitations, hiding transit
23. Be it–humble link
24. Engine disks
25. Foul-weather overshoe
28. Plenty
32. Tijuana two
35. Behave bullishly?
36. Et cetera relative
37. Store sign, hiding transit
41. Hardly bland
42. "Nobel" ending
43. Do likewise
44. Turgenev heroine
45. Like a dive
48. Sound of clothing tags being removed
50. Feature of some boots
54. Unquestioned style, hiding transit

59. Detected
60. On ___ (counting calories)
61. Sail support
62. Cookie magnate
63. Brainy gang
64. Luau root
65. Acoustic measure
66. Favorite of Elizabeth
67. Peevish mood

Down

1. Cookbook instruction, sometimes
2. Part of *The Tempest*
3. Former NYC mayor Abraham
4. Court star Stefan
5. Certain student
6. Savings counterpart
7. Some short months?
8. Quickie portrait, perhaps
9. Monster slain by Hercules
10. It works like a charm
11. Totally wreck
12. While beginning?
13. Puts away the groceries?
21. R.E. Lee's org.

22. Violinist's heirloom, perhaps
26. ". . . ___ flag was still there"
27. Sally Field role
29. Bargain type
30. Pronunciation difficulty
31. Effortlessness
32. Two tablets, maybe
33. Birthstone for 7-Down
34. Golfer Ballesteros
36. Certain levy
38. Meaningless words
39. Coin replaced by the euro
40. Put to the test, in a way
45. Play suit?
46. "B.C." anteater's sound
47. Leavening agents
49. Part of Caesar's boast
51. It covers Congress
52. Nintendo's precursor
53. Also-ran of 1996
54. "Stupid ___ stupid does"
55. Office transmittal
56. Latin American laborer
57. Compartments
58. ___ majeste

1	2	3	4		5	6	7	8	9		10	11	12	13
14					15						16			
17					18						19			
20				21						22				
23								24						
			25			26	27			28		29	30	31
32	33	34			35				36					
37			38	39				40						
41						42					43			
44						45			46	47				
			48		49			50			51	52	53	
54	55	56				57	58							
59				60						61				
62				63						64				
65				66						67				

Puzzle 41: Pantry Raid
Tricky

Across

1. Zig or zag
5. Easily bullied
9. Bit of snowfall
14. Suffix with "corrupt" or "contempt"
15. Follow an order
16. Sheets, tablecloths, and so forth
17. Barker at SeaWorld
18. Heartfelt
19. Preamble
20. Italian meal starter, perhaps
22. Bartletts and Boscs, for example
23. "If all __ fails . . ."
24. Fight, but not seriously
25. "He Ain't ___, He's My Brother"
28. Item in a dentist's office
32. Sister of Emily and Charlotte
33. Card dispenser
35. Prefix for pod or angle
36. Decay
37. Summer outings
38. "When Will ___ Loved?"
39. The "ugly" to Clint's "good" and Lee's "bad"
40. Current terminals
41. Former stitch location, perhaps
42. Dance craze of the '90s

44. Thinks ahead
45. Caesar's bad day
46. Ray of *The Haunted* (1979)
48. Tree with fluttering leaves
50. Period before the Middle Ages
55. Barb-filled ceremony
56. Stovetop items
57. Emotion displayed with hand-rubbing
58. ___-frutti
59. Diabolical
60. Fats Domino's "Blueberry ___"
61. Some swords
62. Tony Curtis classic, *The Great ___*
63. Hawk

Down

1. American Express alternative
2. *Desire Under the Elms* son
3. Israel's southernmost city
4. Substitute for, as a pitcher
5. Ice cream parlor orders
6. Beyond pleasantly plump
7. Pedal pushers
8. Proofreader's find, hopefully

9. Snorkeler's wear
10. One-dimensional
11. Land way down south
12. *From Here to Eternity* actress
13. He had a grandmother named Eve
21. Work busily
24. Glasses
25. Male seal's bevy
26. ___ Gay (infamous B-29)
27. Look forward to
28. Bamboo consumer
29. "I cannot tell ___"
30. Citified
31. Shore platforms
33. Has an elegant meal
34. Financial subj.
37. Word after "in loco," in a phrase
41. Stagnant swamps
43. Carol title word
44. ASAP
46. Where the last flight ends?
47. Cotton thread
48. Johnson of "ver-r-r-ry interesting" fame
49. Liquid nourishment
50. Copycat
51. Spectacular star
52. Tennis champ Nastase
53. "Don't ask, don't ___"
54. Scream

1	2	3	4		5	6	7	8		9	10	11	12	13
14					15					16				
17					18					19				
20				21						22				
			23						24					
25	26	27					28	29					30	31
32					33	34						35		
36				37								38		
39				40						41				
42			43							44				
		45						46	47					
48	49					50	51				52	53	54	
55					56					57				
58					59					60				
61					62					63				

Puzzle 42: Road Rules
Tricky

Across

1. Struggle for air
5. Apple center
9. Actress LuPone
14. *Fort Apache* actor, 1948
15. Sherman Helmsley/Clifton Davis sitcom
16. Ladybug's lunch, perhaps
17. Like the spotted owl
18. Season of penitence
19. Bacteria
20. Song that could carry you away
23. Word before "ignition . . . liftoff!"
24. Screen siren West
25. Tract ending
26. Young feller
29. Song that could carry you away
32. Ranis' garments
35. Grazing land
36. Arcade patron, perhaps
37. Have a bias
38. Out of joint
40. Test answer with a 50/50 shot
41. Garden beauty
42. Wipe lightly
43. Fine rains
44. Song that could carry you away

48. Dry, as in wine
49. Intention
50. *Dr. No* author Fleming
51. Is down with
54. Song that could carry you away
58. Highly proficient
60. Word with cafe or film
61. Tiny Greek letter?
62. Type of train
63. "Great Caesar's ghost!"
64. Today's Siamese
65. Place for a convict's bracelet
66. Cravings
67. ___ Grey (kind of tea)

Down

1. *Ninotchka* actress Greta
2. "You can say that ___!"
3. "Beetle Bailey" character
4. The hunted
5. Opera's Maria
6. Egg dish
7. Where people arrive to split
8. Twists together
9. Heathens
10. High point
11. Mystery novels, for example

12. *A Christmas Carol* boy
13. Personality parts
21. Feathered six-footers
22. Senatorial wraps
27. Northern inhabitant
28. Units of force
29. Belarus capital
30. Excuse
31. *Toys in the ___* (1963)
32. Banana peel mishaps
33. Condor nest, for example
34. Something a fair-weather fan might use?
38. Firefighter Red
39. Emergency cash
43. Musician Manfred
45. Longhorns, and so forth
46. Mystery author ___ Jackson Braun
47. Scottish landowners
51. Uproarious commotion
52. Wedding site
53. Epitome of slowness
55. October birthstone
56. Former Venetian magistrate
57. Quote
58. ___ mode
59. Godfather

1	2	3	4		5	6	7	8		9	10	11	12	13
14					15					16				
17					18					19				
20				21					22					
23				24				25				26	27	28
			29				30				31			
32	33	34						35				36		
37					38	39						40		
41					42						43			
44				45				46	47					
48				49				50				51	52	53
		54	55				56				57			
58	59					60					61			
62						63					64			
65						66					67			

Puzzle 43: Parental Control
Tricky

Across

1. 2,051, in old Rome
5. Play in a mud puddle, for example
10. Madame Bovary
14. "I'm listening"
15. Truant's game
16. Butcher's offering
17. Certain UFO
19. It's found in a round
20. *M*A*S*H* prioritizing system
21. Lab example
23. Gold vein
25. Big name in electronics
26. Detective's assignments
29. *Bonanza* network
32. Aquarium fish
35. Billing unit, for some
36. Like a numismatist's greatest treasure
38. Molder
39. Work unit
40. Spanish clan
41. In the past
42. Words with "loss" or "glance"
43. Gives the heave-ho
44. Pond film
45. Vegetable knife
47. *Fantasy Island* neckwear
48. Bo, Luke, and Daisy

49. "Buenos ___!"
51. Santa ___, Calif.
53. Gourmet onions
57. Appear on the scene
61. Get one's feet wet, in a way
62. Mayor, for example
64. General's gofer, for example
65. Prepare to be knighted
66. Hot streak
67. ___ Mawr College
68. Too sentimental
69. Cornstalk features

Down

1. Ones minding the store (Abbr.)
2. *The Hound of the Baskervilles* locale
3. Viaud's pen name
4. Asthma sufferer's gadget
5. Measure, as of dignity
6. Word with Alamos or Altos
7. Cries of amazement
8. Bounce across water
9. Excessively promotes
10. Marilu Henner's *Taxi* role
11. Certain career path
12. He's not one to talk
13. Soon, ere now

18. Alter ___
22. Terra ___
24. Hard dental layer
26. Penny-pinching
27. Blood vessel that begins at the heart
28. Ingenue's benefactor, perhaps
30. Streisand's *Funny Girl* role
31. John Havlicek was one
33. Scoundrel
34. Molecular components
36. British rule prior to 1947
37. "___-boom-bah!"
40. Like a wild animal
44. Type of pancake (with "crepe")
46. Brennan of *Private Benjamin*
48. Russian parliament
50. Knee-highs and argyles
52. Test a modified paper airplane
53. Mariner's mop
54. Cueball's lack
55. Frank's daughter
56. Resign (with "down")
58. Flightless bird
59. Shifter's selection
60. Flubs it
63. Cowpoke assent

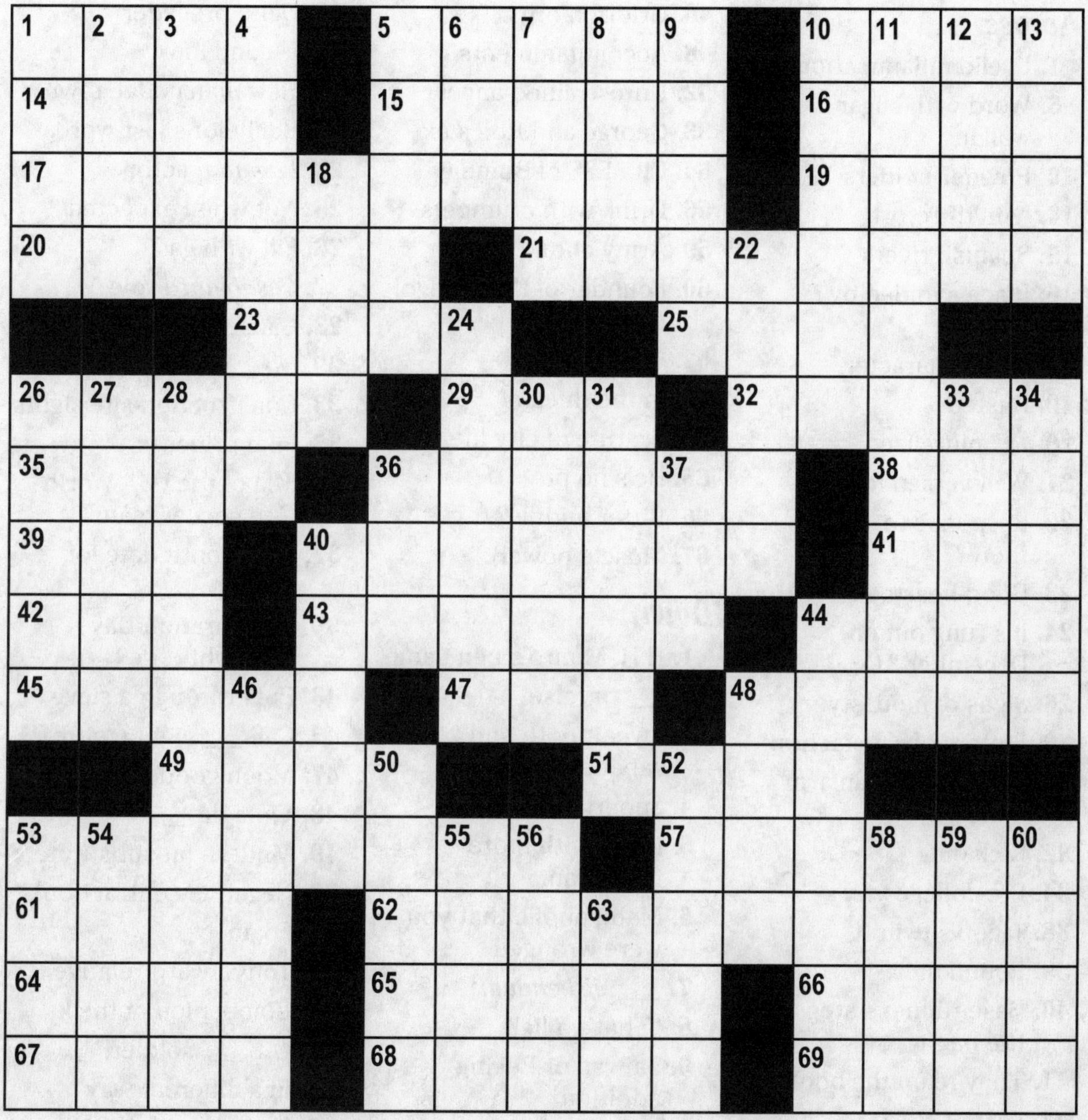

Puzzle 44: 2K Race
Tricky

Across

1. Eyelid inflammations
6. Word with sugar or walking
10. Powder holders
14. "Ain't!" retort
15. Spanish rivers
16. Place avoided by Rushdie
17. *Roots* character
19. Busted
20. "Y" pluralized
21. Well-versed folks?
22. Response to "Who's there?"
23. Good-hearted
24. It's rung out on December 31
26. Signs of modesty
30. Letters of satisfaction
31. Pertaining to an arm bone
32. Kick out
34. Pre-college yrs.
38. Jacob's twin
39. Pound unit
40. Base runner's steps off the bag
41. They're on the books
42. Part of et al.
43. Slick goo
44. Little fox

46. Gridiron orgs.
48. Accompaniments
52. Unrestrained anger
53. George and Rod's ex
54. City ESE of Bombay
56. Drink with crumpets
59. Army chow
60. Founder of the Mongol dynasty
62. Check point?
63. In the thick of
64. Feature of city life
65. He's no pro
66. Bitter middle?
67. Muscle power

Down

1. H.H. Munro's pen name
2. ___ or false
3. Sweet tooth and Japanese coin
4. Superlative suffix
5. Filled with more melodrama
6. Made public that you were wronged
7. ___ *Misbehavin'*
8. "That's a lie!"
9. Taiwan or Peking addition
10. *Jackie Oh!* author
11. Do blackboard duty

12. Delta preceder
13. Unkind look
18. Hawaiian coffee town
22. Bachelor's last words?
23. *Paganini* actor
25. Not when expected
26. Fill with gas
27. *Casablanca* role
28. Cause persistent worry
29. *No ___ Venice*
33. Construction-site sights
35. Film princess
36. Mia of the USA World Cup soccer team
37. Mid-month date for Caesar
39. Inauguration Day highlight
43. Puts through a sieve
45. Call ___ night (retire)
47. Moon goddess
48. Viola da ___
49. Modern fat substitute
50. Negative contraction
51. Foam
55. Tony Award relative
56. Companion of thick
57. "At ___, soldier!"
58. In a different way
60. Krazy of comics
61. Carp in some garden ponds

1	2	3	4	5		6	7	8	9		10	11	12	13
14						15					16			
17					18						19			
20				21						22				
			23					24	25					
26	27	28					29		30					
31					32		33				34	35	36	37
38				39						40				
41				42					43					
		44	45				46	47						
48	49	50			51		52							
53						54	55				56	57	58	
59				60						61				
62				63					64					
65				66					67					

Puzzle 45: Finishing Up
Tricky

Across

1. ". . . and make it snappy!"
5. Young, migrating salmon
10. 455, in old Rome
14. Walt Kelly comic strip
15. Western adventure
16. "King ___" (1950–65 comic strip)
17. About to end
20. Added just before time ran out
21. Machinations
22. Some are three-legged
24. Caboodle's companion
25. Result of baby's first spaghetti dinner
28. Heavy weights
30. Employs an ambulance chaser, for example
34. Buffet selections, often
37. Goat's milk product
39. Plunked oneself down
40. About to end
43. Extra qtrs., for example
44. Piece of window glass
45. "Madness" of a 1936 film
46. Librarian's admonitions
48. Many crossword puzzle themes
50. Word with "fire" or "white"
51. Pickup compartment
53. Joins the choir
56. Some bakery items
60. Gives comfort to
64. About to end
66. Metrical romance
67. Tiny arachnids
68. "An apple ___ . . ."
69. Persuade
70. Keep for later
71. A good cloud to be on

Down

1. Abbey area
2. "Deal!"
3. All ___ (excited)
4. Carpenter's tool
5. Type of boom
6. Powerful attractor
7. Baseball legend Mel
8. Many popes
9. Jesse Owens, notably
10. Some insertion marks
11. Avoirdupois unit
12. *St. Elmo's Fire* actor
13. Some remote abbreviations
18. She's "sweet as apple cider"
19. Greek X
23. Cushions
25. Old PC operating system
26. Home base for everyone
27. Partner of burn
29. Classical prefix
31. Good ol' country, for short
32. Meeting room prop
33. Cubic meter
35. Party snack
36. Some fedoras
38. Baron von Richthofen, for one
41. New homophone
42. A math sign
47. Barely adequate
49. Many a bridesmaid
52. Help out
54. Ominous loop
55. ___ few rounds (spar)
56. Easter fare
57. All hands on deck
58. One of the Simpsons
59. Fit of anger
61. "___ known . . ."
62. Verve
63. Eyelid flare-up
65. Muscle car of the '60s

1	2	3	4		5	6	7	8	9		10	11	12	13
14					15						16			
17				18					19					
20							21							
			22			23		24						
25	26	27				28		29			30	31	32	33
34				35	36		37			38		39		
40						41					42			
43				44				45						
46			47		48			49			50			
			51	52			53		54	55				
56	57	58				59		60				61	62	63
64						65								
66					67						68			
69					70						71			

Puzzle 46: Guy Talk
Tricky

Across

1. Magic Dragon of song
5. Bean spillers
9. It consists of high spirits
13. Ending with "buck" or "stink"
14. Be a verbal rubber stamp
15. Game surface, sometimes
16. *All in the Family* producer
17. Revered expert
18. Sane
19. TOM
22. Hag
23. Valentine's Day's signature color
24. Pampered
27. Fertility goddess
29. Support system?
32. Last of a series
33. One who looks down a lot?
34. "___ here long?"
35. FRANK
38. Change Money?
39. Dwarf's refrain words
40. Paquin and Pavlova
41. Hole that's inhabitable
42. Something to build on
43. In a warm, comfortable way

44. Antagonist
45. Muffled sounds of impact
47. OSCAR
54. Tree that provides for chocoholics
55. Mound miscue
56. The younger Guthrie
57. Tedium
58. "The Lake ___ of Innisfree"
59. Word processor command
60. Boy Scout's undertaking
61. "What happened next . . ."
62. Cubicle fixture

Down

1. Lifeline locale
2. Fertilizer ingredient
3. One with a stable family?
4. Seeing ahead
5. Admiration
6. Sharp or severe
7. CHUCK
8. Like some dough
9. Off one's ___ (crazy)
10. Shortage
11. Canal of song
12. Jacuzzi action
15. Rhythm partner

20. Use a crib sheet
21. *Survivor* group
24. Apt to doodle, perhaps
25. Potassium ___
26. ___ *the Beguine*
28. Manhattan area
29. Extraterrestrial, for example
30. Of the kidneys
31. Tending to fidget
33. Words with "goes" or "seems"
34. Item in some family games
36. Fence supplier
37. Cute zoo bear
42. "Me too" relative
43. Like some treasures
44. Better Business Bureau subject
46. Berry that's easy on the eyes
47. Got a hole in one on
48. Grow faint
49. Troubling marks for high schoolers?
50. Brief note in passing?
51. Item for certain surgeons
52. Automaker Ransom
53. Mobile castle

1	2	3	4	■	5	6	7	8	■		9	10	11	12
13				■	14				■	15				
16				■	17				■	18				
19				20					21					
■	■	■	22					■	23			■	■	■
24	25	26				■	27	28			■	29	30	31
32				■	33				■	34				
35				36					37					
38			■	39				■	40					
41			■	42			■	43						
■	■	■	44			■	45	46			■	■	■	■
47	48	49			50					■	51	52	53	
54				■	55			■	56					
57				■	58			■	59					
60			■	61			■	62						

Puzzle 47: Capital Idea!
Tricky

Across

1. Pieces of two-pieces
5. Small progression
9. Addis ___ (Ethiopia's capital)
14. Tube diameter
15. Popeye, after eating spinach
16. Docket fill
17. Actress Blanchett
18. Complain, complain, complain
19. Pleasant surprise
20. It's a capital place
23. Bradley and Trixie's husband
24. Comstock load
25. Brings to the boiling point
29. Wet, spongy ground
31. Some are natural; some are broken
35. Takes wing
36. Object in a quiver
38. Child seat?
39. It's a capital place
42. Palindromic conjunction
43. ". . . ___ evil, speak . . ."
44. Audio signal receiver
45. Put through the paces
47. Word with "takers" or "day now"
48. Takes the helm
49. They precede mis, on a music scale
51. Haggard work
52. It's a capital place
60. 18 holes, for example
61. "Honeybunch"
62. They may be beaten
64. Compel through coercion
65. No one's in until this is put in
66. Got on one's high horse?
67. Trusty mount
68. Unpleasant situation
69. Otherwise

Down

1. *I, Claudius* network
2. Yellow Brick, for one
3. *Laugh-In* comedian Johnson
4. "As ___ on TV!"
5. Does an office chore
6. They're shed
7. Roberts of *Runaway Train*
8. Game of chukkers
9. Action may make him laugh or cry?
10. Wine container
11. On the Baltic
12. Form droplets
13. Regarding
21. Lawsuit preposition
22. Get ready to surf
25. Coveted quality
26. Dame's introduction?
27. Stares with open mouth
28. Newsworthy period of history
29. Like the ocean
30. Yes ___ (one of two answers)
32. Not with another
33. Spring offering
34. Practices for a boxing match
36. Communicant's word
37. Damper
40. The absolute minimum
41. Cash's boy, in a song
46. Hypnotic sleep
48. Coastlines
50. Finished
51. Part of a full house?
52. Canine sounds
53. Horn sound
54. Work as a barker
55. Father of Cain and Abel
56. Tunney of the ring
57. Horror film fare
58. Adored one
59. Increases (with "to")
63. Figure out

Puzzle 48: Blink, Blink
Tricky

Across

1. Course taken after trig, often
5. January 2 event
9. Bureau
14. Nabisco cookie
15. Product mention
16. Star-crossed lover
17. "___ me up, Scotty!"
18. Indian tourist mecca
19. Allow inside
20. Star of 38-Across
23. Benz ending
24. Cost to be dealt in
25. Fitted within one another
27. Nova follower
30. Brief contact
32. Tin Man's desire
33. Transmission part
34. Electrifying swimmers?
38. Hit show starring 20-Across
41. Plateau relative
42. *London Magazine* essayist
43. Born yesterday
44. Not the final copy
46. School notebook
47. Bedtime recitation
50. Interstate hauler
51. Female octopus
52. Costar of 20-Across
58. Isolated
60. 26 of 32 counties of Ireland
61. Highly rated
62. Beauty parlor
63. Where most humans reside
64. Social blunder for Nanette?
65. Put forth effort
66. Fermented honey beverage
67. Laurel in *The Music Box*

Down

1. *On the Waterfront* star Lee J.
2. Wilderness or staging, for example
3. Shakespearean king
4. Prepared for battle
5. Rival of Athens
6. Pond growth
7. Fly on a hook
8. Yipes!
9. Large waders
10. Mortar tray
11. Irish patriot Robert
12. Parisian waterway
13. Packed a gun
21. Novelist Loos
22. Get used (to) (Variation)
26. Deceitful tricks
27. Wooden gap-filler
28. Relinquish
29. They row, row, row your boat
30. Suit
31. Indian prince
33. It's played in rounds
35. Camelot character
36. Like early television
37. Tarot reader
39. Stiller's partner
40. Opposite of persona
45. Cry uncle
46. Blow the foam off a brew?
47. Distinct stage
48. Hang loose
49. American chameleon
50. It's over Jordan, on a map
53. Twenty quires
54. Ascend
55. Like some points
56. ___ *and the King of Siam*
57. Type of big city light
59. Here–there link

1	2	3	4	■	5	6	7	8	■	9	10	11	12	13
14				■	15				■	16				
17				■	18				■	19				
20			21					22		■	23			
■	■	24				■	■	25		26				
27	28	29			■	30	31				■	■	■	■
32				■	33				■	34	35	36	37	
38			■	39				40						
41			■	42			■	43						
■	■	44	45			■	46							
47	48	49			■	■	50			■	■			
51			■	52	53	54				55	56	57		
58		59		■	60			■	61					
62				■	63			■	64					
65				■	66			■	67					

Puzzle 49: Bird Watching
Tricky

Across

1. Absolute
6. Short distance
10. Very plentiful
14. Upstate New York city
15. Lime cover
16. Egg without a shell
17. Brother on a noted TV sitcom
19. Source of misery
20. Exaggerator's suffix
21. Swarm
22. Sudden emotional pang
24. Like Death's horse
25. Feature of Colorado
26. Jellied side dishes
29. Outlet insert
30. Searched for bugs
31. *The Ghost and Mrs. ___*
32. Rival of Bjorn
36. "... through the air with the greatest of ___"
37. Jazz legend Chick
38. Be a peddler
39. Holiday cherub
40. French articles
41. Desist partner
42. Informal farewell
44. Trust in
45. *Titanic* or *Star Wars*, for example
48. Old salts
49. Maltreatment
50. Evening in Milan
51. Cumberland, for one
54. Word repeated before "pants on fire"
55. *Network* actor
58. Town in Italy, New Jersey, or California
59. Shah's domain, once
60. Humped antelope
61. Suit to ___
62. Brain scans, for short
63. Dude ranch woes

Down

1. Tony-winner Tommy
2. "(Sittin' On) The Dock of the Bay" singer Redding
3. Compete in Camelot
4. Red Baron, for example
5. The end for playwrights?
6. Buying binge
7. Jets, Mets, or Nets
8. Velvet end?
9. Overabundance
10. *A Rage in Harlem* actress
11. Marla's predecessor
12. Toadstools and mushrooms, for example
13. Middle East prince
18. Some Disney collectibles
23. Lose or draw alternative
24. *Carrie* actress
25. Makes an effort
26. Whaling, for example
27. Dog-paddled, for example
28. Item for a Mexican pot?
29. Less sullied
31. "Haystacks" artist
33. Job for Mr. Fixit
34. Start of many words?
35. Ancient garden location
37. Attractive one
41. Wide-mouthed servers
43. Patient replies?
44. *The Belle of Bowling Green* author Amelia
45. Actress Jovovich
46. T.S. or George
47. Forest clearing
48. They're coming of age
50. Deer fellow?
51. Watchdog's sound
52. Dermatology problem
53. Goals for many graduate students
56. "... ___ I saw Elba"
57. U.N. labor arm

Puzzle 50: Buckle Up
Tricky

Across

1. Place for a keystone
5. Fitted by a smith
9. Wound remnant
13. Royal Crown product
14. Prepare mushrooms, in a way
15. Handed-down knowledge
16. Type of ring that goes with bell-bottoms
17. It settles the score
19. Tall, flightless bird
20. *Charlie's Angels* star
21. Gully
22. Condescend
24. It's the key factor in inflation?
25. "I hate to ___ and run"
26. Checkout device
30. Sigourney Weaver classic
31. Woman treated as an object?
32. California campus
36. *Bonnie and Clyde* director
37. Type of semiconductor
39. Part of Indochina
40. Indiscriminating hirers, initially
41. *The Twilight Zone* creator Serling
42. "Father of Impressionism"
43. Darth Vader foe
47. Briquette remnant
50. Romans' caviar
51. From a certain grain
52. Drop off for a bit
54. Jimmy Durante trademark
55. Cyclotron particle
58. Pane frame
60. Pound of poetry
61. Mimicked
62. Bewildered
63. "Able to ___ tall buildings . . ."
64. Capone pursuer
65. Pro votes
66. Not up to much

Down

1. High point
2. Forster's had a view
3. State of bliss
4. "If I ___ a Hammer"
5. Verbally refused
6. Colored
7. Racetrack alternative, briefly
8. Backside
9. Ukrainian, for example
10. Commentator Roberts
11. Site for Globetrotters
12. Che Guevara attire
14. Stiffly theatrical
18. Doo-wop classic "Duke of ___"
20. Lender's backup
23. Still
24. Reading position, sometimes
26. Attire for the Headless Horseman
27. "The low-priced spread"
28. TV's Morgenstern
29. Green Wave school
33. Given sainthood
34. Client for Clarence Darrow
35. Piedmont province
37. Off-street parking area
38. Hawkeye State
42. Apportion
44. Clown of early TV
45. Lasso loops
46. Buckwheat cereal
47. Dam extending across the Nile
48. Take potshots
49. Sharpens, as skills
53. "Against All ___"
54. Space Age org.
56. Type of surgeon
57. Mane spot
59. ___ Anne de Bellevue, Que.
60. Wallach of *The Magnificent Seven*

Puzzle 51: I Want It All
Tricky

Across

1. Data transfer rate
5. Nourishes
10. Festive gathering
14. Adjust, as a motor
15. Garret
16. Nick and Nora's dog
17. In custody
20. Overindulges
21. Bric-a-brac holder
22. Waistcoat
25. Ancient Persians
26. Saint Petersburg neighbor
30. Further away, in a way
33. Local language
34. "___ in a Manger"
35. West in *Night After Night*
38. Flaunt the SEC
42. CPR specialist
43. San Pablo Bay island
44. Long-time Yankee skipper
45. Fragments
47. Boleyn and Hathaway
48. WWII beachhead
51. Sportscast tidbit
53. Dance or music program
56. Underlings
60. Fun standard, traditionally
64. Leif's father
65. Gloomy
66. It has many slots
67. Pops
68. With regard to
69. Yemen port

Down

1. Approx. 252 calories
2. Bea Taylor, to Andy
3. Take down, as hair
4. Not shallow
5. Many a test answer
6. Ike's command
7. Substitute for the unlisted
8. Bank check?
9. Improvise with numbers?
10. Harass
11. Part of FAQ
12. Cubic meter
13. 19th president
18. Bring up to snuff
19. Anthroponym
23. Having only magnitude, but no direction
24. Facing
26. Proverbial healer
27. Famous evictee
28. Excellent condition
29. Hawaiian dish
31. Most current
32. Batiking need
35. "September ___" (Neil Diamond)
36. For some, it could be a lot
37. Achieves with difficulty (With "out")
39. Actress Thurman
40. Borough island
41. 32,000 ounces
45. Avoids work
46. Loathing
48. Formed into a circle
49. Actress/comedian Anne
50. Unpleasantly pungent
52. Nautical direction
54. Portrayer of Pierce
55. Desolate
57. Green pod
58. Have to have
59. "Auld Lang ___"
61. Honorarium
62. Irish Sea isle
63. Gun's offspring?

Puzzle 52: Suits Me Fine
Tricky

Across

1. Aerie area
5. Bit of information
10. Julie's *Dr. Zhivago* costar
14. Sonny of Sonny and Cher
15. Sidestep
16. Windmill blade
17. Suit
19. Similar in nature
20. Where the successful go
21. Bitter end?
23. Guinness World Records suffix
24. Hospital name
28. Threads tennis shoes again
30. Payee of consequences
32. Middlin'
33. Offshore structure
34. Bill attachment
36. Potato sack wt., sometimes
39. ___ uproar
41. Barbary Coast city
43. Suit to ___
44. Incandescent
46. Like a flying carpet
48. One of the Perons
49. "___ I care!"
51. Dogpatch dweller
53. Tenor Andrea

56. Signified
57. Lichtenstein's forte
58. Jennifer on *WKRP in Cincinnati*
60. Then partner
61. Secret retreat
63. Suit
68. Prep school near London
69. Word to the chauffeur
70. Creole vegetable
71. Iniquitous rooms?
72. Goat-legged deity
73. "Read 'em and ___!"

Down

1. *60 Minutes* network
2. 1973 Supreme Court decision name
3. *The Atom ___ Show* (1960s TV cartoon)
4. Bungle
5. Dilapidated
6. Cookbook phrase
7. Rotate
8. It's pulled on a farm
9. Predicaments
10. In vitro items
11. Suit
12. Plant of the carrot family
13. Payments on Boardwalk or Park Place
18. Hindu ascetic

22. Mailbox feature
24. Narrow furrow
25. A noun might be one
26. Suit
27. Autumn Joy
29. Cruising between ports
31. Pertaining to the kidneys
35. Stiff as a board
37. Mississippi restraint
38. Oft-trimmed item
40. Rudolph's prominent feature
42. Hit man's accessory
45. Last ___ and testament
47. Watercraft
50. Annual Nile occurrences
52. Dog's utterance, in kiddie lit
53. Made hay?
54. Pontificate
55. Prefix with "red" or "structure"
59. "___ ain't broke . . ."
62. They may administer IVs
64. Plant that can climb the walls
65. Just manage (with "out")
66. Live and breathe
67. Knock on wood

1 2 3 4 5 6 7 8 9 10 11 12 13
14 15 16
17 18 19
20 21 22 23
24 25 26 27 28 29
30 31 32
33 34 35 36 37 38
39 40 41 42 43
44 45 46 47 48
49 50 51 52
53 54 55 56
57 58 59 60
61 62 63 64 65 66 67
68 69 70
71 72 73

Puzzle 53: School Days
Tricky

Across

1. Apple pie pros
5. They supplied your cousins
10. Roughly
14. "Clinton's Ditch"
15. River to the Rhone
16. Jezebel's deity
17. Corporate big shot
20. "All systems go"
21. Break in friendly relations
22. Models who get a lot of exposure?
23. Prie-___ (prayer bench)
24. Soap and water results
26. Women's volunteer organizations
31. Driver's 180
32. Gomer of classic TV
33. End of many URLs
36. Lay off, to a batter
37. Determine if it's gold
39. Opera goddess
40. Pronoun for a ship
41. Nobel Institute locale
42. Errand boy
43. Rookie of the Year's concern
47. Selected, as straws
48. 1949 peace org.
49. One place to flounder
52. It has a primed and painted body

53. High mountain
56. Congressional rookie
60. British isles
61. Ed with seven Emmys
62. Bindlestiff
63. Civil rights activist Parks
64. The mating game
65. Andy's partner of old radio

Down

1. Flat-topped hill, especially in U.S./Mexican deserts
2. Cookie since 1912
3. Expensive fur
4. Cinque follower
5. More ventilated
6. Serving a purpose
7. Call to the head of the line?
8. Uno + due
9. Wall Street police
10. Angle that's greater than 90 degrees
11. Speak-easy's risk
12. Rescue
13. Barcelona bravos
18. *Men in Black* cat
19. Exceeding what is appropriate or normal
23. Fraught with danger, as some circumstances
24. Dionne Warwick's "I ___ Little Prayer"

25. *The ___ Duckling*
26. Sticks out or protrudes
27. 45th state
28. Microwaves, informally
29. England's ___ Downs
30. Jules Verne milieu
34. Kitchen hot spot
35. Noted critic of capitalism
37. Tennis legend Arthur
38. Tap the brakes
39. Martial arts school
41. *O* founder
42. Advance in age
44. Port city on an arm of the Black Sea
45. Heavy burdens
46. *Consumer Reports* employees
49. A long way off
50. Peter, Paul, and Mary, for example
51. Places for making soaps?
52. Mrs. Shakespeare
53. Fermi's fascination
54. Wolf in the western U.S.
55. Most Masters participants
57. Brit's raincoat
58. It's grate stuff
59. Sound of insight

1	2	3	4		5	6	7	8	9		10	11	12	13
14					15						16			
17				18					19					
20				21					22					
			23				24	25						
26	27	28				29					30			
31						32					33	34	35	
36					37	38				39				
40				41					42					
		43	44				45	46						
		47				48								
49	50	51				52					53	54	55	
56				57	58				59					
60				61				62						
63				64				65						

Puzzle 54: Breaking Bread
Tricky

Across

1. Fish steerer
4. Earth tone
9. What Oscar winners do at the podium
14. "___ matter of fact . . ."
15. Scarlett of *Gone With the Wind*
16. Robinson Crusoe's creator
17. Son of Cratchit
18. William Thackeray hero
20. Rose supporter
22. Fifties automotive clunker
23. Bovine outbursts
24. They may be checked
26. Poe and Pound, for example
28. *Ivanhoe* setting
33. Chili hotness unit
34. Pop up, as a question
35. Catch participant, perhaps
38. Like the Marx Brothers' comedies
39. Instrument with 88 keys
40. Robust
41. Complete
42. Date night option
43. Blue-haired mom

44. It starts January 1
46. Non-European New Zealander
48. Played for a sucker
49. Leader of the masses?
50. Lions and Tigers and Bears
54. Lowly laborer
57. "My dog ate my homework," for example
60. Face off
61. 45-degree serving of pizza
62. Bandleader married to Ava and Lana
63. Winter hazard
64. Elaborate yarns
65. Taxi ticker
66. Took the initiative

Down

1. Jackie Gleason's role in *The Hustler*
2. "Who ___?" (Response to a knock)
3. Familiar trademark
4. Sound of amazement
5. Snappy comment?
6. Something to shake or lend
7. Gets it wrong

8. *The Farmer's Daughter* star Martha
9. Results of some QB passes
10. Surrounded (with "in")
11. Underway, to Sherlock Holmes
12. Restrictions
13. Shoes once made by the United States Rubber Company
19. Westernmost county in Texas
21. Take the plunge
25. High school facility
27. Small bill
28. Labyrinth
29. Panache
30. Born yesterday, so to speak
31. Wood feature
32. ___ one's pockets (profited unfairly)
35. Harum-scarum type
36. Rootless plant
37. The yearling, for one
39. Courteous
40. President after Grant
42. Damage
43. Union label?
44. Bully

45. Outback dweller

46. Bread or cabbage

47. Month known for its showers

49. Verbal elbow in the ribs

51. Major test

52. Land unit

53. Kennel Club reject

55. Uncle Ben's

56. Livestock lunch

58. Ballot option

59. Poetic contraction

Puzzle 55: Ladies, Ladies, Ladies
Tricky

Across

1. "My word!"
5. Org. that gives tips on pet care
9. William Tell's target
14. Test answer, at times
15. It may be read at a fair
16. Old-time newsman
17. Soothing beverage
19. Ship of fuels
20. LAX info
21. Fillable bread
22. Stereo components
23. Part of a rodeo
26. Make the first bid
27. "C'___ la vie!"
28. Cake partner
31. Org. involved with the Scopes trial
34. Accepted as true
36. 1984 Chuck Norris film
40. Commendation
41. Mandlikova of the courts
42. Affectionate name within the family
43. Cable TV news network
44. Song for the fat lady?
47. Utter mayhem
52. What grease monkeys do
55. Theater award
56. "No" to Rob Roy

57. Up in arms
58. What some buy their milk in
60. Revealing skirts
61. Field of study
62. First name in fashion
63. Redolence
64. Sibilant summons
65. Some loaves

Down

1. Mrs. Robert Kennedy
2. The Great Garbo
3. Psychics supposedly read them
4. Ball belle
5. Emulate a film editor
6. George C. Scott's Oscar-winning role
7. Not carrying a piece
8. "I ___ Rock" (Simon and Garfunkel hit)
9. Guitar with no plug
10. Finger attachment
11. Stack
12. Offensive expression
13. Goofs
18. Phrase following dollar amounts, sometimes
22. Electrical pioneer Nikola
24. March king
25. Suffix with "four" or "six", but not "five"

28. Nike competitor
29. Former White House Chief of Staff Panetta
30. Mystery writer Buchanan
31. Gremlins and Pacers
32. 103, in old Rome
33. WWII transports
34. Storage container
35. Wharton's Frome
37. Most restless
38. Forty-___ (gold rush participant)
39. Vanished
44. Strolls leisurely
45. Criticize harshly
46. Prefix with "gram" or "graph"
47. Pillow material
48. Laughs loudly
49. "Have a great time!"
50. It could be made from apples
51. Lily plants
52. Parts of eyeglasses
53. Guitarist Clapton
54. Sheet of stamps
58. It may be between your teeth
59. Point-of-purchase equip. giant

1	2	3	4	■	5	6	7	8	■	9	10	11	12	13
14				■	15				■	16				
17			18					■	■	19				
20			■	21			■	22						
23			24			25				■	■	■	■	■
■	■	■	26			■	27			■	28	29	30	
31	32	33		■	■	34			35					
36			37	38	39									
40						■	■	41						
42			■	43			44	45	46		■	■	■	■
■	■	47			48					49	50	51		
52	53	54		■	55			■	56					
57			■	58				■	59					
60			■	61			■	62						
63			■	64			■	65						

Puzzle 56: Puzzle for Two
Tricky

Across

1. Football gear
5. Twangy, as a voice
10. Some pops end up in here
14. Prefix with ballistic, dynamic, or lite
15. Playground marble
16. Nabisco nibble
17. Caterer's item
18. Mortise connection
19. Three, in a casino
20. Funny dynamic duo
23. *Shogun* belt
24. Kind of maid or moon
25. *Ben-Hur* garb
27. Tennis great Ivan
29. Conscious
33. In the past
34. Row with the flow
36. Place to overnight
37. Bouillabaisse, for example
38. Magical dynamic duo
42. Highland hillside
43. Service charge
44. Charm with flowers and candy
45. For each
46. Make recompense
48. Like the Arctic
52. Oversentimental
54. China's Zhou En-___
56. Lonely number
57. Smoking dynamic duo
62. Ounce of liquor
63. Afghanistan's Karzai
64. Dubai VIP
65. It's pitched
66. Good-night girl of song
67. Surrealist painter Magritte
68. Mosquitoes, to dragonflies
69. Voice between alto and baritone
70. Advantageous position

Down

1. Make the rounds in a police car
2. Bacterium requiring oxygen
3. Attract
4. ___ bean
5. Birth-related
6. To-do list
7. Beach blanket?
8. It may be smashed in a lab
9. Olin in *Romeo Is Bleeding*
10. "Don't tread on me," for example
11. Pipe in water
12. Adolescent
13. Whirligig, for example
21. Pitcher Ryan
22. Short highway?
26. Female pig
28. Ready to serve
30. Enlarge, as a road
31. Formicary resident
32. Was familiar with
35. Castaway's creation
37. Blackthorn fruit
38. One familiar with the Gospel
39. Transistor-radio accessory
40. New prefix
41. Reasoning
42. Modem speed
46. Buccaneer's affirmative
47. Weather whipping boy
49. Was imminent
50. Scorecard division
51. Standard accreditation
53. Small-minded
55. Scotland's only poisonous snake
58. Restaurant check
59. Meadow denizen
60. Prayer finale
61. Word in a James Jones title
62. Auto additive product that is a NASCAR sponsor

1	2	3	4		5	6	7	8	9		10	11	12	13
14					15						16			
17					18						19			
20				21						22				
23				24						25				26
27			28			29	30	31	32			33		
			34		35		36				37			
	38	39				40				41				
42					43			44						
45				46			47		48			49	50	51
52			53					54	55			56		
	57				58	59	60				61			
62					63						64			
65					66						67			
68					69						70			

Puzzle 57: Shark Attack
Tricky

Across

1. Absolutely detest
5. Yin counterpart
9. Certain advanced degrees (Abbr.)
13. All ___ (excited)
14. Sigmund's daughter
15. Get on, as a horse
16. They're a form of consumer protection
18. Ship's lowest deck
19. *Awake, faire Muse,* for example
20. Human ending?
21. Comic strip segment
23. Make tea
25. What a bank becomes, sometimes
28. California white oak
31. One of a temporary 20 in children
33. Join the army
35. Cows' fields
36. Animal facility
37. It can be ear-piercing
38. Goad
40. Tim of *WKRP in Cincinnati*
41. Employment ad letters
42. Ark set
43. First female to swim the Channel
45. She's more than a babysitter
48. Cartoon mirages
49. Hardest hit to get in baseball
50. Pitcher's place
52. Thin nails
54. One-time Camaro rival
55. Denver time zone, briefly
58. Ferber novel
60. Orange-and-black flower
63. Do penance
64. Shamrock isle
65. Preindication
66. Sound that may bring a bad act to an end
67. Hammerhead end
68. Destroyer of sandcastles

Down

1. Angel's aura
2. Added years
3. "Come ___" (Mathis hit)
4. "I" affliction
5. New Haven student, informally
6. Garland for the head, formerly
7. U-turn from SSE
8. Fight for air
9. *West Side Story* star Rita
10. They're used to make the grade
11. A year in the Yucatan
12. "The racer's edge"
15. Some Louvre attractions
17. Students study them
22. Basic hydrocarbon
23. Barely made it home?
24. A Plymouth colony founder
26. French star
27. Sort of scholar
28. Take umbrage
29. One place to promote a new CD
30. County fair award, perhaps
32. Former manager Durocher
34. Like a span of oxen
39. Scala of *The Guns of Navarone*
40. Do one of the three R's
42. Mammal's coat
44. Blood giver
46. Water source or season
47. Type of bag from a restaurant
51. Volunteer state sch.
53. "___ right up!"
55. Mrs. Eisenhower
56. Tireless thing to ride
57. Actress Daly
58. Get droopy
59. Member of a Platte River people
61. Fury
62. Builder's buy

1	2	3	4	■	5	6	7	8	■	■	9	10	11	12
13				■	14				■	15				
16			17						■	18				
19			■	20			■	21	22			■	■	■
■	■	■	23			24	■	25				26	27	
28	29	30			■	31		32						
33				34	■	35				■	36			
37			■	38	39				■	40				
41			■	42				■	43	44				
45			46				47	■	48					
49					■	50		51			■	■	■	■
■	■	52			53	■	54			■	55	56	57	
58	59			■	60	61			■	62				
63				■	64			■	65					
66			■	67			■	68						

Puzzle 58: Verbs on the Run
Tricky

Across

1. A Leeward Island
6. Gaping hole
11. CEO's place
14. Big name in household cleaning
15. Aka Myanmar
16. "___ Daba Honeymoon"
17. Stay in the shade
19. Burns of documentaries
20. Blacken, in a way
21. Atomic energy org.
22. Connecticut collegian
23. Deep cuts
26. Terribly weak, as an excuse
28. AAA recommendation
29. Title for Coptic bishops
31. Ebenezer's exclamation
32. Country in the news
34. Van Gogh had one in his later years
35. Grandparents, often
38. Mixed with water
40. Dictionary
41. Shiny cotton fabric
42. ___ Lingus
43. Wine county
44. *Ben-___*
45. Garlic bulb segment
47. Frat party staple
48. Pollyannaish

51. Wedges in firmly
53. Friend of Wynken and Blynken
54. Like some vbs.
55. Conversation filler
56. Be in the red
57. Be just what the doctor ordered
62. Acapulco aunt
63. Perfect
64. Where to find clowns
65. Sea delicacy
66. "The First Noel," for one
67. The rain here falls mainly on the plain

Down

1. Celebrant's robe
2. "A pocketful of ___ . . ."
3. Country blessed by Lee Greenwood
4. Make a mess of
5. Tennis player Gibson
6. Good buddy, often
7. "What did you say?"
8. Gladiators' milieus
9. Like Mensa members
10. Car maker of note?
11. Be extraordinary
12. Manuscript marks
13. Stock market crash preceder

18. Many a one-hit wonder, today
23. Components of crosswords
24. Heart chambers
25. Make it official
26. Golfer's goal, at the least
27. Eschew the restaurant
30. Dog-scolding word
33. Waiting line
35. Whirling one
36. Captured, at a 64-Across
37. Unexpected obstacles
39. "That's wonderful!"
40. "When I Need You" singer Sayer
42. Nothing counterpart
45. Ringlet-producing gadget
46. Mideast bigwigs
48. Bill worth 10 sawbucks
49. *Deal or No Deal* name
50. Singer in ABBA
52. Jazz genre
55. "___ cost you!"
58. ___-Tse (Chinese philosopher)
59. *Rhoda* mom
60. Wahine's gift
61. Contemporary of Bela

1	2	3	4	5		6	7	8	9	10		11	12	13
14						15						16		
17					18							19		
			20					21				22		
23	24	25					26				27			
28				29		30				31				
32			33		34				35				36	37
38				39				40						
41						42				43				
		44				45			46		47			
48	49			50				51		52				
53				54				55						
56				57		58						59	60	61
62				63						64				
65				66						67				

Puzzle 59: Spy Game
Tricky

Across

1. Beatlesque hairstyles
5. Kind of radio
9. Parts of Scottish accents
14. Moran of *Happy Days*
15. Water or land sport
16. Sci-fi writer Asimov
17. Treble clef reader
18. Dropped leaflets, perhaps
20. See 58-Down
22. Singapore Sling ingredient
23. Center or cure beginning
24. Put down
25. Confirmation phrase
27. Boris Godunov, for example
29. Revolving firework
31. Type of reaction
33. Singer McCartney
34. Sanyo competitor
38. See 58-Down
41. Eye problem
42. Some deer
43. Striped critter
44. ". . . with ___ in sight"
46. Electrical safeguard
47. Big name in small planes
50. ___ Lingus

51. USSR successor
54. Tokyo tie
55. See 58-Down
59. Famed Italian educator
61. Earthenware pot
62. Bar in Fort Knox
63. *Hogan's Heroes* actor Dixon
64. Aquarium problem
65. Some Duma votes
66. "Sighted sub, sank ___"
67. "For ___ — with Love and Squalor"

Down

1. Gettysburg figure
2. Fourth deck of a ship
3. Master gland of the endocrine system
4. Arrogant and annoying person
5. Show up
6. Snakelike fish
7. Beat badly
8. Brood about
9. Foot part
10. Olympic dream team
11. Shortstop's asset
12. Forearm bones
13. Hardly adequate
19. Saintly founder of scholasticism
21. Grassy plain

26. Holds responsible
28. Warning sounds
29. Dwindled
30. Kisses companions
31. The "eye" in broadcasting
32. Castaway's dwelling
33. Subatomic particle
35. Silly individuals
36. Tolstoy title start
37. Chicken-king connector
39. Creates, as havoc
40. Light blue
45. Beginnings
46. Catlike
47. Sam & Dave's "Hold On! I'm ___"
48. Wood from India and Sri Lanka
49. Burn off feathers or hair
50. James ___ Garfield
52. Koran religion
53. Execute an unwritten agreement, in a way
56. Egyptian fertility goddess
57. Astral flare-up
58. This puzzle's underground or undercover thing
60. Rug rat

Puzzle 60: Light Dining
Tricky

Across

1. Pulverize
5. Catches in the act
9. Covered with a hemispherical roof
14. Dealer's call
15. Raines of *The Suspect*
16. Steer clear of
17. Reason to use a clothespin, perhaps
18. Symbol of craziness
19. Use mouthwash
20. Bring-a-dish event
23. Animal's breadbasket
25. Earthquake relief, for example
26. Standard of perfection
27. Tillable
29. Hard-to-swallow verbiage
31. Microwave's nemesis
32. Hunger sign
33. Concert gear
37. Informal event
40. Arthur of the courts
41. Big celebration
42. Mediterranean gulf
43. Gold rush city of 1900
44. More minuscule
45. Printer type

48. Who blows thar?
49. Word with "doctor's" or "greens"
50. Pregame get-together
54. Open-air rooms
55. Shah's homeland
56. Employs a scope
59. Belgian treaty city
60. Partner of a promise
61. Heal, as a radius
62. Bog plant
63. They exist to have a ball
64. Like meringue

Down

1. Longtime Chinese leader
2. As well
3. One's seen on *60 Minutes*
4. White-hat wearer, in stereotypes
5. Nervous one
6. Orally
7. Group that votes alike
8. Went to the bottom
9. Treat with contempt
10. Like a sheep
11. Food from heaven
12. Ford Foundation co-founder

13. Forest ungulates
21. Running total
22. Australian wild dog
23. Venomous black snake
24. Sectors
28. Harden by heat
29. Serve, as stew
30. Peruvian of yore
32. Baby buggy in Hyde Park
33. Cut from the same cloth
34. Changing in form
35. Blender setting
36. Look in wonder
38. Greek marketplace
39. Wickerwork willow
43. Make ineffective
44. They're given in November
45. Bat-maker's tool
46. Broadcasted
47. It supports the cast
48. Michener novel
50. Merchandise markers
51. Arcade foul
52. Buffalo shore
53. Give partner
57. Fighter plane
58. Place to wallow

Puzzle 61: To the Letter
Tricky

Across

1. *Father Knows Best* actress Jane
6. Withhold wages from
10. Sacred bird
14. Be overly attentive, as a waiter
15. First name in scat
16. *Bringing Up Father* girl
17. ". . . and the ___ of defeat"
18. Sprat's preference
19. Hale of *Gilligan's Island*
20. Behave
23. Latish lunchtime
24. Unvaried
25. Spoiler from the sky
28. Prominent span of years
31. Bar choices
35. Barley fibers
36. Finished
38. Neighbor of 12-Down
39. Slap the cuffs on
40. Pencil game entries
42. Beach color
43. Bleak, in verse
45. They're cut by dancers
46. Discovery
47. Sketch over
49. Ring around the collar?
50. Swing a scythe
51. Tournament freebies
53. Before of yore
55. Complete a contract
63. Passing sentences?
64. People shoot it for fun
65. Place for a Chicago touchdown?
66. Glittering vein
67. Popular cookie brand
68. Fracas
69. Satyric stare
70. Swallow flat
71. Rathbone's expression, often

Down

1. Collision noise
2. "Pic-a-nic" basket seeker
3. This company rings a bell
4. Sinews
5. Get a feel for
6. Take-out order?
7. Picador's praise
8. Puts palms together
9. Dorothy's home
10. In a silly manner
11. Font property, sometimes
12. Mideast country
13. Word preceding "souci" or "serif"
21. Requisites
22. Squirrel away
25. Short time off to relax?
26. In the know
27. Under cover
29. Sound from Simba
30. Make void
32. Shaw of swing
33. Prince Harry's mom
34. Wall St. "500"
37. You're tense on this
40. Physician's photos
41. Willow for wicker
44. Dispute settler
46. Add ice, as to an old drink
48. It can be concealed
52. Napper's noise
54. Suite things
55. Kewpie
56. Clarinet cousin
57. Surfer's concern
58. The Johns we don't know
59. Congeal
60. Telemarketer's aim
61. December purchase
62. Soothsayer

Puzzle 62: Eat!
Tricky

Across

1. 4-0 World Series win, for example
6. Abraded
10. Airport queue
14. Co-creator of *The Flintstones*
15. Dead Sea region
16. Peace Prize city
17. Yale of Yale University
18. Bunker buster
19. Where esnes slaved
20. Morning eating place
23. GI with stripes
24. Smaller than small
25. One-time protest site
31. Brothers of soul
32. Island-hopper's stop
33. Brewpub feature
36. Can't do without
37. Mushroom stem
38. Ruinous agent
39. Stumble
40. "I ___ Song Comin' On"
41. Bridge directions
42. Dapper one's wear
44. Just say yes
47. Biblical lifesaver
48. End-of-the-day noshes
55. Fall into a chair
56. "Waiting for the Robert ___"
57. Dazzling effect
58. Roll call yell
59. Reporter's quest
60. Fuel-yielding rock
61. Service closer
62. Big top, for example
63. Creedal statement

Down

1. "The Purple People Eater" singer Wooley
2. A ridge, especially on cloth
3. *Idylls of the King* character
4. Highlighted
5. Corpulent
6. Friday on TV
7. Shark stimulus
8. City on seven hills
9. Fortify, as a town
10. Strongbox
11. Like the yak
12. Smile on
13. Sentimental soul
21. Happy associate
22. Stem-to-stern part
25. Come-on
26. Web surfer
27. Cub or Met, for short
28. Granola-like
29. Being of service
30. Like some stock
33. Tedious undertaking
34. Kick in to a pot
35. Royal pain
37. Feeling
38. It could cause one to lay down on the job
40. Huckleberry or Mickey
41. Heartfelt
42. Intensify
43. Bk. after Hebrews
44. Omega's antithesis
45. City of witch hunts
46. Part of some chains
49. Exultation
50. Chopped down
51. Crammer's concern
52. Family group
53. Crinkly cabbage
54. Leave in after all

Puzzle 63: Comet Watching
Tricky

Across

1. Bibliographic space saver
5. Crude dwellings
9. Nat and Natalie
14. Abnormal breathing
15. Brilliantly colored food fish
16. Worship
17. Flowering plant from South Africa
18. Burrowing insectivore
19. Leg bone
20. Comet
23. Stolen, slangily
24. Anti-price-fixing agcy.
25. Cable channel
28. Physicist Niels
31. Old undergarment
36. *Coffee, Tea ___?*
38. Angora output
40. It was given statehood in 1820
41. Comet
44. Milo or Tessie
45. Powerful shark
46. Some female parents
47. Like a cloudless night
49. Bart's sister
51. Corned beef holder
52. Gumshoe
54. Shade provider
56. Comet
65. Vocally
66. Nondairy spread
67. Folk singer Mitchell
68. Crown
69. Barbecue offering, perhaps
70. Final notice, briefly
71. It's a crying need
72. British nobleman
73. Wagers

Down

1. Estrada of TV
2. Kind of dancer
3. Returned to the perch
4. *Lifestyles of the Rich and Famous* host
5. Everybody has one
6. Well briefed about
7. Baby powder ingredient
8. Rock ledge
9. Underground burial site
10. God of war and poetry
11. Evert specialties
12. Pennsylvania county
13. Cook quickly
21. Fireplace ledge
22. And so on (Abbr.)
25. Santa remarks
26. French seaport
27. Creighton University site
29. 1947 Oscar winner Celeste
30. Part of RCMP
32. Event at Minsky's
33. Lute of India
34. Foe
35. Concise
37. Always
39. Norse god of discord
42. Environmentalists' celebration
43. Big game in college
48. Vote for
50. Chicken ___ king
53. Like some calls
55. Low-paying employment, slangily
56. Shower alternative
57. Pelvic bones
58. Shark's offering
59. Wait in hiding
60. Jazzy Fitzgerald
61. Planetary revolution
62. Honshu seaport
63. Air conditioner, for example
64. Cherry parts

Puzzle 64: You Bet!
Tricky

Across

1. George Herman Ruth, familiarly
5. Burn slightly
9. MacKenzie of old beer ads
14. Curtain color
15. *This Gun for* ___
16. Rabbit fur
17. Surgery reminder
18. Monumental
19. Elroy Jetson's dog
20. Toss the dice, for example
23. Use an ax
24. Disrespects verbally
25. This and that
27. Aviation-related prefix
30. Executor's concern
33. Surmise
37. Matures
39. Camelot lady
40. Payment for a crossing
41. Shirley Temple trademark
42. Prep school since 1440
43. Charles Lamb
44. Pub potables
45. Rock concert venue
46. Predatory bird
48. What Sinbad sailed
50. *The Tortoise and the Hare* writer

52. Not just again
57. "Big" burger, at McDonald's
59. Bet a long shot
62. "Love"-ly word in a Stevie Wonder song
64. Sponge or facial feature
65. They make waves
66. ". . . miss is as good as ___"
67. Related by blood
68. It may be about a foot?
69. Hall of *Let's Make A Deal*
70. Baker's dozen of popes
71. Male turkeys

Down

1. Outperforms
2. Ghana's largest city
3. Donkey sounds
4. Transnational money
5. Kind of cake
6. A 36 of a famous measurement
7. Seed sheath
8. Divide the deck again
9. Satisfies the thirst
10. Faux ___
11. Call one's bluff
12. Fraught with danger, as circumstances
13. It may be on the mountaintop
21. Close by

22. Game that features mating
26. Rodeo attendee
28. Brother of Fidel
29. Mythical meanies
31. Suffix used to form abstract nouns
32. *Show Boat* playwright Ferber
33. Road for Nero
34. Vincent Lopez song
35. One way to make a decision
36. Tickle pink
38. "Is there anything ___?"
41. Yuletide song
45. Arthur, the tennis legend
47. Sea bird
49. Greek capital
51. Like some Vatican bulls
53. Chickens come home to do it
54. State known for potatoes
55. Kind of drive, in a computer
56. Letters that create hurdles for lispers
57. Polite palindromic address
58. Bullets and such
60. Pair up, as oxen
61. Group of three
63. Farthest or highest, briefly

1	2	3	4	■	5	6	7	8	■	9	10	11	12	13
14				■	15				■	16				
17				■	18				■	19				
20			21					22		■	23			
24					■		25			26		■		
■	■	■	■	27		28	29	■	30			■	31	32
33	34	35	36		■	37		38		■	39			
40				■	41				■	42				
43				■	44				■	45				
46			47		■	48		49		■	■	■	■	■
■	■	50				51	■		52		53	54	55	56
57	58		■	59			60	61						
62			63	■	64				■	65				
66				■	67				■	68				
69				■	70				■	71				

Puzzle 65: Look Up
Tricky

Across

1. Lad's sweetheart
5. Decrease in intensity
10. Famous literary bear
14. Ruler part
15. Sticky substance
16. Highest or lowest in the deck
17. TV twosome (1975–79)
20. Postulation
21. Goddess of abundance and fertility
22. Linda Lavin's sitcom role
23. Songbird
25. Sporting spots
26. Road danger
31. Tristan's love
32. Fifth and Sixth, in N.Y.C.
33. Janitor's closet item
36. It's all three words of a liar's policy
37. End ties
39. Variety of cotton
40. Before, poetically
41. Brogan, for example
42. Insightfulness
44. Working a second job
46. Retirement option
49. More than want

50. Some stuff stuffed in tubs
51. Clothe
53. Wedding vow word
57. Trendy theme restaurant
60. Scope lead-in
61. Blackfoot's abode
62. *Key of Valor* author Roberts
63. Montgomery's ___ *of Green Gables*
64. Tom Mix prop
65. Goblet part

Down

1. Santa's got a long one
2. Opening chip, in poker
3. Read rapidly
4. In a cunning way
5. Lifesaving craft?
6. Above partner
7. "Right now!"
8. Cookie holders
9. Wind up
10. Overly aggressive fighter
11. Join the cast of
12. Holiest city of Islam
13. Powdery remains
18. Valuable violin, briefly

19. Rabbit relatives
24. Range of vision
25. Batting statistic
26. One of two in a game
27. ___-friendly
28. What the "poor dog" got
29. "Concerto for the Left Hand" composer
30. Suffix with "correct"
33. "La Bohème" soprano
34. Prophetic sign
35. Hunger feeling
38. Many millennia
39. Insults
41. Drench
43. Like gummy bears
44. Unification Church follower, informally
45. Hearths
46. Momma's guy
47. Tim or Steve
48. Long for
51. "Take ___ Train"
52. Utterance after a spill
54. Tooth or hair part
55. Very painful
56. Dutch cheese
58. Final amt.
59. MGM mascot

1	2	3	4	■	5	6	7	8	9	■	10	11	12	13
14				■	15					■	16			
17				18						19				
20					■	21			■	22				
■	■		23		24			■	25				■	■
26	27	28					29	30				■	■	■
31					■	32				■	33	34	35	
36			■	37	38				■	39				
40			■	41				■	42	43				
■	■		44				■	45						
46	47	48				■	49				■	■	■	■
50				■	51	52			■	53		54	55	56
57				58				59						
60				■	61				■	62				
63				■	64				■	65				

Puzzle 66: Feeling Lucky?
Tricky

Across

1. *Psycho* actress Miles
5. Knitted blanket
11. Barbecue offering
14. Yoked pair
15. City on the Rio Grande
16. Night before
17. Poker dealer's command
19. Didn't get bought
20. Bye, in France
21. Fateful Roman date
22. Some are cooped up
23. Roscoe ___ Brown
24. Wharton deg.
26. Rude and sullen
27. What to do to a Vegas slot machine
31. Two-wheeled carriage
34. "O ___ Night"
35. A Beatle's spouse
36. Gave a buzz
37. Bloodline?
39. Provides succor
40. Creative result
41. Unpopular spots
42. Acts the drum major
44. Roulette maneuver
47. Reach a higher level?
48. 2002 Winter Olympics host

49. Place for losers?
52. Crazy as a ___
53. Bolshevik target
56. Hollow-fanged snake
58. So-so link
59. What crapshooters do
61. Bridal bio word
62. Brooks Robinson was one
63. Low in fat
64. Filling degree?
65. Greater in excellence
66. *Show Boat* author Ferber

Down

1. Not shy with one's opinion
2. Discharge gradually
3. Fix a loose shoelace, for example
4. Poker buy-in
5. Guinness specialty
6. Beauty parlor treatment
7. Degree holder, for short
8. Where I wish you were
9. Makes a contribution
10. Refusals
11. Water tower
12. Three-time U.S. Open champ
13. Famous seamstress

18. Partially decomposed organic matter
22. Shade
25. Laundry additive
26. Kind of dog
27. Pot-bellied critter
28. Lost on purpose
29. Very popular
30. Gladdens the heart
31. Bad way to touch down in a plane
32. Speared, as a whale
33. Direct opposites
38. "Take ___"
39. Have a bug
41. Tennis tour letters
43. Bob's partner?
45. Woman of habit?
46. Rush violently
49. Went undercover
50. Pie choice
51. Sports center
53. Ran like the dickens
54. Skirt vent
55. Jillions
57. Sitting on one's hands
59. Mary's *Dick Van Dyke* hubby
60. Yonder damsel

1	2	3	4	■	5	6	7	8	9	10	■	11	12	13
14				■	15						■	16		
17				18							■	19		
20				■		21				■	22			
23			■	24	25		■			26				
■	■	■	27				28	29	30					
31	32	33			■	34				■	35			
36				■	37	38				■	39			
40			■	41				■	42	43				
44			45				46				■	■	■	■
47					■	■		48			■	49	50	51
52				■	53	54	55		■	56	57			
58			■	59					60					
61			■	62					■	63				
64			■	65					■	66				

Puzzle 67: On Tap?
Tricky

Across

1. Hinged implement
6. Industrial haze
10. Like Dorothy's slippers
14. Certain Nordic person
15. River to the Rhine
16. Big pot of stew
17. Draft
19. E pluribus ___
20. Judge Lance
21. Resort town near Santa Barbara
22. Joe-to-go packets?
24. What two fins equal
26. Go well together
27. Norse god of war
28. Post-arson markdown
32. Victrola successor
35. Push-button predecessor
37. Firmaments
38. "Oh, you wish!"
39. Bee "bite"
41. Significant times, historically
42. Office workers, collectively
44. Disaster ___
45. Proof goof
46. Unwanted overhang
48. Fond du ___, Wisconsin
50. Lean (on)
51. Seasoned vet
55. San Fernando Valley city
58. Ignored the limit
59. Peeples or Long
60. Ellery contemporary
61. Draft
64. Actress Cameron
65. Lady who rings doorbells
66. What a glass of warm pop has?
67. Treater's words
68. They have many teeth
69. Knight's mare

Down

1. Implicit
2. Stand up and speak
3. Synthetic textile
4. Cowpoke's sweetie
5. Charles Schulz character
6. 1978 co-Nobelist Anwar
7. Wailuku's isle
8. Food scrap
9. Yellowstone attraction
10. Draft
11. Elbow-to-wrist bone
12. Obscure
13. Oft-candied tubers
18. Norwegian bays
23. Plays for a sucker
25. Good thing for a cooling-off period?
26. Creator of a storybook Robin
28. Kind of tale
29. Well-ventilated
30. Clear a hurdle
31. Old gas station identification
32. Padlock mate
33. "That's all there ___ it!"
34. Royal order
36. Boot-shaped country
40. Ship's mess
43. Satellite transmission
47. Andean beasts
49. Enhancing accessories
51. Hangs out one's shingle
52. Bill's *Groundhog Day* costar
53. Sibling's daughter
54. Had the nerve
55. Go back to the drawing board
56. Green land?
57. It's grand in baseball
58. What a plow plows
62. Reproductive cells
63. Fall into decay

Puzzle 68: Tricky Situation
Tricky

Across

1. Concerning the ear
5. They can be programmed
9. Four-flusher
14. "___ contendere" (no contest plea)
15. Quaker State port
16. Mend the lawn
17. ___ the Red
18. Preakness entries
20. Swindles
22. Waste allowance
23. Prefix for field or stream
24. Response to a weak joke, perhaps
27. Chamberlain epithet
30. OB-GYN's org.
33. Habitations at high altitudes
35. Anger
36. Words with "pour" or "pass"
37. Swindles
40. Seth's son
41. Vitiate
42. Literary ridicule
43. Domestic retreat
44. Largest African nation
46. Word with "common" or "horse"

47. Frazier or Friday
48. Doing business
50. Swindles
56. What some speculate in
57. 1948 film *The Fallen* ___
59. Make a change
60. Wee thing
61. Bad thing to be under
62. Some stingers
63. Telescope part
64. Sasquatch's kin

Down

1. Hydrogen's number
2. Cause for civil action
3. Operatic Trojan princess
4. Some mixed drinks
5. Chapter and ___
6. Arts companion
7. *Miami Vice* cop
8. Farsighted one?
9. Loss's opposite
10. Salome's royal audience
11. ___ buco (trattoria dish)
12. December song
13. QB's gain or loss
19. Small villages
21. Bald eagle's cousins
24. Displayed a big mouth?

25. Go back to school, in a way
26. Sweater material
28. Coronation coronet
29. It's so taxing!
30. Ordered out
31. Peatlands
32. Parisian's year
34. Clemens and Gompers
36. Grow stronger
38. It's all the craze
39. Desert meccas
44. Detoxifies (with "up")
45. Carney's *Honeymooners* role
47. Mint ___
49. They rhyme with reason
50. Creme-creme center
51. Nosebag filler
52. Bibliographer's abbr.
53. Oscar nominee Blanchett
54. Adams in *The Apartment*
55. Put into piles
56. Like the fish in sashimi
58. Lanai necklace

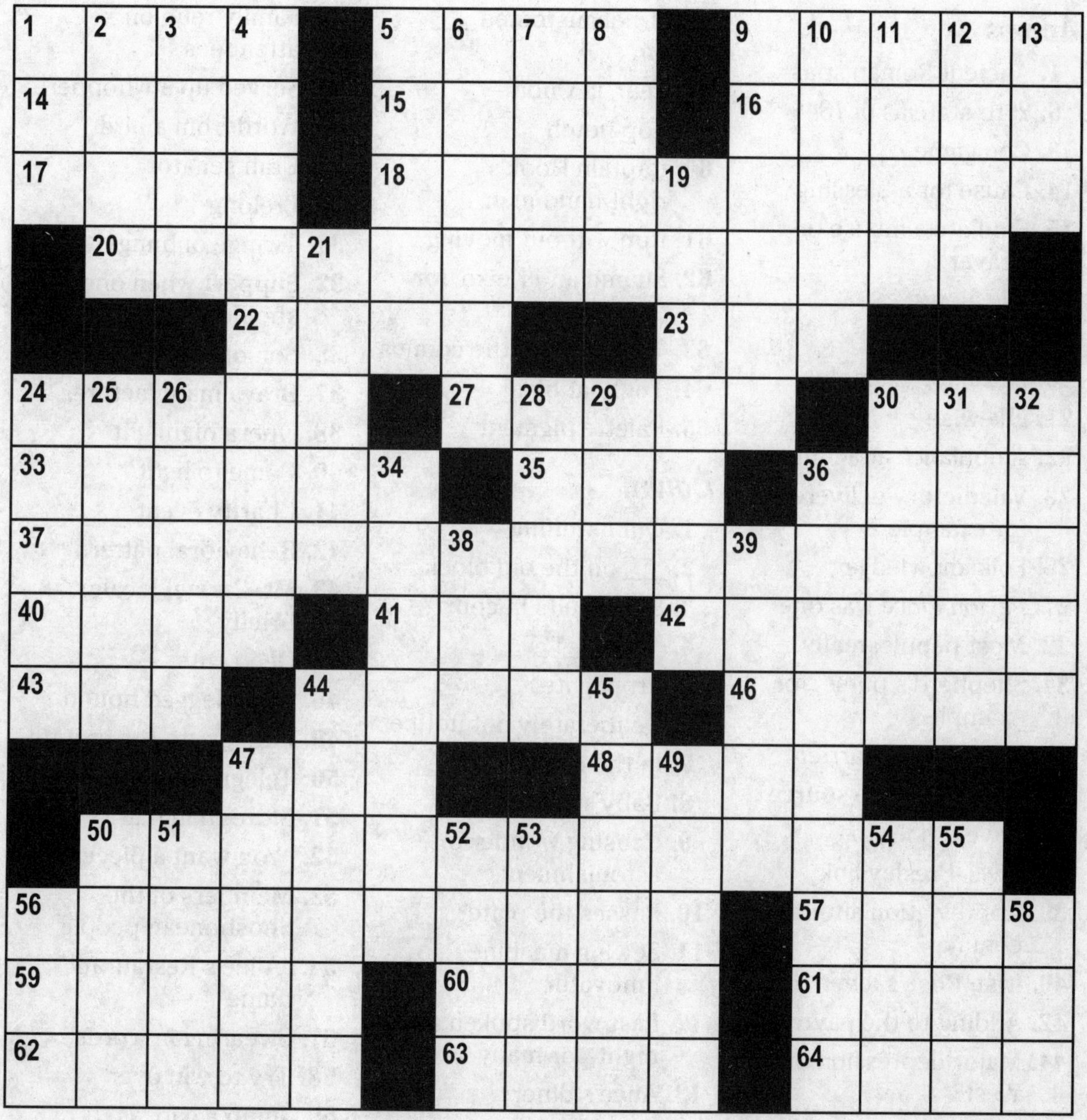

Puzzle 69: Clean Up
Tricky

Across

1. Ancient Roman spas
6. 29th state as of 1846
10. Con game
14. Cause for a blessing
15. Emulate a mouse or beaver
16. Tag along
17. Cry "uncle!"
20. 20-20, for example
21. Likewise
22. Ambulance attachments
23. Valedictory deliverer, for example
26. Folk knowledge
27. *Peyton Place* was one
32. Most people, really
34. Shepherd's purse, for example
35. Genetic info carrier
36. Healthful juice source
37. Gave dinner to
38. Elvis–Presley link
39. Abbreviation after a comma
40. Irish Rose's lover
42. Adding to the payroll
44. Major depression out West?
47. "That ___ hay!"
48. Uncle of Lot
51. Hair care concoction
54. "Unaccustomed ___ am . . ."
55. Year, in Cuba
56. Top-notch
60. Captain Hook's right-hand man
61. Run without moving
62. Shamu and Keiko, for example
63. Trueheart of the comics
64. Tugboat blast
65. Palette pigment

Down

1. Quilt stuffing
2. ___ off the old block
3. Some suits in court?
4. "Yoo-___!"
5. Propagate
6. Deliberately not notice
7. In the know about
8. Baby's cry
9. Causing wonder or astonishment
10. Passes the plate?
11. Sewing machine innovator
12. Last word spoken at night, for many
13. Alice's diner
18. Newsy nuggets
19. Hackneyed, as a joke
24. "I smell ___!"
25. Family reunion attendees
26. Served up a whopper
28. Word from a bird
29. Utah senator
30. Erelong
31. Twinge of hunger
32. Support when one shouldn't
33. Son of Adam and Eve
37. Brava manufacturer
38. Opera highlight
40. Come to light
41. Charity event
42. Behavioral pattern
43. Mt. Carmel locale, briefly
45. Deep cuts
46. Short-legged hound
49. Puts ___ to the ground
50. Telegraph inventor
51. More than half
52. "You want a piece ___?"
53. Members of the Shoshonean people
54. "Alice's Restaurant" name
57. Swearing-in words
58. Try to win over
59. Jump a gap, as electricity

Puzzle 70: A Shrilling Puzzle
Tricky

Across

1. ". . . the gamut of emotions from ___"
5. Helvetica, for example
9. Enterprise medical officer
14. Site of Samson's jawbone slaughter
15. French cheese
16. Geneva's river
17. Smart as a whip
19. Bone below the femur
20. It emits a shrill warning
22. Those in favor
23. Piece of the whole, briefly
24. Utterly unyielding
26. Mark of the serpent?
29. British alphabet enders
32. Moo ___ pork
33. Natural cattle pen
36. Feeling of foreboding
40. Mediocre
41. Board projection
43. Signing gorilla
44. They pull their load
46. Game based on following directions
48. Femur's upper end
50. Dynamic start?
51. Electric guitar pioneer Paul
52. Perch atop
56. It's omitted in alphabetization
58. *Panic in the Streets* director Kazan
59. High-pitched signal device
65. Gracefully slender
67. Trash bag closers
68. Hold in high esteem
69. Kind of formality
70. Feline film heroine
71. *Let's Make ___*
72. Irish singing star
73. Ides of March rebuke

Down

1. Priestly garb
2. Tenure
3. Glenn's home state
4. Fleeces
5. Special investigator
6. Word with "history" or "hygiene"
7. Member of a famous sailing trio
8. Popular aquarium fish
9. "I pity the fool" speaker
10. Shrill singers
11. Snake preyed on by the mongoose
12. Bulb vegetable
13. Brewery need
18. TV hostess Gibbons
21. Rx writers
25. "I knew it!"
26. Is retrocessive
27. Destructive rodent
28. Word with "eye" or "final"
30. Goes platinum?
31. *The Merry Widow* role
34. It makes a shrill noise for attention
35. Coastal Alaskan city
37. World Cup announcer's cry
38. Scottish isle
39. Eighty-six
42. Oil production area
45. Swill opposite
47. Like seven Ryan games
49. Group of seals
52. Brazilian rainforest
53. Troy story?
54. Every song has one
55. One reply to "Who did this?"
57. First name in cosmetics
60. *Damn Yankees* dancer Verdon
61. Lean and sinewy
62. Medieval contest
63. "___ we forget . . ."
64. Jacob's brother
66. Underwater shocker

Puzzle 71: Community Puzzle
Tricky

Across

1. Dromedary features
6. Get out of its way!
10. Word with "electrical" or "red"
14. Take by force
15. "Garfield" canine
16. Land of plenty?
17. Southern Indian
18. Type of balloon
19. Proofreader's notation
20. Oscar vehicle for Jack Palance
23. Florida retirement mecca, informally
26. Seasoned sailor
27. Big name in TVs
28. Bert of *The Wizard of Oz*
29. Defense org. since 1949
32. Unexpected sports result
34. Neck of the woods
35. Historic introduction?
36. Hilo souvenir
37. Pitney title song for a movie
43. Rummy-player's word
44. Work unit
45. Mountain stat.
46. Judge's need
49. Like the Chrysler Building

50. One way to transfer money
51. "Hail, Caesar!"
52. Cause damage to
54. Chase-scene noises
56. New York weekly since 1955 (with *The*)
60. Gutter locale
61. Complain violently
62. Nonsensical
66. Checklist detail
67. Author Gardner
68. Linen shades
69. Shows a profit of
70. They may be black or private
71. Gable's Butler

Down

1. Primitive shelter
2. Olympic basketball team
3. With mouth shut
4. Buyer's minimum-to-maximum
5. Acrobatic maneuver
6. Sacred
7. Fruity drinks
8. Theater district
9. Image-maker's tool
10. Chore
11. Fall flowers
12. Puncture

13. Annoys
21. Bowling target
22. Salad oil holder
23. Blinds piece
24. Hawaiian tuber
25. Narrow escape exclamation
30. Word with 49-Across
31. Snickering sound
33. Plumber's tool
36. Bela of *Dracula*
38. First name in Bedrock
39. Mythical monster
40. Nastase of tennis
41. Fork-tailed shore bird
42. St. Laurent of fashion
46. Cried "Uncle!"
47. Fly an aircraft
48. Luxurious fabric
49. Like a dismal day
53. Fail to clash
55. More likely to cause a skid
57. Moon-landing transports
58. Repulsive
59. Spanish cheers
63. Will be now?
64. Pistachio, for one
65. Ultimate suffix

1	2	3	4	5		6	7	8	9		10	11	12	13
14						15					16			
17						18					19			
			20		21					22				
23	24	25						26				27		
28					29	30	31			32	33			
34				35				36						
37			38				39				40	41	42	
			43				44			45				
46	47	48				49				50				
51				52	53				54	55				
56		57				58	59							
60				61				62		63	64	65		
66				67				68						
69				70				71						

Puzzle 72: Hi, Chum!
Tricky

Across

1. Dinnertime annoyances
6. Tell good jokes
11. Help wanted notice?
14. The Beatles' "Eight Days ___"
15. Saunter
16. Classic TV mom
17. TV landlady
19. *A ___ of Flanders*
20. Before, in poesy
21. Loserless outcomes
22. Ballpark figures
24. Eden denizen
26. Nixon said he was not one
27. Keogh plan relative
28. Some sharp turns
31. Walks in the water
34. Cooking or sewing term
35. Forbes profilee, sometimes
36. Cabbie of old radio
37. In need of paving, perhaps
38. Card game for three
39. Thieves' hideout
40. Martinique landmark
41. Musical interludes
42. Old-time school desk features

44. What did ewe say?
45. Peter and a Wolfe
46. Shipping measure
50. Part man, part machine
52. Miner matters
53. Mauna ___, Hawaii
54. Statute
55. TV surgeon
58. Realtor's offering
59. Agenda details
60. Actress-dancer Champion
61. Powerful pols
62. Twins share them
63. Web destinations

Down

1. Bat hideouts
2. *Bird on ___* (Gibson film)
3. Prying bar
4. Sweet-smelling necklace
5. Figure-eight performers
6. WWII GI, today
7. Extinct, flightless birds
8. "Anchors Aweigh" grp.
9. Word with "blanket" or "guard"
10. Unsightly sight
11. Potential theme for this puzzle

12. "Phew!" inducer
13. Bends in the middle under weight
18. La ___ (weather influence)
23. '50s high school event
25. Slapstick props
26. Societal division
28. Abhors
29. Orderly
30. Overdrinkers
31. Sahara depression
32. Service sign-off
33. TV lawman
34. Optimistic traders
37. Move
38. Actor Penn
40. Old-fashioned topper
41. Kidnappers' demands
43. Benign growth
44. Certain South African
46. Lock not on a door
47. Ready for anything
48. Deep ravine
49. Relieves, as pain
50. ___ *Ha'i*
51. Computer image
52. Treater's announcement
56. Japanese capital
57. Moo goo ___ pan

1	2	3	4	5	■	6	7	8	9	10	■	11	12	13
14					■	15					■	16		
17				18							■	19		
20			■	21				■	22		23			
24			25			■	26					■	■	■
■	■		27			■	28						29	30
31	32	33			■	34				■	35			
36				■	37				■	38				
39			■	40				■	41					
42			43				■	44			■	■	■	■
■	■	45				■	46				47	48	49	
50	51				■	52				■	53			
54			■	55		56				57				
58			■	59				■	60					
61			■	62				■	63					

Puzzle 73: To the Letter
Tricky

Across

1. Go back and forth
5. Physical beginning
9. Grill meat
14. Use an IBM Selectric
15. Nutritive mineral
16. Spine information
17. Mann's *The Magic Mountain* locale
18. "Open 24 hours" sign material, perhaps
19. Liszt piece
20. Thanksgiving dessert
21. G?
23. Ears or eyes?
25. Kind of temper or treatment
26. *Lady Sings the Blues* star
27. Royal Leamington feature
29. Renaissance name of fame
33. "It" girl Bow
35. Persona's opposite
37. Female military gp.
38. B?
41. Line of dramatic development
42. Gardener's support
43. Vegetable spreads
44. Woods' pocketful
46. Word of encouragement
47. Count calories
48. Umbrage
50. De Klerk's successor
53. T?
58. Negative joiner
59. Unconcerned
60. Bit of urban noise
61. Creature not welcomed on Wall Street
62. Lacking sense
63. Without repetition
64. Briny bully
65. At a different time
66. Jury member, in theory
67. Pallid

Down

1. Kind of infection
2. Poet Elinor
3. First sighting
4. Thumbs-up
5. Flirtatious females
6. In an upright position
7. Hammer, for one
8. Grandma Moses
9. Great bargain
10. Diacritical dot
11. Small ornamental case
12. Ray of *The Marrying Kind*
13. Intellectually acute
21. Some English compositions
22. Home of the Dolphins
24. Mi-fa lead-in
27. Serpentine
28. Air freshener scent
30. Further inducements
31. Tampico lunch, perhaps
32. Immature newts
33. Gabfest
34. Myth kin
35. Yonder
36. Consecrate with oil
39. Playful water animal
40. Tireless carrier
45. French writer Beauvoir
47. Gloomier
49. Send, as to a specialist
50. Recipe directive
51. Slender freshwater fish
52. Orderly grouping
53. Harness the wind
54. Bone in the arm
55. Castle guard
56. Boutique
57. Perfect, as one's skills
61. Muscular snake

Puzzle 74: Get a Job
Tricky

Across

1. Omit, in diners
5. Began playing on Broadway
11. Tackle
14. Young Mayberry resident
15. Copy illegally, as software
16. Dijon water
17. Type of help wanted
19. Wire measure
20. Chicago sightings
21. Little wave
23. Melville effort
24. Furnish for free
25. Informs, fink-style
28. Hollered
31. *Clash by Night* playwright
32. Track tipsters
33. Short highway?
34. They may be strained in young families
35. Amusingly outlandish
36. Comic vignette
37. Tree with tough, useful wood
38. Impressionist Claude
39. Knight or rook, for example

40. They're cold-blooded
42. Common aquarium fishes
43. Aviation hero of '27
44. Surround
45. Dumas dueler
47. Retirement incomes
51. Typical question
52. Type of help wanted
54. Riddle-me-___ (children's book catchword)
55. Build a fire under, say
56. Greek goddess of marriage
57. Babi ___ (historical WWII site)
58. Complicated situations
59. Tick-___

Down

1. Hydrant hookup
2. Foreign car make
3. Tuneful cadence
4. Does a freezer-related chore
5. Cruise control or CD player, for example
6. It might be grand
7. Plays a wrong note
8. Rebel slave Turner
9. It goes on and on

10. Mocks
11. Type of help wanted
12. Transportation mode
13. Season to be jolly
18. Greek island
22. Group of seals
24. Emulate Dante's Peak
25. *Three's Company* landlord
26. An Astaire
27. Type of help wanted
28. ___ *a Horseman*
29. New York city
30. Heads of France?
32. U.S. chief justice 1836–64
35. Fever blister
36. "Be patient!"
38. Lightweight recorder
39. Intrinsically
41. Dickens child
42. Traces of color
44. Web-footed honkers
45. Off-course
46. Ostrich look-alike
47. Summer's sign?
48. Cookie snack
49. Decoy to dealers
50. Coyote St.
53. ___ Gatos, California

1
2
3
4
5
6
7
8
9
10
11
12
13
14
15
16
17
18
19
20
21
22
23
24
25
26
27
28
29
30
31
32
33
34
35
36
37
38
39
40
41
42
43
44
45
46
47
48
49
50
51
52
53
54
55
56
57
58
59

Puzzle 75: Shake!
Tricky

Across

1. Yields, as territory
6. Elephant baby
10. Chowder favorite
14. Of a central line
15. Skin cream ingredient
16. Surrounding glow
17. Panorama
18. Agree, with allies
20. Abbreviation meaning "plus additional things"
21. Restaurant bill
23. Steep in brine
24. Like an old bucket of song
26. Give off
28. Agree, in business
33. Small and sprightly
34. *Bus Stop* playwright
35. Large tub
37. King of beasts
38. Peninsula in northeastern Egypt
40. Natalie Wood's sister
41. Average score for the golf course
42. Vehicle for the golf course
43. One type of bear
44. Agree, as in a gentlemen's agreement
48. Roman poet

49. From another planet
50. Goteborg resident
53. Distinctive and stylish elegance
54. First name among baseball ironmen
57. Agree, as in negotiations
60. Resort lake
62. Tandoor, for one
63. Peruvian capital
64. Happening
65. Notable exploit
66. Good earth
67. Stopwatch button

Down

1. Bat hideout
2. Sign by a door
3. Pain, for example
4. Absorb, as a loss
5. Become looser
6. Place to gamble
7. Hit the runway softly
8. Birling surface
9. Low, swampy marsh
10. He wrote *In Cold Blood*
11. Waikiki wingding
12. Pendulum paths
13. Last word in a chess match
19. Stage whisper

22. Yon lady
25. Ugandan despot, Idi
26. It blew its stack in Italy
27. Bethlehem trio
28. Beatles album
29. Rap sheet name, perhaps
30. Kings Peak range
31. Snow disasters
32. Hawaiian isle
36. Cascades lake
38. Hector Hugh Munro
39. Made angry
40. Theater box
42. Musky cat
43. Laser or inkjet
45. Rat or beaver, for example
46. Fir tree
47. Pie ___ mode
50. Component of urban air
51. Whitecap
52. Just gets by (with "out")
53. Peel, played by Rigg
55. Top-notch
56. Riga denizen
58. Corner letter?
59. *Blame It on ___*
61. Old greeting for Caesar

Puzzle 76: Look Here!
Tricky

Across

1. Prerecorded
6. Baseball's Ripken
9. Joplin of ragtime fame
14. Honshu port
15. Stretch the truth
16. Movie tough guy Peter
17. Summer Olympics event
19. Merger
20. Before, formerly
21. "___ the season . . ."
22. Neaten, as a napkin
23. Break in the action
25. Minor transgression
28. Immigration island
30. Word with "fly" or "clap"
31. One 'twixt 12 and 20
32. Term of affection
34. 90 degrees from norte
36. AARP members
37. Words after the end of 17-, 25-, 53-, and 62-A
40. K.C. time zone
43. One way to get to elementary school
44. Workers' incentives
48. Sounds of insight
50. Curved molding

52. "You've got the wrong guy!"
53. Monaco resort
56. Bum, to some
57. Fertilizer ingredient
58. Italian monk
60. Order to a firing squad
61. French states
62. Banded beast
65. Sidewalk show
66. Cooked–turn link
67. Xenophobe's fear
68. Musial and Getz
69. Tub trio
70. Does a darn good job?

Down

1. Dried (off)
2. Generally speaking
3. Kneecap
4. Barely manage (with "out")
5. Kind of board
6. Skeleton site
7. Feel malaise, for example
8. MGM's lion
9. Swerved
10. Meat cooked and preserved in its own fat
11. Some birds

12. Certain fisherman
13. Sinews
18. Apple seed, for example
22. Bird of prey
24. Former Italian bread
26. Spreading plant
27. Like some transactions
29. Absolution targets
33. Former Gracie Mansion resident
35. Distinctive flair
38. Nickname of Aqueduct Racetrack
39. Name that's quite fashionable
40. Some park dwellers
41. Try for
42. Clarion blast
45. Arrive quietly
46. Sent via a click
47. Some weekly messages
49. New York island
51. *Dharma & Greg* star
54. Steven Spielberg openings?
55. ". . . man ___ mouse?"
59. First of all
62. Bread box?
63. Lobster coral
64. Project end?

1	2	3	4	5	■	6	7	8	■	9	10	11	12	13
14					■	15			■	16				
17				18					■	19				
20			■	21			■	■	22					
23			24	■	25		26	27			■			
28				29	■	30				■	31			
32					33	■	34			35	■	36		
■	■	■	37			38				39	■	■	■	■
40	41	42	■	43			■	44			45	46	47	
48			49	■	50		51	■	52					
53				54				55	■	56				
57					■	■	58		59	■	60			
61				■	62	63				64				
65				■	66			■	67					
68				■	69			■	70					

Puzzle 77: Oh Baby
Tricky

Across

1. Washed out
6. WWI art innovation
10. Revered expert
14. Spry
15. Notable Haymarket Square event
16. ICBM launcher
17. Game that leaves you strung out?
19. Son and son-in-law to Claudius
20. Toll rd., perhaps
21. Princely
22. Smiley novel *A Thousand ___*
23. Builders of military bases
25. Tangled tale
27. Enticed deceptively
29. World's third-largest island
33. Stretch for the stars?
36. Seek redress, in a way
37. Join formally
38. It can bring tears to your eyes
40. Price fixer?
42. Bond investor's concern
43. City ravaged by a 1666 fire
45. River into the Gulf of Tonkin

47. Sad comment
48. Rundown condition
49. Olympic gymnast Kerri
51. Labor Dept. watchdog
53. Genealogist's quest
57. Spare-time filler
60. Raisin cousin
62. Poet Sylvia's poet husband
63. Laotians' neighbors
64. Batter's change of mind
66. Rumor propagator
67. Reply to a pen pal?
68. Hairlike cell growths
69. Rich vein
70. Circular current
71. Sleek, furry swimmer

Down

1. Particulars
2. Surprised-looking
3. Bears Super Bowl coach
4. Some monorails
5. Order from on high
6. Prolongs
7. Opera's slave princess
8. Madame Alexander creations
9. Downed
10. Artillery mount
11. Product endorser, hopefully
12. Once-in-a-lifetime

13. Sci-fi sights
18. Oboe parts
22. Intense suffering
24. Red Cross vehicle
26. Nickname associated with honesty
28. Closes in on
30. Carol word
31. Singer with Louis and Duke
32. Henry Ford rival
33. Singer/dancer Falana
34. Party to
35. Salt source
39. In need of a muffler
41. Hit the jackpot, say
44. "I'd rather not"
46. Imbibe
50. World org. based in Paris
52. Crop pest
54. Leaning
55. It might come out with a rub
56. Ventriloquist Bergen
57. WWW language
58. All-Amerian Soap Box Derby state
59. Minus locks
61. Rip apart
64. British miler Sebastian
65. Cleverness

Puzzle 78: It's About Time
Tricky

Across

1. Sail support
5. Wall of earth
9. Clavicle cover
14. Wash up, for example
15. 1997 role for Peter Fonda
16. Abode above
17. Two-dimensional calculation
18. Repair
19. Static attraction
20. Captain Kirk's command, perhaps
23. "___ Loves You" (The Beatles)
24. First name in daytime talk
25. Source of a princess's discomfort
28. Round figure
30. Common street name
31. Bloodletter?
34. Type of alert
36. Cushiness
38. Fable, for example
39. Literary listing
42. Doesn't dawdle
43. Kilmer creation
44. The Tin Woodsman's quest
45. Kind of dog

46. Title for Walter Scott
47. Otic organ
49. Install, as tile
50. Zeros (in on)
52. Burgle
54. Globe-trot
60. Texas cook-off dish
61. Little dipper?
62. Level
63. Throw with force
64. Get exactly right
65. Group with a common ancestor
66. Coastal cove
67. Spiral
68. Parade recipient, perhaps

Down

1. Corned beef sandwich go-with
2. Start to sail?
3. Orate with assurance
4. Collects, as wheat
5. Type of crop
6. Robert of the CSA
7. Taylor or Adoree
8. Intrusive
9. Indian chief
10. Spartan queen
11. Diva's deliverance
12. Tighten a spring

13. Pants part
21. Word with "patrol" or "leave"
22. First *Tonight Show* host
25. Primrose and bridle, for two
26. Compaq communique
27. Westminster, for one
29. Shortly
31. Ear area
32. Prefix meaning "extremely"
33. On edge
35. The six of *Little Nellie Kelly*
37. Deck denizen
38. Start of a giggle
40. Express one's view
41. Kind of pillow
46. Part of USSR
48. Ring of color (Var.)
50. Split
51. Go off the path
53. Screw up
54. Afterwards
55. Iran currency
56. Realm recipient
57. Get one's goat
58. Shakespearean King
59. Feared Fleming foe from fiction
60. Greek "X"

Puzzle 79: Join In
Tricky

Across

1. Online journal
5. Electric stun gun
10. Rude and insensitive one
14. Pan counterpart
15. Be taken with
16. It may be uncontrollable
17. No longer one-sided
18. *Star Wars* director
19. Company's alternative to bankruptcy
20. Gradually decrease
21. Hebrew judge
22. Followed unobserved
24. "Wreck" or "car" preceder
26. Fay's role in *King Kong*
27. Take back
30. Made varsity
35. Rustic poems (Var.)
36. Fever fit
37. Conserve
38. ___ colada
39. Chip off the old urn?
40. Blade of yore
41. They're offensive and looking to score
42. Latin bandleader Puente
43. Alter to make better
44. Father of basketball

46. Dieter's bane
47. L-o-n-g time
48. Big name in cosmetics
50. Eggnog enhancement
53. Norma or Charlotte
54. Have problems sleeping
58. Fine steed
59. Cream of the crop
61. Cowell's show, familiarly
62. A sudden numbing dread
63. Kidney-related
64. Bump on a log, for example
65. Friend in need
66. Indications
67. Reunion attendee

Down

1. Start to form, as a storm
2. Source of basalt
3. Pizza producer
4. United Nations group
5. Scout's discovery
6. Insect stage
7. Gregarious get-together
8. Period of distinction
9. Put another way
10. Use for the conference room

11. Like some vaccines
12. Eye unsubtly
13. Accordion component
23. Formicary member
25. Three for nanny?
27. Become edible, in a way
28. *Absolutely Fabulous* character
29. Grammy winner Lauper
31. Bologna buck
32. Hindu royal (Var.)
33. Fight card listing
34. Papers signifying ownership
36. "We want ___!" (baseball fans' chant)
39. Brandy-based drinks
43. Gape producer
45. Man among Stooges
46. Hardens
49. *Paradise Lost* character
50. ___ Valley, Calif.
51. Russian river or mountains
52. Skyscraping
55. Fish market feature
56. Kind of cracker
57. Runners support it
60. Lanai ring

1	2	3	4		5	6	7	8	9		10	11	12	13
14					15						16			
17					18						19			
20					21				22	23				
			24	25					26					
27	28	29					30	31				32	33	34
35						36					37			
38					39						40			
41					42					43				
44				45					46					
			47				48	49						
50	51	52					53				54	55	56	57
58					59	60					61			
62					63						64			
65					66						67			

Puzzle 80: Having Fun
Tricky

Across

1. Lip cosmetic
6. Bible book
10. One of 39-Across
14. Sing at Sing Sing?
15. Fans do it!
16. Short-tailed wildcat
17. Teddy Roosevelt's daughter
18. Minor land?
19. Fontainebleau lady friend
20. One of 39-Across
22. They're non grata at some motels
23. Do the wrong thing
24. Curing agent
26. Bargain hunter's scene
31. Famous Ford
35. Farm creature
36. Distribute
38. Baseball as opposed to football
39. They're fun for all
43. Pig sound
44. Pad site, perhaps
45. Hadrian's hello
46. Last six lines of poetry
48. Tailor
51. Like half of all major league baseball games

53. Abundance
54. Bambi, notably
57. One of 39-Across
63. Cassini of fashion
64. Inventor's specialty
65. Egyptian Nobelist, 1978
66. Moon valley
67. Hunan, Keemun, etc.
68. Irregularly notched
69. Diminutive suffix
70. Afflictions
71. One of 39-Across

Down

1. Snatch
2. "Deck the Halls" syllables
3. Mayberry character
4. Clobbered
5. Villainous visages
6. Fine equine
7. ___ Nostra (crime syndicate)
8. Works a double shift, for example
9. *Hogan's Heroes* setting
10. Pretentious talk
11. Type of tick-borne disease
12. Type of pricing
13. Simple signatures

21. Role for Chaplin
25. ___-majeste
26. Safecrackers
27. On the qui vive
28. Uncle of *Song of the South*
29. Bulb related to onions
30. Some waist-length jackets
32. Musical key
33. Take off
34. Launderette purchase
37. Olympic blade
40. Knot up
41. Slow-cooked meal
42. Office user's deal
47. Papeete is its capital
49. Made chaotic (with "up")
50. World's largest desert
52. Sing Swiss-style
54. Golfer's call
55. Returned to the perch
56. Raised stripe
58. Kind of estate or time
59. Answer with attitude
60. Wood pussy's defense
61. Map section
62. Jeanne d'Arc et al.

1	2	3	4	5	■	6	7	8	9	■	10	11	12	13
14					■	15				■	16			
17					■	18				■	19			
20					21					■	22			
■	■	■	23			■	■	24		25		■	■	■
26	27	28				29	30	■	31			32	33	34
35			■	36				37	■	38				
39			40	41					42					
43					■	44				■	■	45		
46					47	■	48			49	50			
■	■	■	51			52	■	■	53			■	■	■
54	55	56		■	57		58	59				60	61	62
63				■	64				■	65				
66				■	67				■	68				
69				■	70				■	71				

Puzzle 81: Facing Bills
Tough

Across

1. It's nothing to Pedro
5. Acknowledges applause
9. Allays
14. *Aeneid* figure
15. Song for Callas
16. Deplete
17. Rainier locale
20. Abbr. before an office number
21. Game with matadors
22. Thought
23. Storm start
24. One destined to receive?
25. Italian tenor of note
28. New Year's Eve word
29. Withdraw (with "out")
32. They have pull
33. Breathing apparatus
35. "Hubba hubba" sayer
37. A capital place
40. Standoffish
41. Denuded
42. Barnstorming feat
43. Flat sound
44. Fall short
46. Witchlike women
48. Gulf War missile
49. Large, round, wicker basket
50. It can be concealed
53. Computer symbol
54. Stable bit?
57. Canadian industrial center
60. City on the Penobscot
61. God's was little, in fiction
62. Nightingale's symbol
63. One who wants to know something
64. *We the Living* author
65. Last word in an ultimatum

Down

1. Cronkite's delivery
2. Smell ___ (detect wrongdoing)
3. 10 cc, perhaps
4. ___ Lawn (James Monroe's home)
5. Finance
6. Church staple
7. Two-time figure-skating gold medalist of the 1980s
8. Paulo lead-in
9. Oater saloon feature
10. Awake and moving about
11. Meat type
12. Trumpet accessory
13. Risked getting points
18. "Stupid ___ stupid does"
19. *Pomp and Circumstance* author Coward
23. Con game
24. More gargantuan
25. Pepsi and Coke, but not 7UP
26. Botanical angles
27. Former attorney general and Nevada city
28. Yearly record
29. '50s middleweight champ Bobo
30. Superior grade of black tea
31. Game keepers?
34. Not an auctioned suit, in cards
36. Lively dance in duple time
38. Bawdy
39. Summoned silently
45. *Travels with My* ___ (Graham Greene)
47. $50 Boardwalk outlay
48. Body part mentioned in "That Old Black Magic"
49. Show contempt toward
50. Horse halter
51. "I'm all ___"
52. Without self-control
53. Peruvian Indian
54. Like some confessions
55. Uses a scope
56. Drink like a fish
58. Pole
59. Hearty drink

1	2	3	4		5	6	7	8		9	10	11	12	13
14					15					16				
17				18					19					
20				21					22					
			23					24						
25	26	27				28						29	30	31
32				33	34				35	36				
37			38					39						
40					41					42				
43				44	45				46	47				
			48				49							
50	51	52				53					54	55	56	
57					58				59					
60				61				62						
63				64				65						

Puzzle 82: Write On!
Tough

Across

1. Bugaboo
5. Habitation
10. Home economics' counterpart
14. "Hard ___!" (helm command)
15. Carpenter's tool
16. Knitting term
17. Arsonist's cry?
19. Substitute spread
20. Long-eared equine
21. Desiccated
22. City of Brotherly Love, briefly
24. Margin mark, perhaps
25. Sleuth Vance
26. Braved the rapids
29. Water quantity, often
32. It has a very large floor
33. Wheat husks, for example
34. Back
35. Gregory Peck role
36. Council of ___ (1545–1563)
37. Creche trio (with "the")
38. No-frills resting place
39. Celestial ram
40. Microwave feature
41. Bamboozle
43. Mousetrap temptation
44. Monk's mantle
45. Kicker's target, sometimes
46. Italian island
48. Moisturizer ingredient, perhaps
49. Contender for your title
52. Seek opinions
53. Gun storage for ewe?
56. Catchall Latin citation
57. Commonwealths
58. Swiss chard, for example
59. Means partner
60. Notched and jagged
61. Noted volcano

Down

1. *Ali ___ and the 40 Thieves*
2. "'Tis a pity!"
3. Front-page stuff
4. Sniggler's quarry
5. Wayne's butler
6. Suit
7. "Art of Love" poet
8. "___ Rosenkavalier" (Strauss)
9. Mammoth's kin
10. Victors' reward?
11. Place for the greatest nut-shellers?
12. City south of Moscow
13. Stratagem
18. Like granola
23. Vent sound
24. Seize with a toothpick
25. Schemata
26. *Our Gang* producer Hal
27. Word preceding a blessing, perhaps
28. What a great sculpture may be?
29. What unintelligible writing is to me?
30. Prompts
31. River in France
33. Threshold
36. Velocipede
37. Personal appearance
39. MP's prey
40. Recipient of a stop order?
42. Fire safety activities
43. Pick partner
45. Snow conveyances
46. Eject, as molten lava
47. Whit
48. "___ extra cost to you"
49. Be a worrywart
50. Good sign or bad sign
51. Spanish 1 verb conjugation
54. Skiff need
55. Mount Rushmore man, honest!

Puzzle 83: Or What?
Tough

Across

1. ". . . and to ___ good night"
5. Dish for Twist
10. Tumultuous sit-down
14. "Tres ___!"
15. Above average in size
16. Tear asunder
17. Words with "here I come"
19. Often used Latin abbreviation
20. Forbidding
21. Reflexive pronoun
23. Horse course
24. Odorize by burning
26. Wedding cake feature
29. Piper's due
30. Spot for shots
34. Low in fat
35. Approximately
37. Eruption fallout
38. They're hot south of the border
39. Move aimlessly
40. "Last chance!"
42. Acronymic computer truism
43. It may be light or grand
44. Back muscle, to weightlifters
45. They sometimes accompany ejections
46. Respond to, as information
48. ___ Salvador, El Salvador
49. Brunei's island
52. Priest's simple ceremony
56. All het up
57. When to call me?
60. Editor's option
61. Certain Alaskan
62. First of 13 popes
63. Sniggler's haul
64. "The Winding Stair" poet
65. Masher's look

Down

1. Part of a hocus-pocus phrase
2. "In ___ of flowers . . ."
3. Areas between woods
4. Words with "now"
5. Denzel Washington film
6. Infrequent
7. Caterer's vessel
8. Psyche division
9. Admit
10. Find a buyer beforehand
11. A type of beer
12. Shape of the old pigskin
13. Filthy lucre
18. Orbital period
22. Ivan and Peter
24. Camel string
25. Shoelace place
26. Steppe sister?
27. Fable composer
28. A name for the God of the Old Testament
29. Grapefruit relative
31. Initiate
32. English teacher's concern
33. It was opened before Windows
35. Homo sapiens
36. ". . . ___ the fields we go"
38. Use caller ID
41. They are often juggled
42. Saloon
45. Cower
47. It's here before tomorrow
48. Puts first things first
49. Beseeched
50. S-shaped molding
51. Paper-towel unit
52. Stumblebum
53. *The Morning Watch* author
54. Clog, for example
55. Prepare paint
58. XXX drink, in the comics
59. A floor vote

1	2	3	4	■	5	6	7	8	9	■	10	11	12	13
14				■	15					■	16			
17				18				■		■	19			
20						■		21	22					
■	■	■	23			■	24	25				■	■	■
26	27	28			■	29			■	30		31	32	33
34				■	35				36					
37			■	38							■	39		
40			41						■	42				
43					■	44			■	45				
■	■	■	46		47			■	48			■	■	■
49	50	51			■		52					53	54	55
56				■	57	58	59							
60				■	61					■	62			
63				■	64					■	65			

Puzzle 84: Open Wide
Tough

Across

1. Basilica projection
5. Standard
10. *Green* ___ *and Ham*
14. Fifth Avenue retailer
15. Part of UNCF
16. Butler, for Gable
17. Fodder for Freud
20. Bo Derek's number
21. Telephone line acronym
22. They may fall over the crowd
23. Ad agency award
24. It may be checkered
25. Get in the way of
28. Classify
29. ___ Tome and Principe
32. Carolers' selections
33. Diva ___ Te Kanawa
34. They lay around the farm
35. With nothing in reserve
38. Ages upon ages
39. Golfers' props
40. *Victory* ___ (1954 film)
41. Docs' helpers
42. Argued, as a case
43. Like the knoll associated with J.F.K.
44. "Ah, those were the days"
45. Boats like Noah's
46. Mythical inferior deity
49. "That makes sense"
50. Something the picky pick?
53. Ready for battle
56. Equestrian's grip
57. Like Harvard's walls
58. Costa ___
59. ___ and features
60. Street-smart
61. K–12, scholastically

Down

1. Abbr. in many job titles
2. Color-deficient
3. Largest human organ
4. Clairvoyant skill
5. Word on strikers' signs
6. Heated argument
7. Exclamations of disgust
8. *Bells* ___ *Ringing* (Judy Holliday's last film)
9. Fictional ladies' man
10. ___ & Young (accounting firm)
11. Vincent van ___
12. Model airplane kit requirement
13. Visualizes
18. Wise, presumably
19. Give the boot to
23. Placates
24. Docking locales
25. Make a deduction
26. Dummkopf
27. Lowly workers
28. Blind or broad attachment
29. *Cat in the Hat* author
30. Adds to the kitty
31. Western comic strip "Rick ___"
33. Believers may fall on theirs
34. Words before "Hades" or "a pistol"
36. Ocean off Maine
37. Grocery store
42. Walk heavily
43. Wanting it all
44. Revival shouts
45. Showing evidence of fright
46. Pub missile
47. Environs
48. Kuwaiti noble
49. "Put ___ writing"
50. First name among moonwalkers
51. Cast wearer's problem
52. It's the talk of Bangkok
54. They travel through fallopian tubes
55. Before, in poesy

Puzzle 85: A Trio of Trios
Tough

Across

1. "___, poor Yorick . . ."
5. Classic TV show, *F* ___
10. ___ *at Sea* (Laurel and Hardy movie)
14. Wax bananas?
15. Start to be sorry?
16. *Doctor Dolittle* actress Pratt
17. Sarah McLachlan hit or an opera backwards
18. *M*A*S*H* extra
19. *Woman of the* ___ (Tracy/Hepburn film)
20. TV trio
23. *Wheel of Fortune* buy
24. Dressing may make it better
25. Jerry Lewis film, *The* ___ *Professor*
27. Nickname for Hemingway or Haydn
30. Rita of *West Side Story*
33. *Othello* conspirator
37. Just-for-fun activity
39. Attorney played by Raymond Burr
40. TV trio
43. Begin, as winter
44. Philip of *From Here to Eternity*

45. Civil War side (with "the")
46. Nancy Reagan's designer
48. Michelle of *Crouching Tiger, Hidden Dragon*
50. Loses one's footing
52. *Meet the* ___
56. Paul's *Exodus* co-star
58. TV trio
62. "___ a man with seven wives"
64. Very practical
65. "Lamp ___ My Feet"
66. Dibs on collateral
67. Windward Island Saint ___
68. *Law & Order: Special Victims* ___
69. Retained
70. Satisfy the store owner
71. "Auld Lang ___"

Down

1. Saroyan's *My Name Is* ___
2. "The ___ Got Potential" (Song from *Evita*)
3. Hill who went to Capitol Hill
4. Lesley of *60 Minutes*

5. Emmy-winning *Cagney & Lacey* costar
6. Libertine
7. *Yours, Mine and* ___
8. James of *The Andromeda Strain*
9. Fully attended meeting
10. It's above us all
11. Sailor's response, perhaps
12. ___ *9 from Outer Space*
13. *Two Mules for Sister* ___ (Clint Eastwood movie)
21. ___ sheet (police arrest record)
22. Leaf pores
26. Police adversary of 39-Across
28. El ___, Texas
29. "The Sheik of ___"
31. Mrs. Nick Charles
32. ___ *Angels Have Wings*
33. ___ *Mad Mad Mad Mad World*
34. Stunned
35. Enter Dreamland
36. *Darby* ___ *and the Little People*
38. "Trick" joint
41. Not suitable

42. Insult or a "gorgeous" introduction

47. *Letter from an Unknown Woman* director Max

49. Mins. and mins.

51. Put together

53. Richard Burton film

54. Favorable forecast

55. Sleek fabric

56. Another sleek fabric

57. She's a sweetie in Tahiti

59. *Of ___ and Men*

60. Lena of *Havana*

61. Act like a grandparent

63. You'll get a bang out of it

1	2	3	4		5	6	7	8	9		10	11	12	13
14					15						16			
17					18						19			
20			21						22		23			
	24					25			26					
			27		28	29		30				31	32	
33	34	35	36		37		38		39					
40			41				42							
43					44				45					
46		50			47	48		49						
		50			51		52		53	54	55			
56	57		58			59	60					61		
62		63	64						65					
66			67						68					
69			70						71					

Puzzle 86: In the Waiting Room
Tough

Across

  1. Pantomimist Jacques
  5. Warn a la Lassie
 10. Envelope feature
 14. Arabian Sea gulf
 15. Counting word
 16. "I lack iniquity" speaker
 17. The Islamic community
 18. Asian weight units
 19. Minks and sables
 20. Spicy stews
 22. QED middle
 23. Create a yen
 24. Couturière Schiaparelli
 26. Fuel source
 30. Cosmonaut's home away from home, once
 33. Central, for one
 36. Actor who played Oskar in *Schindler's List*
 37. Form of quartz
 39. Embryo-sac encloser
 41. What this puzzle is about, briefly
 42. Garrisons
 43. Many end in .com
 44. Meaningful
 46. Cognac rating
 47. "That's a funny one!"
 48. Child's wonderland
 51. Certain draft
 53. Like some enemies
 57. ___ and away
 59. Simple questions
 63. Bring the house down
 64. Made an "oopsie"
 65. Tyrrhenian Sea island
 66. Knock for a loop
 67. Creator of Peg Woffington
 68. Part of a jukebox
 69. *Trinity* novelist
 70. They have their ups and downs
 71. Lat. and Ukr., once

Down

  1. Gray-brown
  2. They create spots
  3. Play the siren
  4. Up the creek
  5. "Be serious!"
  6. Collect with a harvester
  7. "__'Clock Jump"
  8. Basketball's Chamberlain
  9. Abate
 10. Shrill woodwinds
 11. Faye Dunaway role
 12. Uttar Pradesh city
 13. Last name in etiquette
 21. *The Name of the Rose* writer Umberto
 25. A new one may be turned over
 27. Watergate figure
 28. Former fillies
 29. "No thanks!"
 31. "Tell ___ the judge"
 32. Poll answerer (Abbr.)
 33. Ritzy
 34. Sneaker brand
 35. *Laugh In* regular
 38. Nanny
 40. Where el sol rises
 45. Ointments for ducktails?
 49. Cantankerous
 50. Louis XIV, for example
 52. They're crossed in Olympic competition
 54. Goes public
 55. Resting place in a garden
 56. Future attorneys' exams
 57. Language of Pakistan
 58. The Jack before Johnny
 60. Twist-off snack
 61. Give a hee and a haw
 62. Fix over

¹	²	³	⁴	■	⁵	⁶	⁷	⁸	⁹	■	¹⁰	¹¹	¹²	¹³
¹⁴				■	¹⁵					■	¹⁶			
¹⁷				■	¹⁸					■	¹⁹			
²⁰			²¹							■	²²			
²³					■	■		²⁴	²⁵			■	■	
■	■		²⁶		²⁷	²⁸	²⁹			■	³⁰	³¹	³²	
³³	³⁴	³⁵		■	³⁶			■	³⁷	³⁸				
³⁹			⁴⁰	■	⁴¹			■	⁴²					
⁴³				■	⁴⁴		⁴⁵	■	⁴⁶					
⁴⁷			■	⁴⁸	⁴⁹			⁵⁰		■	■			
■		⁵¹	⁵²			■	■	⁵³			⁵⁴	⁵⁵	⁵⁶	
⁵⁷	⁵⁸			■	⁵⁹	⁶⁰	⁶¹	⁶²						
⁶³				■	⁶⁴				■	⁶⁵				
⁶⁶				■	⁶⁷				■	⁶⁸				
⁶⁹				■	⁷⁰				■	⁷¹				

Puzzle 87: Smooth Landing
Tough

Across

1. Candied tuber
4. *Casablanca* cafe
9. Native plant life
14. ". . . man ___ mouse?"
15. Moral code
16. Hood of renown
17. "Ick!"
18. Land depletion
20. "Equatorially" ample
22. Things stacked in a parlor
23. He anointed Saul and David as kings
25. Sold out, as an arena
30. Like some criticism
32. Follow suit
33. H.S. dropouts' achievements
35. Southeast Asian language
37. A dropped pop, for example
38. Once around the block
39. Street gang combat
42. Grenade ingredient, perhaps
43. Heep of fiction
45. Whimsically strange
46. "Take ___ Train" (Duke Ellington song)
47. Melancholy poems
50. Make obscure

52. Like a ghost town
54. Spanish wife
57. Makeshift money
59. Someone who makes a lot?
60. Ducks for cover
65. Serpent's mark?
66. Sporting wings
67. Beethoven's last symphony
68. Bank worry
69. Andrew ___ Webber
70. Diminutive suffixes
71. Last word of "America the Beautiful"

Down

1. Acts unpredictably, as a stock price
2. Antilles resort
3. Prepare faux chocolate pastries?
4. Tend to the bird feeder
5. "How was ___ know?"
6. Elegantly stylish
7. Drug smuggler's measures, perhaps
8. Act start
9. Less genial
10. Article for Alamos
11. It's fit to be tied
12. Bravo or Lobo
13. Massachusetts cape

19. Paper measure
21. Grabs some rays
24. Ripsnorter
26. 8½-x-11-inch size, briefly
27. Bulldozers, for example
28. Item used in curling
29. Sealy competitor
31. Drop target, sometimes
33. Bonded, in a way
34. Bogart's role in *High Sierra*
36. Switch setting
39. Hungered partner
40. Fly catcher
41. Supporting ballots
44. Survey blank
46. Rocker Turner
48. Impress indelibly
49. Calm and unruffled
51. Plumb-line measures
53. "I ___ my way . . ." (famous lyrics)
55. Las Vegas show, perhaps
56. Boxing locale
58. Pub serving, sometimes
60. Actor Holbrook
61. Not well
62. It's universal, in Chinese philosophy
63. Shoat place
64. Map abbreviation

1	2	3	■	4	5	6	7	8	■	9	10	11	12	13
14			■	15					■	16				
17			■	18					19					
20			21		■	22				■	■	■	■	■
23					24	■	25			26	27	28	29	
■	■	30				31	■	32						
33	34			■	35		36	■		37				
38			■	39				40	41		■	42		
43			44		■		45			■	46			
47				■	48	49	■	50		51			■	■
52							53	■	54				55	56
■	■	■	■	57				58	■	59				
60	61	62	63						64		■	65		
66					■	67					■	68		
69					■	70					■	71		

Puzzle 88: Temperature Rising
Tough

Across

1. Expect anon
6. Piano exercise
11. Racer's relative
14. California city or cotton cloth
15. House components
16. Seashell seller
17. Showed trepidation
19. Lion or Tiger
20. *A Midsummer Night's Dream* quartet
21. Downhill racer
22. Completely unfamiliar
24. Jocular Johnson
25. Burly
26. Gangster's weapon
29. Fleming characters
31. Poetry Muse
32. Hood
33. Bit of mosaic
37. Lost one's temper
40. Responds in *Jeopardy!*
41. Eye of ___ (part of a *Macbeth* recipe)
42. Be fearful of
43. City near Brigham City
45. Lengthy recitation
46. Withered hags
49. Granola ingredients
50. Fastener for Rosie
51. Cookie sheetful
53. Follow a Vail trail
56. Gardner of Hollywood
57. Compassionate
60. Scuff up, for example
61. Rub out
62. Herman's Hermits' leader
63. Layer
64. Bocelli's pitch
65. "Nifty!"

Down

1. Feel pain
2. *Batman* sound effect
3. Assists
4. *Monsters, ___*
5. Machine shop area
6. Marsh growth
7. Java joint
8. State with conviction
9. Poe's "Annabel ___"
10. What you will?
11. Jellied garnish
12. Ogre of note
13. Flashy flower
18. Mandolin cousin
23. Skills of yesterday
24. Display unity
25. Lovelorn's utterance
26. Country's McEntire
27. Cinnabar, taconite, and so on
28. Potato holder
29. Displayed
30. Masters' stroke
32. Archaic pronoun
34. Invention beginning
35. Mean partner
36. Little whirlpool
38. Drops the curtain on
39. Lily Tomlin character
44. Jump in the pool
45. *Arsenic and Old ___*
46. Swimmer's bane
47. Romantic competitor
48. Part of a floral carpel
49. It may be just past significant
51. Fiber source
52. "Are not!" retort
53. Classical colonnade
54. Superman, most often
55. Lead-in for "gram" or "graph"
58. Were now?
59. Lobster coral

1	2	3	4	5		6	7	8	9	10		11	12	13
14						15						16		
17					18							19		
20				21						22	23			
			24						25					
26	27	28					29	30						
31						32					33	34	35	36
37				38					39					
40				41					42					
			43	44				45						
46	47	48						49						
50						51	52					53	54	55
56				57	58					59				
60				61					62					
63				64					65					

Puzzle 89: Rules are Rules
Tough

Across

1. *Call Me* ___ (Hope film)
6. "What a pity!"
10. Strike breaker
14. Ticks off
15. Type of defense
16. Glee club member
17. International hold-up man?
18. Wedding cake layer
19. Word with "base" or "summer"
20. By any means
23. Rumanian coin
24. Congenial
25. No so great
28. Polished off
29. Gangster's gun
30. TV actress Charlotte
31. Not yet solidified
34. Kind of alert
36. Scholarly book
37. However one can
40. Oracle's sign
41. Ultimatum word
42. Delineates
43. Go ___ (freak out)
44. Uh-huh
45. Someone or something special

46. Give a pounding
48. Molecule piece
50. Pressure unit
53. Without constraint
56. Exploitive fellow
58. Light green legume
59. Stocking shade
60. Musical pause
61. Arab ruler
62. Nepal's neighbor
63. Agcy. known to shoot for the stars
64. Elbow benders
65. Advantageous purchase

Down

1. Donnybrook
2. Slender branch
3. Reduce, as fears
4. Full-strength, as a drink
5. Give one's approval for
6. People conquered by Cortés
7. French wine valley and river
8. In a fresh way
9. Blood bank science
10. Gives the axe
11. Teacher's milieu
12. Bread machine?

13. Monk's style
21. Engage in a contest
22. Warning hue
26. Ireland's De Valera
27. Smells awful
28. Eternity
29. Friar's attire
31. WWII predator
32. Insect larva
33. Transparent quality
34. Flatfish
35. Bride's new title
36. Even off
38. Peepers' places
39. Ornamental flowering vine
44. Cinder
45. Old salt
47. Heart line
48. Own up to
49. Some past despots
50. Goody-goody
51. Rich brown pigment
52. Standard of perfection
54. VIP transport
55. Babble angrily
56. Footed vase
57. Bounding main

1	2	3	4	5		6	7	8	9		10	11	12	13
14						15					16			
17						18					19			
20					21					22				
23				24					25				26	27
			28					29				30		
31	32	33				34	35				36			
37					38					39				
40					41					42				
43				44					45					
46			47				48	49				50	51	52
		53				54					55			
56	57				58					59				
60					61					62				
63					64					65				

Puzzle 90: Water Ways
Tough

Across

1. Some cantata singers
6. Fine-grained mineral
10. "Want to hear a secret?"
14. Small hand drum
15. Truant, in the USMC
16. Blues singer James
17. It doesn't leave a paper trail
18. Linda Ronstadt hit
20. Olfactory stimuli
22. Parking lot topper
23. Hosp. employee
24. Brainstorm
26. Sweetest and kindest
28. Bobby Darin hit
33. It could be stuffed
34. Actor Erwin
35. Stadium sounds
39. Fall, while surfing
42. Finch
44. Glance impolitely
45. U.S.A. defense agency
47. Diamond-studded topper
48. Part of an Otis Redding hit
52. Puget Sound city
55. Combat for two
56. Familiar vow
57. Exist
59. Footwear giant
63. Henry Mancini hit
66. Got into pitch
68. Gardner of fiction
69. Roman ruler
70. Step into
71. Lull
72. Trouble persistently
73. Pitiless

Down

1. "It must have been something I ___!"
2. Spiritual leader
3. A winter lift
4. Miscellanea
5. *Rebel Without a Cause* actor
6. Programmed command for fixed indentations
7. Leatherworker's tool
8. Big galoot
9. Makes quite a profit
10. Word with "soup" or "shooter"
11. Vogue
12. F3.5 and F4.0
13. Reproach bitterly
19. It's cheesy
21. Cookbook direction
25. Patient sounds?
27. King novel
28. Big sports event
29. Peace Nobelist Wiesel
30. "Oh, my!"
31. Strain one's muscles
32. Toy store aliens
36. League type
37. Israeli dance
38. Oscillate
40. Not concerned
41. "For shame!"
43. They participate in big games
46. Icelander's catch
49. Tent tycoon
50. Plow line
51. Start of a giggle
52. Official recorder
53. Hold precious
54. Chills
58. Free from fluctuations
60. It can be a drag
61. Understanding
62. Quick-witted
64. Spiker's barrier
65. Historic time
67. Unbuttered

Puzzle 91: Who's Trying Now?
Tough

Across

1. Jazz variation
6. Word with "bar" or "binary"
10. Little bits
14. Roll with the punches
15. Cutlass, for one
16. Heir to the Ponderosa
17. Try
19. Diving position
20. Counterfeiters' nemeses
21. Japanese Prime Minister Hirobumi
22. "It's been ___ pleasure"
23. Try
27. Certain woodwind player
29. Comparer's words
30. Plays in city after city
31. Places for idols
36. "___ the season to be jolly"
37. Buenos ___
38. Bud's funny bud
39. White-flowered shrubs
42. Fife player's percussion
44. Track-and-field contest
45. Cause to expand, as pupils
46. Try
51. 007, for example
52. Guy who's all thumbs
53. Foot portion
56. Cape Town cash
57. And try again . . .
60. Lid irritation
61. Asia's shrinking sea
62. Smooths, as the way
63. ___ over heels
64. Like an owl, supposedly
65. Mules, hinnies, and such

Down

1. Sheet of matted cotton
2. Coated dairy product
3. Where breads, cakes, and pastries may be made
4. Kind of concert or market
5. "Harper Valley ___"
6. Raccoon relative
7. James of *The Andromeda Strain*
8. Outlawed pesticide
9. Suffix with Taiwan or Peking
10. Carrot's principal feeder
11. "Farewell" from France
12. Capital of Senegal
13. Small, silvery fish
18. Pinball violation
22. *Hamlet* fivesome
24. Naval monogram on many ships
25. *The Prince of* ___
26. "Sweet" suffixes
27. "Beetle Bailey" dog
28. A way to cook eggs
31. Michelangelo work
32. Make a faux pas
33. Obstacle to success or large sea bird
34. Burglar's swag
35. Completely convinced
37. Middle East gulf
40. Changed for the better
41. Nice and tidy
42. Comedian Conway
43. Llama cousins
45. Resist with boldness
46. Swampland
47. Fine print, perhaps
48. Safari country
49. Old Roman wraps
50. *Knights of the Round* ___ (1953)
54. Canadian Native American
55. Pianist Dame Myra
57. Like most fish in sushi
58. "Mentalist" Geller
59. Red or Dead body of water

1	2	3	4	5		6	7	8	9		10	11	12	13
14						15					16			
17					18						19			
20						21					22			
		23		24				25	26					
27	28						29							
30						31	32					33	34	35
36					37						38			
39			40	41					42	43				
			44					45						
46	47	48				49	50							
51						52				53		54	55	
56				57	58				59					
60				61					62					
63				64					65					

Puzzle 92: Check Out the Joint
Tough

Across

1. Frost in the air
4. Thespian's trophy
9. Type of position
14. Suffix with "hero"
15. Stuff in the attic?
16. Word with "zinc" or "nitrous"
17. It may be pulled or bent
18. Cockney's challenge
19. Jewish calendar month
20. Bumbling ones
23. Close again, as an envelope
24. Gray's area?
28. City south of Moscow
29. Downright unpleasant
32. Prefix for "term" or "wife"
33. Movie critic Roger
35. Flower holders
37. Pasta choice
41. *Meet the ___*
42. Metric measures
43. "I love" to Latin lovers
44. She vanted to be left alone
46. Freelancer's enc.
50. Endangered Florida creature
53. Motion of the ocean result

55. Hilarious
58. So old that it's new
61. Stringed Renaissance instruments
62. Actress Gretchen
63. "The Hollow Men" poet
64. Escape detection
65. Miner's discovery
66. *Divine Poems* author
67. Scotch partners?
68. Chocolate factory need

Down

1. Pitching brothers Joe and Phil
2. More mindless
3. Examine closely
4. Bay of Japan
5. Not yet used
6. ___ d'Azur
7. Gothic doorway shape
8. Prepare leftovers
9. *The Grapes of Wrath* actor
10. Occupy time and space
11. "___ better to have loved . . ."
12. This org. has a lot of pull
13. Cariou in *The Four Seasons*
21. Famous folks
22. "___ other questions?"

25. Writing on the wall, for example
26. *La Boheme* heroine
27. PGA measurements
30. Kind of wrestling
31. Garden support
34. Diddley and Derek
35. BO sign
36. 50-50 chance
37. *At Wit's End* author Bombeck
38. Former heavyweight champion Spinks
39. Op. ___ (footnote abbr.)
40. Star of a classic sitcom
41. Grier or Shriver
44. "Wow!" to Beaver Cleaver
45. Passes a rope through
47. *The Gods Themselves* author Isaac
48. Lady in Spain
49. Aerie newborn
51. Ohio's rubber city
52. Gov't security
54. Cathedral parts
56. Minuteman's home?
57. With the volume on 10
58. Roulette play
59. "Turn to Stone" group
60. Oz woodman's composition

1	2	3		4	5	6	7	8		9	10	11	12	13
14				15						16				
17				18						19				
20			21						22					
23								24				25	26	27
28					29	30	31				32			
			33	34					35	36				
	37	38					39	40						
41						42								
43				44	45					46	47	48	49	
50			51	52				53	54					
			55			56	57							
58	59	60				61					62			
63					64						65			
66					67						68			

Puzzle 93: Bye Bye!
Tough

Across

1. Wryly amusing
6. Swedish import
10. Abbr. in a real estate ad
14. Like *The Twilight Zone*
15. "___ boy!"
16. Moreno or Hayworth
17. Ward and June's decision?
20. *Monty Python* star
21. With 53-Across, a Beatles song
22. More than required
23. Kind of vibes
24. Start with school
25. Used "th" in place of "s"
29. Do home work?
34. "___ nous" (confidentially)
35. Brewer's kiln
36. Opposite of stet
37. Lose one's cool
40. It may be tall
41. Aft
42. Heathen
43. They may travel by butterfly
45. Balance sheet item
46. Brian of rock
47. Ring cheer
48. Bogart's role in *Casablanca*
52. Caesar's welcome
53. See 21-Across
57. Use up all the alibis
60. "That makes ___ of sense"
61. Neighbor of Turkmenistan
62. Dear, as a price
63. Sandwich staple
64. Pullman and passenger, for two
65. Type of bear

Down

1. Bagel source, often
2. Bassoon part
3. Verbalized
4. "___, from New York . . ."
5. *To Kill a Mockingbird* author
6. Full and satisfied
7. Member of a bar assoc.
8. Start of a vol. 1 heading
9. Yankee legend
10. Bric-a-___
11. Low-class joint
12. 66 and others
13. Utopia Plains setting
18. "If ___ a Hammer"
19. Farrow and Gardner, in Sinatra's life
23. "Where's the ___?"
24. Tough question
25. Some turns
26. Nonblood relative
27. Record groove cutters
28. Introduction
29. Punch-line payoff
30. Best and Ferber
31. Marsh plant
32. ___ ease (uncomfortable)
33. High schoolers
35. Alamogordo's county
38. Frantic
39. Church section
44. Computer selection screen
45. Author Haley
47. Many operate on gas
48. Obnoxious young'un
49. Pip
50. Many a lit. author
51. Jot
52. Not nearby
53. Burlap ingredient
54. Secondhand
55. Exploit
56. Catch sight of
58. Man-mouse filler
59. Chicago clock setting

Puzzle 94: Gardening 101
Tough

Across

1. Mr. Bean portrayer Atkinson
6. FBI agt.
10. Our portliest president
14. Europe's second largest lake
15. Declaim wildly
16. Out of work
17. Animal in a roundup
18. "Pretty maids all in ___"
19. Timely benefit
20. "Auld'" land
21. Stop at the outset
24. Elevator inventor Otis
26. Old West tales
27. Kind of saw or tire
29. Colonial insect
30. Love deity
31. Very light brown
34. Operating room substance, once
39. Make a bust?
41. Van Gogh's sacrifice
42. It's full of holes
43. Lugs around
44. First word in many letters
46. Biblical utopia
47. Orangutan
49. Displaced person
51. Historic Harlem theater

55. *Seinfeld* friend
57. Celeste Holm musical
59. ___ *Lucky Night* (1945)
62. Smoky mist
63. Glossary entry
64. Semiconductor device
66. Unnamed people or things
67. Brainstorming session result
68. NBA Hall-of-Famer Baylor
69. McCarthy's prey
70. Barracks beds
71. Bowler's button

Down

1. Betsy or Diana
2. "Hang ___ your hats"
3. Remove unwanted elements
4. "Act your ___!"
5. Land in C.S. Lewis's *Chronicles*
6. Economics textbook feature
7. *West Side Story* song
8. Shakespeare's river
9. "Danke Schoen" singer Wayne
10. *Seven Years in ___*
11. Baked brick building
12. Bakery staple

13. Works the garden
22. ___ of Wight
23. Finds intolerable
25. Tightly twisted thread
27. Take a breather
28. With the bow, in music
29. Surrounding glow
32. Formally hand over
33. *Diff'rent Strokes* actress Charlotte
35. Promotional link
36. Large rodents with sharp bristles
37. ". . . lived happily ___ after"
38. Actress Russo
40. Verse from King David
45. Raise children
48. Kind of justice
50. Weather forecast word
51. More than dislike
52. Carpenter's tool
53. Seeped slowly
54. Rich soil deposit
55. Everglades resident
56. Succotash beans
58. Decorate anew
60. Entertaining Adams
61. Monthly expense, for some
65. ___ de France

1 2 3 4 5 6 7 8 9 10 11 12 13
14 15 16
17 18 19
20 21 22 23
24 25 26
27 28 29
30 31 32 33 34 35 36 37 38
39 40 41 42
43 44 45 46
47 48 49 50
51 52 53 54 55 56
57 58 59 60 61
62 63 64 65
66 67 68
69 70 71

Puzzle 95: Try It On
Tough

Across

1. 1 on the Mohs scale
5. Former NATO Mediterranean headquarters
10. Gravy spoiler
14. Black-and-white delight
15. Therapeutic plants
16. Translucent gem
17. A car might have one on it
18. Puts on the market
19. 1995 Dodger phenom Hideo
20. Massive
22. Summer pest
23. Chef's catch phrase
24. Thurston Howell III type
26. Bonnie's tie with Clyde?
29. Secured, as a deal
32. Base individuals?
36. Apply paint hastily
38. Spielberg soldier
40. Poetic Dickinson
41. Kachina fashioner
42. Trial companion
44. Become hazy
45. Symbol for electrical resistance
47. Site of the fabled forges of the Cyclopes
48. Teamster's truck

49. Hora's featured shape
51. Brood overseers
53. Initials of a crack team?
54. Vent sound
56. Noche's antithesis
58. Building location
61. Difficult tasks
67. Hole in a sweater?
68. Universally accepted principle
69. Have ___ in one's bonnet
70. Inflammation suffix
71. Describing pitch
72. Blame bearer
73. Anthroponym
74. Antagonist
75. Denouements

Down

1. Crossing cost
2. Domingo piece
3. Disconcerting look
4. "1-2-3-kick" dance
5. One-sided contest
6. *Tess of the D'Urbervilles*' cad
7. Entertainer Falana
8. Acts the stoolie
9. Thumbs-up
10. Acts of desperation on the gridiron

11. Conversant about
12. Cradle call
13. It sometimes thickens
21. "Y" wearer
25. Pitchblende is one
26. For this purpose only
27. Ruth's mother-in-law
28. Super conclusion?
30. Jane of fiction
31. First name among film villains
33. Lubricated
34. Fashionable feather
35. UAR component
37. High muck-a-muck
39. ___ the wiser
43. With no apparent pattern
46. Fatima's husband
50. What you will, perhaps
52. Knight, by definition
55. The "S" of WASP
57. Traditional truism
58. *Wheel of Fortune* option
59. Cyclops's I?
60. Minimal haircut
62. Waiter's place
63. Good soil
64. Dark, poetically
65. Library byword
66. They're erected on Broadway

1 2 3 4 5 6 7 8 9 10 11 12 13
14 15 16
17 18 19
20 21 22
23 24 25
26 27 28 29 30 31 32 33 34 35
36 37 38 39 40
41 42 43 44
45 46 47 48
49 50 51 52 53
54 55 56 57
58 59 60 61 62 63 64 65 66
67 68 69
70 71 72
73 74 75

Puzzle 96: New Approach
Tough

Across

1. *East of* ___
5. Speaker go-with
8. Co-Nobelist with Begin
13. Baltimore Colt Hall of Famer Marchetti
14. Remarkable deed
16. Prepare for painting
17. Deserves a slap, perhaps
19. Red Square mausoleum occupant
20. Have the same views
21. "Take This Job and ___ It"
23. Carbon-14 determination
24. *Hee Haw* banjoist Clark
25. Right from the oven
28. Net gains?
30. End of a college address
31. Existed
33. Where Ivory soap and the pop-top can were invented
37. Desert spot
41. It flows through a conductor
44. English test, perhaps
45. Four-footed friends
46. *Two Years Before the Mast* writer
47. Gym alternative
49. "Hey there"

51. "Not a minute afterward"
57. Contemptible fellow
60. Encouraging word
61. "Is that your ___ answer?"
62. Idolize
64. What the fat lady sings
66. One-time paperback
68. Combat doctor
69. *Call of the Wild* vehicle
70. Melodious Horne
71. Condensed but memorable saying
72. Some NCAA basketball players
73. Carhop's load

Down

1. British actress Samantha
2. Mexican artist Rivera
3. Contestants' costs
4. Race-winning margin, sometimes
5. Neighbor of Eur.
6. Reagan attorney general
7. Ottoman official
8. Display of grandeur
9. *Butterflies* ___ *Free*
10. Talk-show hostess Shore
11. Southwest sidekick
12. Group principle

15. Shoe man McCann
18. Parker of *Old Yeller*
22. Go for the gold
26. Thursday is named for him
27. Property protectors
29. One way to pay
31. Quilters' get-together
32. Singh rival
34. Place to shoot from
35. It may be crushed
36. World Series mo.
38. Auto sprucer-upper
39. Country lodging
40. RR stop
42. Word processing decision
43. Org. that delivers the goods
48. Clay, today
50. Cutup with Oliver
51. Fragrance
52. For later viewing
53. Screen vixen Bara
54. Sentence joiners
55. Coin toss choice
56. Glue name
58. *Gladiator* setting
59. Postponement
63. Numskull
65. Predetermine the outcome
67. Sullivan and Koch

1	2	3	4		5	6	7			8	9	10	11	12
13					14			15		16				
17				18						19				
20						21			22			23		
24				25	26					27				
		28	29						30					
31	32				33	34	35	36		37		38	39	40
41				42				43						
44					45					46				
			47		48				49	50				
51	52	53				54	55	56				57	58	59
60				61						62	63			
64			65			66			67					
68						69					70			
71							72				73			

Puzzle 97: Masterpiece!
Tough

Across

1. Critically injure
5. More, to minimalists
9. Relieve of weapons
14. Major suffix
15. Differential-gear locale
16. Salk's conquest
17. Run wild
19. Native of Peru
20. Touch lightly in passing
22. Some like it felt
23. Beehive State tribesman
24. Maternally related
28. *It Wasn't All Velvet* autobiographer
31. "Spring forward" letters
34. It became independent in 1821
36. Place to find a porter
37. Its tail flaps in the wind
38. Party hearty
41. It's supportive for those eating in bed
42. Start of the Lord's Prayer
43. Encircled and attacked
44. Fashion monogram
45. Lose one's mind
47. In the poorhouse
48. Music scale note
49. Former name of Tokyo
51. Brilliant idea
59. Sports complex
60. Group of street musicians from 34-Across
62. Clerk of the 4077th
63. Midmonth day
64. Foreign currency
65. To the left, to sailors
66. Abound
67. Tool repository

Down

1. One of the "Little Women"
2. Get from ___ (progress slightly)
3. *Ripley's Believe ___ Not!*
4. It's got food all over it
5. Shaping machine
6. Old-fashioned stage direction
7. Prelude to a duel
8. Word sung by Doris Day
9. Awake into the wee hours
10. "Honest!"
11. Alda of *M*A*S*H*
12. Eyeglass frames
13. Castle defense
18. Facet
21. Cajun concoctions
24. E, on a gas gauge
25. Closes in on
26. Located around a central hub
27. Like Ho's bubbles
29. Reason to buy Met tickets
30. Same old grind
31. Mournful melody
32. One of *The Avengers*
33. White House nickname
35. *My Favorite Year* star
37. Cap site
39. What you want your car engine to do
40. Ryder of Tinseltown
45. Racing vehicle
46. Extent
48. Coast Guard equipment
50. Certain religious philosophy
51. Title sister in an Eastwood film
52. Links hazard
53. More than patch up
54. Leave unsaid
55. Age blue jeans
56. Cold confections
57. "Nope"
58. Mudder's father
61. Turf

Puzzle 98: Just Be U
Tough

Across

1. You may want more for your buck
5. Well suited to the task
10. Wimbledon score
14. Get an ___ effort
15. "Message received"
16. Two-dimensional measure
17. Place of Scarlett fever?
18. Grouse
19. Potatoes partner
20. U
23. Bambi's mother
24. Bummed
25. Some Gillette razors
28. Erie Canal mule, of song
31. Showed concern
35. Emulated Ederle
36. Napoleon cousin
38. June phrase, for many
39. YOU
42. It's average for students
43. Tranquility
44. Make an artistic impression
45. The Buckinghams hit, "Kind of ___"
47. Suggested object for a tit for tat
48. Toyota model
49. Laughing substance
51. Inner-tube innards
52. EWE
60. Delivery at a nightclub
61. Catchers do it
62. Privy to
63. One of the great wet ones
64. Prevention measure?
65. It may leave its mark
66. Decimal units
67. Doctor locator
68. Backtalk

Down

1. Mongol conqueror, Khan
2. Like Churchill's country
3. Ibsen's *Doll*
4. Some Pontiacs
5. Make a case
6. Campus quarters
7. Plate armor
8. ___ up (energizes)
9. Long baskets, in basketballese
10. Greek letter
11. Cookie often eaten inside out
12. Piccata meat
13. Don the feedbag
21. One of the Cyclades
22. PC shortcut
25. Animal support org.
26. Certain jacket
27. Closer to extinction
28. Land's end?
29. Pewter or brass
30. Subscription termination
32. Protests gone awry
33. Draw out
34. Hawaiian warbler
36. Lansing-to-Flint dir.
37. Fury
40. Heart, but not soul
41. Close call
46. Is in sync
48. Word with "sugar" or "cream"
50. Bulletin board overseer
51. Diet ad caption
52. Party pooper
53. Similar in nature
54. Lung opening?
55. It can help you reach the next level
56. Bait fish
57. Crooner Paul
58. Clark's colleague
59. Partner of odds
60. *West Side Story* gang member

1	2	3	4		5	6	7	8	9		10	11	12	13
14					15						16			
17					18						19			
20				21						22				
			23					24						
25	26	27				28	29	30		31		32	33	34
35					36				37			38		
39				40							41			
42				43						44				
45			46			47				48				
			49		50				51					
	52	53				54	55	56				57	58	59
60					61						62			
63					64						65			
66					67						68			

Puzzle 99: And the Band Played On
Tough

Across

1. Piglet's mom
4. Milan's La ___
9. Scarlett O'Hara, for one
14. Rapa ___ (Easter Island)
15. Weighty books
16. Time partner
17. SSTs once crossed it (Abbr.)
18. Bakers, really
19. Intimidated
20. Dated "Darn!"
23. Hidden
24. Big Ten sch.
25. Disencumber
28. Child's play
30. Fried Japanese dish
33. Skirt shape
36. Catch
38. Musical Copland
39. Change of heart?
43. Some waves
44. "Scram!"
45. Choice word
46. Less lenient
49. Source of a blast?
51. It adds 10 to 8?
52. Caribbean liquor
54. Reciprocal
58. Symbol of abundance
61. Fabled fabulist
64. Symbol of strength
65. Partner of wide
66. Regular writing
67. Spanish diacritic
68. Blind rage
69. Not leftover
70. Quite a bit
71. "My country, ___ of thee"

Down

1. Major malfunction
2. ___ the open
3. Uninhabited regions
4. Swiped
5. Formal agreement
6. "My Cup Runneth Over" singer
7. Slow, in music
8. Lend a hand
9. Forth partner
10. Some may be gigantic in Hollywood
11. Order partner
12. Cypress Point placement
13. Word with "tight" or "loose"
21. Hopelessness
22. Word with "ball" or "card"
25. Bucolic
26. Removes clotheslines?
27. Divine poet?
29. What golfers try to break
31. Where you may be given some latitude?
32. Color range
33. Word with "saw" or "sea"
34. Wax eloquent
35. Dandy poet?
37. Do a supermarket job
40. Alternative to smoking?
41. Tuck partner
42. Bull rush?
47. Blow it
48. Seeks solace from
50. Dour
53. Unifying theme
55. Ill-suited
56. Arcade game pioneer
57. Ancient instruments
58. It may wind up on the side of a house
59. Sesame starter
60. Sensed
61. King Kong, for one
62. Distinctive time
63. Lush

1	2	3	■	4	5	6	7	8	■	9	10	11	12	13
14			■	15					■	16				
17			■	18					■	19				
20			21					22			■	■	■	■
23					■	24			■		25	26	27
■	■	■	28			29	■	30		31	32		
33	34	35		■	36		37	■	■	38			
39			40				41	42				
43				■	■	44		■	45				
46				47	48	■	49		50		■	■	■
51			■	52		53	■	54		■	55	56	57
■	■	■	58	59			60				
61	62	63			■	64			■	65			
66				■	67				■	68			
69				■	70				■	71			

Puzzle 100: Ringing in the Ears
Tough

Across

1. Leisurely stroll
6. "Pipe down!"
11. Serpent's warning
14. Beat
15. Opera set in Rome
16. Russian Blue, for example
17. Clock radio feature
19. Spanish river
20. Schedule letters
21. Perry's creator
22. River in New York state
24. Beans go-with
25. Short-tempered one
26. Island country in the eastern Mediterranean Sea
29. Easy mark, slangily
30. Sign a new lease
31. More robust
32. Where Daniel was placed
35. Some batteries
36. Theme of this puzzle
37. Came apart at the seams?
38. Humorously ironic
39. Brings under control, as a horse
40. Liquor measures
41. Clears a disk
43. Lady Godiva got them
44. It looks good when ripped
46. ___ monde (high society)
47. Intimate address
48. Kind of insurance
49. Blonde shade
52. Hospital dept.
53. Many look up to her in N.Y.
56. Leg, in slang
57. Where troops camp after a day's march
58. Advantage
59. Crystal ball, for example
60. *The Magnificent ___*
61. Shorelines do it

Down

1. Mug for the camera
2. Jemima or Millie
3. Greek promenade
4. Tokyo, long ago
5. Seep slowly, as ketchup from a bottle
6. Celery unit
7. Deep impression
8. Surfin' locale of song
9. Christmas season grumps
10. Popular house pet
11. Mosquito season need
12. Steppe antelope
13. Offered one's seat
18. Flubs it
23. Doctor of sci-fi
24. Veep's superior
25. Components of rolling landscapes
26. Bird's pouch
27. Wine connoisseur's concern
28. Acted as if one was in the dark
29. Looks inferior by comparison
31. Macho guys
33. *Harper's Bazaar* illustrator
34. Robert Stack role
36. Standard amount, as interest
37. "How do you like ___?!"
39. South of the border orders
40. Trip and almost fall
42. Caviar, for example
43. Delhi dress
44. Spanish friend

45. One way to get around town

46. Troy beauty

48. Eschew the mouse

49. Fleece-bearing craft

50. Type of diamond earring

51. Exaggerated publicity

54. Org. for warwounded

55. Suffix with "rocket" or "profit"

Puzzle 101: Keep Trying
Tough

Across

1. *Duck Soup* brother
6. Hook alternatives
10. ___ mater
14. Chili-hotness unit
15. Surface extent
16. Hamburger grade
17. Change careers, for example
20. Barely conceal one's anger
21. Clapping animal
22. Symbol of easiness
23. Acerb
25. Done up in braids
27. Like Granny Daisy Moses
30. Certain *Badge* color
32. Northern diving bird
33. Coaching great Parseghian
34. Irritated
36. Printed goofs
40. Try again
43. Become unsteady applying lipstick
44. Stats for hats
45. Old cloth measure
46. Chester White's home
48. New York athlete
49. Baited a trooper
50. War memorials, for example
54. Emptied a barrel?
56. Dawn personified
57. Violist's clef
59. Develop over time
63. Begin anew
66. Pre-owned
67. Two-tone snack
68. Found pleasant
69. Gardening supplies
70. *The Absent-Minded Professor* actor Keenan
71. Contents of some packets

Down

1. Actors who mug
2. Aves have them
3. Autumn tool
4. "___ Woman" (Orbison tune)
5. Brando's birthplace
6. It holds the mayo?
7. *Iliad* figure
8. Assailed on all sides
9. Arid area in Africa
10. PC keyboard key
11. Bounds companion
12. An Osmond
13. Pitched in, and got a hand
18. Rabbit chaser
19. Holmes and Chan, for two
24. State number 28
26. Terrier breed
27. Hangs heavy
28. Proper partner
29. Carry on wildly
31. The best overall material?
34. Type of reality
35. Catches a few winks
37. Attend Andover, for example
38. Let one know you're interested
39. Completely convinced
41. Word with "Anglia" or "Berlin"
42. Restraint
47. Green component
49. Prop for George Burns
50. Arrange, as a blind date
51. Ruin of a statue, perhaps
52. Heretofore
53. Building level
55. Deformed circles
58. Where one's goose is cooked?
60. One place to get fresh water
61. Contended
62. Wraps up
64. Some paper rectangles
65. Period of many years

Puzzle 102: Parts of the Body
Tough

Across

1. Adenoidal
6. Short-winded
11. X-ray cousin
14. "Be-Bop-___" (Gene Vincent hit)
15. Perceived by the ear
16. Auric's creator
17. Strenuous exertion
19. Set afire
20. Carreras, for one
21. Tax type
23. When DST begins
25. Kind of cheese
28. Rider's handful
29. Thumb (through)
31. Snoop
34. *House & Garden* topic
36. Word with "chuck" or "covered"
37. Being tested or tried
40. Grammy winner Manchester
44. Ancient Hebrew prophet
46. Dud on wheels
47. Assent without action
52. What Babe Ruth was, sometimes
53. Feverish chill
54. Java emanation
56. Bad thing to break
57. "I don't believe my eyes!"
60. Word with "basin" or "wave"
62. Fingerlings-to-be
63. Pedestrian shoppers
68. Bard's before
69. Two to one, for one
70. Noted game show announcer
71. Paced the field
72. Time after time
73. Lovers' rendezvous

Down

1. Glasgow turn-down
2. One hundred percent
3. Take away
4. Burn balm
5. Some bowling sites
6. Bodega setting, perhaps
7. Quebec street
8. Keogh relative
9. Alleviate
10. Show muscle?
11. Environment
12. Cookie addition, perhaps
13. Denote or connote
18. Word with "evening" or "night"
22. Political pals
23. Tough-guy actor Ray
24. Claw alternative
26. Chicago-to-Memphis dir.
27. It's in stitches
30. Emulate Cassandra
32. Get more mature
33. Turn over and over
35. Work up
38. Cause of inflation
39. Hawaiian bubbly?
41. Pip-squeak
42. Couch potato's place
43. With a clean slate
45. Title for Arthur Conan Doyle
47. Hardy partner
48. Pay no heed to
49. Put through a blender
50. T-shirt material
51. Kuwaiti head
55. Rewrite for Hollywood
58. Voluminous do
59. Lounge around
61. Off in the distance
64. Baseball great Mel
65. Casual Friday castoff
66. Bouncers read them
67. Barracks bed

Puzzle 103: PC
Tough

Across

1. ___ and all (as is)
6. Draw in
10. Word of hearty concurrence
14. Ready for anything
15. Made cheddar better
16. Sheltered spot
17. Weathercaster's tool
18. Plug in the mouth
19. Delineated
20. Gifted child's performance, perhaps
23. Compass heading
24. On a roll
25. Star of the rotation
28. Tang anagram
31. Tyrannous type
36. Apple or pear
38. Face-to-face exam
40. Alan Ladd classic
41. Some are unsuitable for children
44. "Uncle!"
45. Grain storage locale
46. Give a hand?
47. Ogles
49. Hebrides hats
51. Resort in the Ardennes
52. It has a wet floor
54. NASA thumbs-up
56. Construction superintendent's nightmare
65. Auspicious
66. Wart cause, in folklore
67. Private preceptor
68. Assures, in slang
69. "Not ___ many words"
70. Chopin piece
71. Urbane fellow
72. Dear partner?
73. Compensate

Down

1. *Star Trek* speed
2. Apple treatment, once
3. Change the look of
4. Word with "secret" or "school"
5. Kind of bikini
6. Full of frills
7. Sounds of disgust
8. Arm's length
9. Depp role
10. Current choice
11. Oliver Twist's request
12. From now on
13. Ex-speaker's name
21. Salami city
22. 1998 headline event in India
25. Doctor repellent?
26. Comic "Professor" Irwin ___
27. Get melodramatic
29. Two of all fours
30. Unspoken
32. Tool repository
33. Glass squares
34. Ready for use
35. Current wizard
37. Poacher's needs?
39. Marlene Dietrich role in *Blue Angel*
42. Play reveille
43. Start of a Donne quote
48. Jelly ingredient
50. More malleable
53. Words before "time" or "another"
55. Fonda-Sutherland film
56. Libertine's opposite
57. Wedding shower?
58. Candid
59. Wisecrack
60. Hombre's dwelling
61. Landfill problem
62. Words with "live" or "give"
63. Sonata finale
64. Part of a low straight

1	2	3	4	5		6	7	8	9		10	11	12	13
14						15					16			
17						18					19			
20					21				22					
			23					24						
25	26	27		28		29	30		31		32	33	34	35
36			37		38			39		40				
41				42					43					
44						45					46			
47					48		49			50		51		
				52		53			54		55			
56	57	58	59				60	61				62	63	64
65					66					67				
68					69					70				
71					72					73				

Puzzle 104: Take Off
Tough

Across

1. Distinctive clothing
5. A lot, for many?
9. Ignominy
14. Lotion lily
15. Timely blessing
16. Word with "cap," "bear," or "Regions"
17. Discovery zone?
19. Place setting?
20. Minor planet
21. Manet or Monet, for example
22. You can dig it
23. Caesar's penultimate words
24. Exorcist's adversary
28. Ignore, as an insult
33. Wear away, as popularity
34. James of *The Godfather*
35. Red or White baseball team
36. Quote
37. Squatter's right
39. Miss Kitty's friend
40. Outstanding tennis serve
41. Head of 42-Across
42. Stout cousin
43. To be classified as
46. Word with "soap" or "grand"
47. Greek god of war
48. Last qtr. kickoff
50. Loud and blaring
53. Type of relationship
58. Up the ante
59. Mythical place where sleep is paramount
60. Pearl Mosque country
61. *The Grapes of Wrath* character
62. Horsewhip
63. Ford failure
64. Took advantage of
65. "Auld Lang ___"

Down

1. Type of affair
2. Shakespearean "Bummer!"
3. Decisive defeat
4. "Stand By Me" singer ___ King
5. More than dislike
6. Workplace fixture
7. Hope/Crosby film title word
8. Windup
9. Marked by frugality
10. Spa amenity
11. "___ want for Christmas is . . ."
12. *The Valachi Papers* author Peter
13. Formerly, formerly
18. Old hag
21. Special Forces unit
23. Actor Morales
24. Coffee type, briefly
25. *Fear of Fifty* writer Jong
26. *Psycho* setting
27. Horatian creation
29. Caesar's "veni"
30. Midwest native
31. Campaign target
32. More than required
37. Rock rabbit
38. Young men
39. Where X marks the spot
41. Marine mammal
42. State revenue generator
44. Timmy's pal
45. Former White House nickname
49. Handed over
50. Soft cheese
51. *The Fountainhead* novelist Ayn
52. Pitches in
53. Tara's neighbor, Twelve ___
54. Does in, mob-style
55. Word of exclusivity
56. When two hands meet?
57. What trained athletes look for
59. Bud's partner

Puzzle 105: What's Your Rank?
Tough

Across

1. Operatic villains, often
6. Bit of a tiff
10. Oration location
14. Sneak ___ (look quickly)
15. Mark's successor?
16. Early South American
17. Yukon hero
20. Jack London sailor
21. Tick's cousin
22. Dry with a twist
23. Tater topper, perhaps
25. Elation
27. Good, on the street
30. Bring to a boil?
32. Skip a turn
36. Diminish, in a way
38. Commandment violation
39. Mezzo's colleague
40. Medical soap?
44. 1961 chimp in space
45. Precious eggs
46. At pique's peak?
47. Tropical root
48. Dis
51. Do followers on a music scale
52. Starring role
54. Small paving stone
56. Bit of broccoli
59. Wife of Charlie Chaplin
61. Be a little hoarse
65. Long-running kid's show
68. *The African Queen* screenwriter
69. First name in game show production
70. Neptune's realm
71. Marsh plant
72. Say grace
73. Feature on an old Lincoln?

Down

1. Camden Yards marker
2. Followed suit
3. Withering
4. Musical repeat sign
5. Musician Turner
6. Junior's namesake
7. Minor stroke
8. Chord whose notes are played in rapid succession
9. Rocky peak
10. Condition of needing to be fixed
11. Member of the opposition
12. Elvis, to many
13. Ratted, in mob lingo
18. Preacher's closing
19. Meadow mother
24. Stare amorously
26. Telescope piece
27. Procreate, biblically
28. Sphere of competition
29. Generous sort
31. Fire proof?
33. Setting for a bachelor's last day
34. Washington, for one
35. Pumps have them
37. Depopulated
41. La Scala show-stopper
42. Tube patron
43. Brad of Hollywood
49. Seabees' branch of the military
50. Like Jack Sprat's diet
53. Notable time
55. Slightest evidence
56. Rhinoplasty reminder
57. Capitol Hill worker
58. Cousin of a foil
60. Gumbo pod
62. ___ code
63. Fly high
64. Fishing hole, perhaps
66. Street urchin
67. Whipped cream serving

Puzzle 106: Finding Felines
Tough

Across

1. *Arabian Nights* flying creature
4. Agenda contents
9. Pie choice
14. Santa ___, Calif.
15. What the Beatles inspired
16. Battery terminal
17. N.Y.C. subway
18. It features catkins
20. Second-longest human bone
22. Most microscopic
23. Important business to many states
26. Boxing officials, briefly
27. Establish a better foothold, as with plants
29. Miniature golf club
33. Special-interest grp.
35. Kama ___
37. First name in hoteliers
38. Part of a tooth or orange
40. Participant in a confidence game
42. Give off, as rays
43. Turn swords into plowshares, for example
45. Beverages from Japan
47. Audiophile's stack
48. Daytime showing
50. Very energetic person
52. Jagged rock
54. Type of egg
57. Precipitating in winter, in a way
61. Impolite looker
62. Diagonally
65. Bit of financial planning, for short
66. Loud, as the surf
67. Delicate purple
68. Little bit of liquor
69. Strong tastes or pungent odors
70. Fix firmly in place
71. Wait partner

Down

1. "Nick of Time" singer Bonnie
2. *Blame It* ___ (Michael Caine film)
3. Sneaky thief
4. Makes inoperable
5. Athenian T
6. Nearly half of 99?
7. Atomizer output
8. Nay follower
9. Sore
10. Volunteer recruit
11. Merry king
12. Commotions
13. Colorful amphibian
19. What to do after you "read 'em"
21. Dander
24. Old French coins
25. Emperors in the closet?
28. Three-tone chord
30. Mixologist's creation, perhaps
31. *National Velvet* author Bagnold
32. Exterminator's targets, sometimes
33. Musical composition
34. Ancient alphabetic character
36. Substance used in adhesives and paints
39. Place to check for a markdown
41. What an actor may flub
44. Sufferers for causes
46. Took pleasure in
49. Worldly rather than spiritual
51. Russian fighter
53. Dwarf of fable
55. Macabre
56. Hang loosely
57. Three-handed card game
58. Italian coin of old
59. College on the Thames
60. Metric system unit
63. Pencil stump
64. Halloween, to All Saints' Day

Puzzle 107: Problems, Problems
Tough

Across

1. Cotton seed pod
5. Individual
10. Confession confessions
14. Vicinity
15. City on the Ruhr
16. Medicinal plant
17. Difficult spot
20. The first of September?
21. Cultivates, perhaps
22. Steinway product
23. Tailless feline
24. Not as spicy
26. Show up
29. Pirate treasure
30. *Cannery Row* character
31. Spiral-shelled gastropod
32. *Sanford and ___*
35. Words after "Well, ain't that"
39. Something to do for the camera
40. Hack's passengers
41. Comes to the rescue
42. Worked diligently
43. Respectful gesture
45. Rabbit ears
48. Towel word
49. Inclination
50. Starship hit

51. Hardwood variety
54. Equally unattractive choices
58. Piece of fencing?
59. Paycheck
60. It might wind up on a lake?
61. Geeky guy
62. Clear the board
63. Baxter of *The Ten Commandments*

Down

1. Pedestal part
2. Food scraps
3. Souvenirs with scents
4. Lancelot du ___ (knight of the Round Table)
5. Over and above
6. English county on the Thames
7. Egyptian goddess
8. Shrimp snare
9. Large African antelope
10. Lustrous and smooth
11. Story of Achilles
12. Nary a soul
13. Tijuana title
18. Mongol chieftain
19. Unconcern
23. Malicious

24. Adherences
25. Out of one's mind
26. Rodin sculpture
27. Bean curd food
28. Math course, for short
29. Showed obsequiousness
31. Nuclear reactor parts
32. Word with "monkey" or "birthday"
33. Race track figures
34. Meddlesome
36. Some score notes
37. Flag Alex Rieger's vehicle
38. Galley gear
42. Held to the mat
43. Cherry red
44. Asian range
45. Drained of color
46. Split to unite
47. Not as well-done
48. Charon's underworld
50. The Forsytes had one
51. Sign for a seeress
52. Last word in Bibles
53. Leafy greens
55. IOU component
56. Kind of cry
57. Historic time

Puzzle 108: Glad Inside
Tough

Across

1. Glaswegian headgear
5. Flat-bottomed freight boat
10. Tasty paste
14. Berth place
15. Judge's decision, sometimes
16. German industrial valley
17. Growth-regulating spray
18. Migratory tribesman
19. School founded by King Henry VI
20. Fighter of yore
23. Work period
24. Farm machinery company
25. The Gold Coast, now
28. Coastline feature
32. First houseboat
35. Republic in southern Asia
38. Tropical fruits
41. Gracefully agile
42. Florida national park
44. Word in the society pages
45. Stairway post
46. Part of a willing trio
49. Brainy bunch
52. Russian spirit?
56. Useful items for painters
60. Edible tubes
61. Maker of cameras and copiers
62. Black, in verse
63. Seamus Heaney's land
64. On twos, rather than fours
65. Point-to-point connector
66. Mysterious loch
67. Tend to a loose shoelace
68. Gang follower?

Down

1. Former Winter Palace residents
2. Distribute proportionately
3. Home of the Heat
4. Bounded
5. Explosive sound
6. Too far off base?
7. Sacred Islamic month
8. Evaluate eggs, for example
9. *Leave It to Beaver* character
10. Puts on an act
11. Train alternative
12. Norse god of thunder
13. South end?
21. To the ___ degree
22. Cantata vocal solos
26. Famous murder victim
27. They were responsible for finding Atlantis?
29. Revolutionary Trotsky
30. *For ___ – With Love and Squalor*
31. Quaker pronoun
32. The last word in worship
33. Enthusiastic review
34. Was acquainted with
36. Type of singing club
37. Da Vinci model
39. 1984 comic horror film
40. Gave the twice-over
43. Jack Webb show
47. Home entertainment system component
48. Sings in peak form?
50. Miss Congeniality, compared to the others
51. Part of a drummer's kit
53. Bookkeeper's entry
54. Danish coin
55. Moore's TV editor
56. Marshmallow toaster's necessity
57. He gave us a lift
58. Centers of great activity
59. Poker buy-in
60. Branch of Buddhism

Puzzle 109: Material World
Tough

Across

1. Recurrent theme
6. Capital of Manche
10. Lofty peaks
14. "Maria ___" (Dorsey tune)
15. Use the maxilla and mandible
16. Bring exasperation
17. Printing technique
19. Fastening item
20. Fa-la link on a musical scale
21. Terms of enlistment
22. Place for hope?
23. Demonstration site, 1965
24. Blackball
25. Be agreeable
28. Children's classic
32. Phony deal
33. ___ Raymond Cobb of baseball fame
34. Sixth word of the Gettysburg Address
35. Meet, as expectations
38. Lacking zest
40. First name in cotton gins
41. Nixon's undoing
43. Editing mark
44. "Charge of the Light Brigade" poet
46. Mushroom cells

48. Lose freshness, as lettuce
49. Crocodile drops?
51. Lightweight fabric
53. Down Under dog
54. "Breastwork"
57. Sudden transition
58. White-scutted creature
60. Roofer's concern
61. Give wolfish looks
62. Set apart as sacred
63. Frankfurt's river
64. Cold one
65. Wax eloquent

Down

1. Army chow
2. Vaudeville shtick
3. Break the news
4. It looks good on paper
5. Secure, in a way
6. Rugby formation
7. Psychologist's prescription
8. Bottom-of-the-barrel stuff
9. Have exclusively
10. Literary king
11. Writer's supply, perhaps
12. "And . . ."
13. Paving stone
18. Belmont entry

22. Game believed to be of Indian origin
23. Truck stop sight
24. Cause to be immobile
25. Thing of value
26. Deli counter item
27. Interlacing technique
29. Goddess with a golden apple
30. Light on one's feet
31. Bumps on a log
33. What thsi is
36. Counterpart of substance
37. Eschew edibles
39. Wedding vows
42. Give the right to
45. *His Master's Voice* pooch
46. Pudding base
47. In nothing flat
50. "Come in!"
51. Singer Laine
52. Do one of the three R's
53. Former Genoese magistrate
54. *Ali ___ and the 40 Thieves*
55. Wild disorder
56. ___ vera (lotion plant)
58. Corn-eater's throwaway
59. Adhesive for feathers

1	2	3	4	5		6	7	8	9		10	11	12	13
14						15					16			
17					18						19			
20				21						22				
			23						24					
25	26	27					28	29					30	31
32						33						34		
35				36	37			38			39			
40				41			42				43			
44			45						46	47				
		48					49	50						
51	52					53						54	55	56
57					58						59			
60					61					62				
63					64					65				

Puzzle 110: On the Sea
Tough

Across

1. One of the Marx brothers
6. QED verb
10. Depletes
14. Group of Coral islands
15. Jazz singer Horne
16. ___ Mountains (Eurasia divider)
17. Vatican-related
18. *Jeopardy!* first name
19. Animal ethics org.
20. Sound advice for fishermen
23. Cracker's focus
26. Result of a witch's hocus-pocus
27. Clear the boards
28. Went silent (with "up")
30. Obsessive whaler of fiction
32. Not just feuding
33. Page with views, briefly
34. Turndowns
37. Sound advice for rowing crews
41. Snake's sibilant sound
42. Some retirement accts.
43. Crimea conference attended by Churchill
44. Lugosi's *Son of Frankenstein* role
45. Tax loophole
47. Wife of Abraham
50. Consumed consomme
51. Study surface
52. Sound advice for deck hands
56. Hip to
57. Reverse, as a typo
58. Billionaire with a book club
62. Possessive declaration
63. Naval rum
64. Blue-blooded
65. Defendant, to a juror
66. Bronte's Jane
67. Avocet's cousin

Down

1. Last sound some bugs hear
2. Schedule letters
3. Weasel sound?
4. Diner souvenir
5. Bulging earthenware vessel
6. Tickled pink
7. Partner of sit back
8. From scratch
9. Urban conveyance
10. First-rate
11. Site for Globetrotters
12. Cracker spreads
13. Party's pick
21. "Thar ___ blows!"
22. Nickname for a sharpshooter
23. Hordes
24. Some hers singing hymns?
25. Gushes (over)
29. He's out there, hopefully
30. Appropriate
31. Cynical laugh sound
33. Green-lights
34. *Cape Fear* star
35. "Maneater" duo Hall and ___
36. Kind of contrast
38. ___ y Plata (Montana motto)
39. Jam ingredient?
40. Unmopped area?
44. Tedious affair
45. Shemp, for one
46. Like cool cats
47. Pinch pennies
48. Broadway orphan
49. *Wide World of Sports* creator Arledge
50. Gusto
53. Unusually large
54. Professor 'iggins, to Eliza Doolittle
55. Billion-year increments
59. A homer provides at least one
60. Alternative to nothing
61. Riled (up)

1	2	3	4	5	■	6	7	8	9	■	10	11	12	13
14					■	15				■	16			
17					■	18				■	19			
■	■	■	20		21					22				
23	24	25		■	26			■		27				
28				29			■	30	31			■	■	■
32					■		33				■	34	35	36
37				38	39					40				
41			■	42				■		43				
■	■	■	44			■	45	46						
47	48	49			■	50			■	51				
52				53	54			55			■	■	■	
56			■	57			■	58			59	60	61	
62			■	63			■	64						
65			■	66			■	67						

Puzzle 111: Mother of Invention?
Tough

Across

1. Lava forerunner
6. Sneak ___ (look quickly)
11. TV watchdog
14. Stern with a bow
15. Painter Matisse or Rousseau
16. Result of raising hackles
17. Workshop machine invented by Tabitha Babbitt
19. Bled in the laundry
20. Legal right of passage
21. Least at risk
23. Finish
24. Lacking natural light
25. Straighten, in a way
29. Satellite radio name
30. They serve up whoppers
31. First ruler of all Egypt
32. El ___ (Spanish hero)
35. Plot size, perhaps
36. Shows concern
37. Moon shot org.
38. Pen tip
39. 20 Mule Team product
40. One of Snow White's seven
41. Slanted type
43. Grumpy "old" men

44. *Honeymooners* star
46. In good shape
47. St. John's player
48. Degas subject
53. "Long, Long ___"
54. Typist's fluid invented by Bette Nesmith Graham
56. Kilmer of *Batman Forever*
57. Tease
58. Base eight system
59. Building wing
60. Flounder through water
61. This and that

Down

1. *Of ___ and Men*
2. Large land mass
3. Needlefishes
4. Nutmeg-based spice
5. Insights
6. Lend ___ (help)
7. Impudent
8. Printer's measures
9. Blackboard deletions
10. Community group since 1915
11. Lifesaving invention of Anna Connelly
12. Uncouth
13. Word on a nickel

18. Give for a while
22. Type of vaccine
24. Vicks spray brand
25. ___ Bator
26. Heading on Santa's list
27. Ruth Handler's invention that girls love
28. Before, poetically
29. Block of ice on a glacier
31. Actor Cheech
33. A Cosby show
34. Fortnight's 14
36. Pre-Revolutionary period
37. Faultfinder
39. Volcanic rocks
40. Popular club
42. Scottish topper
43. Real bargain
44. Final resting place
45. Corporate department
46. Hope and charity partner
48. Presses for cash
49. Apiece
50. Words with "the minute" or "no good"
51. Seven on a map
52. First name in courtroom drama
55. "___ Vadis"

Puzzle 112: Sea to Shining Sea
Tough

Across

1. Capital of Ghana
6. Not proximately
10. Farmer's yield
14. One a'courting
15. Pickling veggie
16. General feel
17. Made a boo-boo
18. Meal with mutton
20. Blind alley, for example
22. Carson's sidekick
23. Large ocean vessel
24. *Who's Who* entry
25. Whispered call
27. Dangerous emission
29. Cook's meas.
33. Actor Sir McKellen
34. Comic canine
35. Popular garden flower
37. It's fit for a queen
39. Major broadcaster
41. Singer Rimes
42. Capital that replaced Istanbul
44. Word with "horse" or "human"
46. Garfield or Morris
47. Watch part
48. Fabric pattern

50. Biathlon gear
51. Candied tuber
52. Abhorrence
54. Highlight
58. Bureaucratic runaround
61. 1990s campaigner
63. German pistol
64. "Lonely Boy" singer Paul
65. Eye desirously
66. Susan Lucci role
67. SALT I signer
68. Network signal
69. Knocks to the canvas

Down

1. Made one's jaw drop
2. Seedy place?
3. Colorful slitherer
4. Make additional corrections
5. *Our Miss Brooks* star
6. Harmful downfall
7. PETA peeve
8. With hands on hips and elbows bent outward
9. Cancel, as a law
10. Cuban's house
11. Babe that's famous
12. Popular cookie since 1912

13. Expendable chess piece
19. Med. group
21. Unlikely prom king
25. They're pocketed in delis
26. New Orleans athlete
28. Actress Winger
29. "T" in "GWTW"
30. Sorcery
31. Biblical mountain
32. Suit part
34. Low-tech propeller
36. Steak and ___
38. Zodiac creature
40. Frolicked
43. Informed about
45. Hand over
49. Come forth
50. Hospital stitch
51. Uh-huh
53. Ran in neutral
54. German Mrs.
55. Many, many millennia
56. Seeks permission
57. Russian Revolution victim
59. Eight quarts
60. Historical periods
62. Grand ___ Opry

1 2 3 4 5 6 7 8 9 10 11 12 13
14 15 16
17 18 19
20 21 22
23 24
25 26 27 28 29 30 31 32
33 34 35 36
37 38 39 40 41
42 43 44 45 46
47 48 49 50
51 52 53
54 55 56 57 58 59 60
61 62 63
64 65 66
67 68 69

Puzzle 113: The Works
Tough

Across

1. Aeries, for example
6. Something to bank on
9. Hoity-toity type
13. *Silas Marner* novelist George
14. Crow
16. Hand over
17. Orphaned boy of comics
18. Type of type
19. First name among the *Cheers* cast
20. Tomatoes
23. Fallopian tube travelers
25. Watch chain
26. Commotion
27. Lettuce
31. ". . . the ___ of defeat"
32. Third largest city in South Korea
33. "Hogwash!"
36. Enticement
37. Like two of Beethoven's symphonies
38. Cello music marking
39. Poker option
40. Like the Smoky Mountains
42. Search high and low
43. Pickles
45. Even though
48. Preposition in poetry
49. Zuider ___
50. Mustard
54. Snip a snap
55. Plunder
56. Lady's beau
59. Authentic
60. Like a fashionable arrival
61. British actress Samantha
62. Prelude to a deal, perhaps
63. Word with "flung" or "fetched"
64. Plow pioneer

Down

1. Beatty in *Network*
2. "Don't Bring Me Down" rock band
3. Destination of the first Hope/Crosby "Road" picture
4. Well-___ (wealthy)
5. Utilize a wok
6. Fit
7. The Andrews Sisters, for example
8. Ginobili of the NBA
9. Theater hangings
10. Jacket of the '60s
11. *The Life of Riley* character
12. Admirer of Beauty
15. Attend sans date
21. Part of TGIF
22. Revered leader
23. Some gemstones
24. Ambiguous
28. Elmira-to-Syracuse dir.
29. Hawaiian island
30. Where many doubles land
33. Early period of civilization
34. Like some angles
35. Centaur, in part
38. Biggest diamond
40. Facial contortion
41. Spin the same yarn
42. Did refinery work
43. Streisand classic
44. ___ de Triomphe
45. Port city of Ghana
46. Filmdom's Sophia
47. Puff up, as an ego
51. Plenty of bread
52. Very small amount
53. Egg on
57. Scratch the surface?
58. "View" start

1	2	3	4	5	■	6	7	8	■	9	10	11	12
13					■	14			15	16			
17					■	18				19			
■		20			21				22				
23	24		■	25			■	26					
27			28			29	30				■	■	■
31				■	32				■	33	34	35	
36				■	37			■	38				
39			■	40	41			■	42				
■			43					44					
45	46	47			■		48			■	49		
50				51	52				53		■	■	
54			■	55			■	56			57	58	
59			■	60			■	61					
62			■	63			■	64					

Puzzle 114: B Hive
Tough

Across

1. "Arrivederci ___"
5. Pythias' partner
10. Sheffield stroller
14. ___ Bator, Mongolia
15. *The Life of ___ Zola*
16. Philbin's sidekick
17. Big top B's
20. Terrestrial amphibian
21. Hit bottom
22. Where to begin negotiating from
23. Give way
24. Charged atoms
26. B's on the table
32. Music to a comic's ears
33. It lands at Ben Gurion
34. Bale fodder
35. Checked out
36. Herculean types
38. Gael's language
39. Balderdash
40. Place for an ace
41. Does the get-away driving, for example
42. B's 1948 Oscar-winning song
46. Double-curved molding
47. Mediterranean gulf
48. Pleasant scent
51. "___ plaisir!"

52. Type of station
55. B's roadside stop
59. Give off
60. Antelope with twisted horns
61. Song for Madama Butterfly
62. Rat Pack nickname
63. Map collection
64. Roentgen discovery

Down

1. Hayseed
2. Scandinavian name
3. K follower
4. Abby's twin
5. Strong request
6. Kitty of *Gunsmoke*
7. Ritzy wrap
8. Timeworn
9. Bird's honker
10. A man of the cloth
11. Provoke
12. Mimicked
13. Baseball's "Say Hey Kid"
18. "___ directed" (Rx order)
19. Void, as a marriage certificate
23. It's drawn with a rifle?
24. Not up to anything

25. Firth of Lorn resort
26. Marshy arm
27. Gable role
28. Ancient Greek games site
29. Hurled
30. Some bridge players
31. Food grains
32. Parsley or peppermint, for example
36. Make perfect, as one's skills
37. "Anything ___?"
38. Dark, poetically
40. Incredible Hulk?
41. Sternward
43. Pizza paste
44. Nine days of services
45. Doesn't look forward to
48. Tucked in
49. Do followers
50. Frigg's husband
51. Asian salt sea
52. She had a *Tootsie* role
53. Where the Amur flows
54. Reprieve from the governor
56. Fed watchdog
57. Short order?
58. Office staple

1	2	3	4		5	6	7	8	9		10	11	12	13
14					15						16			
17				18						19				
20				21						22				
			23					24	25					
	26	27					28					29	30	31
32							33					34		
35					36	37					38			
39				40						41				
42			43					44	45					
			46					47						
48	49	50					51					52	53	54
55					56	57					58			
59					60						61			
62					63						64			

Puzzle 115: Toasty
Tough

Across

1. Pincushion alternative
5. Rajiv Gandhi's grandfather
10. Slightly open
14. Former German capital
15. In great haste, at sea
16. Drawn fish
17. Love-in-a-mist bouquet
19. Hit the ground
20. Lounging locale
21. Love of life
22. Club that sings
23. Smoke detector
25. Off the beaten track
27. Veto
30. Cast of characters?
34. Stat that's good when low
35. "Stormy Weather" singer
37. End, in the Bible
38. Word with "base" or "summer"
40. It's removed by a stripper
42. *Cutty* ___ (historic ship)
43. Sure-footed creatures
45. *The Love Boat* employee
47. Old name preceder

48. Security feature
50. Cockscombs
52. Child's reward, perhaps
53. Proper word, at times
54. Tableland
56. Muse of history
59. Humidified
63. Czech runner Zatopek
64. Term of endearment
66. Without self-control
67. Massey of old movies
68. You can stick with it?
69. Turns into leather
70. Fine and ___
71. Powerful emotion

Down

1. Goes back to sea?
2. Track tipster
3. "___ Thee Oh Lord"
4. Vocalize, as in James Earl Jones
5. Veep under G.R.F.
6. One who runs the show
7. Heist tally
8. Gifford's successor
9. Open, as a change purse
10. Word games
11. Reagan's love
12. Tahiti sweetie

13. Memorization method
18. Historic time
24. Telegram punctuation
26. One of the five W's
27. Go over again
28. Do blackboard duty
29. Impromptu jazz performance
30. Cookie flavoring
31. See 35-Across
32. Plume's source
33. Confiscates
36. Guard on the deck
39. Morale builders
41. Sandwich with a crunch
44. Doo-wop syllable
46. Morsel
49. Greenhouse plant
51. "Stop it!"
53. ". . . with ___ in sight"
54. Food group
55. 1816 Jane Austen novel
57. Singer Falana
58. Barge ___ (interrupt)
60. *To Live and Die* ___ (1985)
61. Bunny tail
62. "Of ___ I sing"
65. "Yippee!"

Puzzle 116: B Exterminator
Tough

Across

1. Put in a snit
5. Suffer from self-pity
9. Dropped in importance
14. ___ Fjord (inlet of the Skagerrak)
15. In business right now
16. Accustom to hardship
17. Beer-swilling sailor?
20. Just put on the market
21. Wampum in Yemen
22. Assists
23. Ones going through a stage?
24. Clinic or spread
25. Participate in a limping contest?
32. Shampoos tell you to do it twice
33. Coffee variety
34. Offer
35. Forget to include
36. The time of one's life?
37. Summoned the butler, for example
38. Detectives, for short
39. Measly problem?
41. Italian bowling game
42. Trips on some garden tools?
46. First-rate
47. Oxford feeder
48. Foam
50. Potato holder
51. Word on either side of "-a-"
54. Like Dick Button?
57. Transform
58. Pout
59. *The Little Red Hen* denial
60. Is ahead
61. Doesn't shut up
62. Hog filler

Down

1. Groan associate
2. Wight, for one
3. Rode the wind
4. Watch pocket
5. In the current fashion or style
6. Poppy plant derivative
7. Lime cover
8. Keyboard key
9. Blotto
10. Not digital, as a watch
11. Group (together)
12. Memorable times
13. Home of the cubs
18. Speak pompously, for example
19. Disgrace
23. Dermatologist's concern
24. Riot-subduing stuff
25. Stage objects
26. Constrain
27. Spice for absinthe
28. Traffic signal
29. One way to be taken
30. Slice and dice
31. Borders
36. Adolescent affliction
37. Multihued horse
39. Some similar chemical compounds
40. Buffed
41. Tamed, as a horse
43. Stopped
44. Intensify
45. Engraves
48. Fish entree
49. Middle Eastern bread
50. Ancient Greek colonnade
51. 16th-century stringed instrument
52. Engrossed with
53. Hop-jump connector
54. Buddy
55. Dickens's Little Dorrit
56. They may administer IVs

Puzzle 117: Nice Arrangement
Tough

Across

1. Part of DJ
5. Dazzling display
10. International marketplace
14. Kings Peak locale
15. Looking-glass girl
16. Collapsed under pressure
17. Melchior's trio
18. Fabric in an Ellington title
19. Multiply
20. Daisy's cousin?
23. Went underground, for example
24. Adam's third son
25. North Dakota neighbor
30. Reason for a temporary shop closure
34. Get long in the tooth
35. Walleye or white cloud, for example
37. Scratching-post scratchers
38. Bearer of bell-shaped flowers
42. God in the Quran
43. Without moisture
44. Neither fold nor raise
45. Human rubber stamp
47. Bilko or Pepper
50. Diagnostic scanners, briefly
52. Slangy name for a stranger
53. Wild carrot fit for royalty?
60. Contented tabby sound
61. Electricity, slangily
62. Haley of *Roots* renown
63. Adjutant
64. Scent source
65. Puddle-jumper's destination, perhaps
66. Tater
67. Forward-looking group?
68. Putrefies

Down

1. Type of bell or waiter
2. Sloping type, briefly
3. Narrative of heroic exploits
4. Trendy dresser
5. Gave some slack
6. Ali, once
7. Beer choice
8. Etcher's supply
9. Grammar topics
10. Shade of white
11. Silent star Theda
12. "___ calling!"
13. Arrow wood
21. Drum set, for example
22. Ancient neighbor of Carthage
25. Asia's ___ Peninsula
26. Sure-footed
27. Gwyn and Carter
28. Quarter halves?
29. Volcanic emissions
31. Popular condiment
32. "'Twixt" partner
33. To date
36. Roll call response
39. Complained whiningly
40. Windy City landing site
41. 17th-century Dutch painter's masterpieces
46. Japanese mercenaries
48. Nitrous oxide, for example
49. Filled pastry
51. Pan-fry
53. Clever remark
54. Pakistani tongue
55. Evening, on Nickelodeon
56. "Tar Heels" state, briefly
57. What's more
58. Irish or Welsh, for example
59. Mates, once
60. ___ de deux

Puzzle 118: Off the Market
Tough

Across

1. Palm whack
5. Shopping excursion
10. Holds title to
14. Give a mighty heave
15. Labyrinth locale
16. Lucy Lawless character
17. In international waters, for example
18. Totaled, as a bill
19. Put out the candle
20. Start of a riddle
23. Up to
24. ___-doodle-do
27. Riddle (Part 2)
33. Knot on a tree
34. Birthstone for 36-Across
35. ___ the Explorer
36. What 10 may stand for, briefly
37. Low-altitude cloud formation
40. Weekly NBC offering
41. That alternative
43. Global Surveyor subject
44. Heat headliner
46. Riddle (Part 3)
49. Ball partner?
50. Schedule abbr.
51. Answer to the riddle

59. Give away, in poker
61. Lead car, sometimes
62. Say positively
63. Sheltered
64. Revolted
65. Ruffle some feathers
66. SALT participant
67. Residence of a clergyman
68. Party to a defense pact

Down

1. *Pygmalion* playwright
2. Rife with vegetation
3. Length times width
4. It may be uncovered before use
5. Dead Sea document
6. Make pleas on one's knees?
7. Nevada town
8. Famous last words?
9. Anti-discrimination agcy.
10. Dress shoe color, sometimes
11. Carefully selected, as in words
12. St. Louis-to-Chicago dir.
13. Toothed tool
21. How some numbers were entered, once

22. Oldenburg exclamation
25. Egyptian temple near Luxor
26. "Big ___ outdoors"
27. Popeye's tattoo
28. Reasons
29. Synagogue item
30. Eyeball-bending drawings
31. ___ Rizzo ('69 Hoffman role)
32. Lexington, Virginia inst.
33. Must, informally
38. HBO competitor
39. Somewhat, informally
42. More petite
45. Popular honeymoon spot
47. Prop in many action films
48. Wall hanging, often
52. Unwelcome e-mail
53. Fictional plantation
54. Computer symbol
55. Scottish Loch of renown
56. It's not good
57. *Gimme a Break* star Carter
58. Domino with three pips
59. Sigma follower
60. Chi-town trains

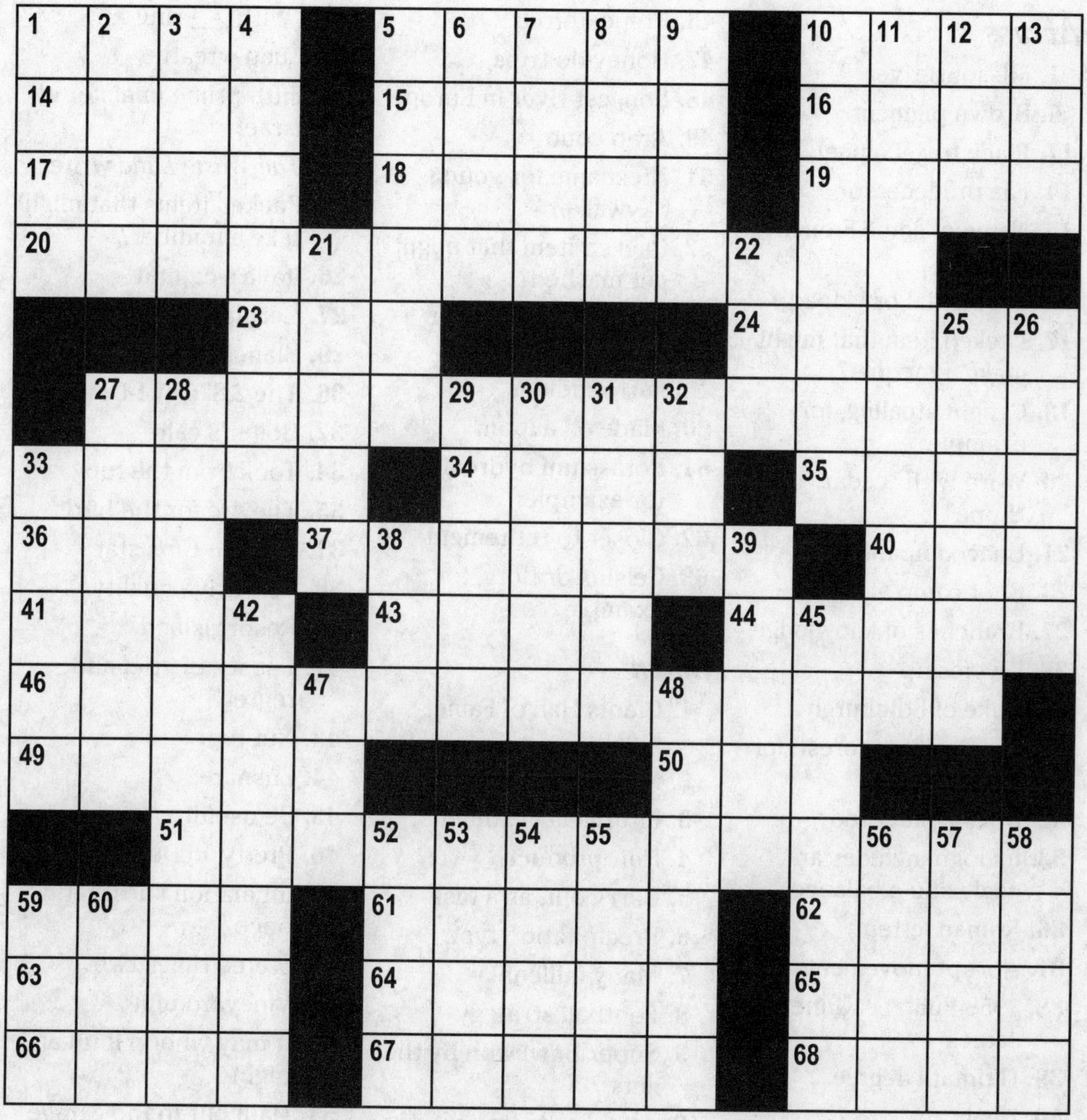

Puzzle 119: Moving Crew
Tough

Across

1. Missouri river
6. Brown pigment
11. Place to get a peel
14. Fax predecessor
15. Name of some French kings
16. Proverbial brickload
17. Packed item that might make a racquet?
19. Caught stealing, for example
20. Word with "cedar" or "hope"
21. Unaccompanied
23. Boot camp attendee
27. Branches of knowledge
28. Divvies up
29. Duke of Edinburgh
31. Tropical rain forest, for example
32. Doesn't succeed
33. Its logo includes an eagle and a balance
36. Roman letter
37. Abrupt movements
38. 1958 Pulitzer winner James
39. Ultimate degree
40. Heals
41. Leather with a napped surface
42. Circumvents
44. Ring-shaped surface

45. Preposterous
47. Honey-do trips
48. Longest river in Europe
49. Arab country
51. Nickname for young Skywalker
52. Packed item that might get mashed?
58. It's kept by a keeper
59. Cognizant of one's surroundings
60. Made on a loom
61. Potassium hydroxide, for example
62. Closer to retirement
63. Celsius or Borg, for example

Down

1. Giants Hall of Famer Mel
2. Melville's inspiration
3. Liturgical vestment
4. Hair product
5. Carry out, as a task
6. Precipitation type
7. Many millennia
8. Football strategy
9. Super Bowl won by the Jets
10. Attacks vigorously
11. Packed item that might fly away?
12. 100 pence
13. Initial contributions

18. "With ___ ring . . ."
22. Luau wreath
23. Fifth prime minister of Israel
24. *The Waste Land* writer
25. Packed items that might take a number?
26. Italia's capital
27. German river
29. Blanches
30. The 2,876 of 1-Down
32. Golfer's call
34. Took from the top
35. They're for the birds
37. *Kiss the Girls* star
38. Pervasive quality
40. Resort island
41. Causes of grief and regret
43. Nut type
44. Ensnare
45. Be useful
46. Pretty, in Dundee
47. Inhalation anesthetic, once
49. Stereo times two
50. Vineyard unit
53. It may whoop it up at night
54. Haul out to the garage
55. Reverential salutation
56. WJM's Baxter
57. It's for the money?

Puzzle 120: In the Pocket
Tough

Across

1. Public person?
6. Frasier's first sister-in-law
11. Bottom line?
14. Parting remark
15. "___ you the lucky one!"
16. Latin 101 word
17. Island near Miami
19. Pvt.'s superior
20. Period of note
21. It may come after life?
22. Suburbanite, on some autumn days
24. Zaragoza's river
25. Accepted a proposal
27. Not blatant
30. Cream serving
31. Danish fruit
32. Thicket of trees
33. Subsidy, for example
36. Movie mutt
37. Markedly masculine
38. Opposing voice
39. Create using shuttles and thread
40. Unskilled writers
41. Ollie's cohort
42. Mitchell clan
44. Stevenson character
45. Make sudden impact
47. Prepares for feathering?

48. Was in need of a good rubdown
49. Humorist Bombeck
50. Chess pieces
53. Far–many link
54. Variety of hibiscus
58. Debut of 10/11/75, briefly
59. Friend, slangily
60. Kind of tube
61. It is its own square root
62. Mature, as fruit
63. Sans clothing

Down

1. Boxing's LaMotta
2. Baltic Sea tributary
3. Informal greeting
4. Buzzard's beak, for example
5. Split hairs
6. Former Portuguese territory (Var.)
7. "I smell ___!"
8. Marina del ___
9. Bethlehem sellout
10. Clinically clean
11. Mischief
12. Roast host
13. Heather-covered lands
18. Word with "thumb" or "loser"
23. Hustle and bustle
24. Lab burner

25. Some undergrads
26. Likewise
27. Petty quarrel
28. Celestial bear
29. Corner for talking purposes
30. Marina features
32. Source of chocolate
34. Contraction with "do" or "work"
35. It had all your telephone numbers
37. Shopping place
38. Northern seafowl
40. Railroad worker's transport
41. Hair protein
43. Leave quickly
44. Tight spots
45. Dustin's role in *Midnight Cowboy*
46. Coll. with a husky named Jonathan XII
47. Check the fit of
49. Slight advantage
50. Expensive coat
51. Type of sword
52. Overly bookish sort, stereotypically
55. Start of Cain's query
56. Tuck partner
57. Letters with "messenger" or "transfer"

Puzzle 121: Give Me a Break
Treacherous

Across

1. "Cloud hoppers"
5. ___ Zapata!
9. Antler-bearers
14. Result of splitting hairs?
15. All tied up
16. Vietnam capital
17. Short break
20. Hush-hush
21. Marksman of Swiss legend
22. Peg of Woods
23. Fancy jug
25. Bears the expenses of
27. Saintly circle
30. Malevolent
32. Stout cousin
33. Silver Gavel Award org.
34. Buttinsky
36. Opening words
40. Clean break
43. Pupil of Socrates
44. Soothing substance
45. Tony winner Brooks
46. Key on a keyboard
48. Palter
49. Start from scratch
50. Drawing rooms
54. Yggdrasill, for example
56. *The Soul of a Butterfly* memoirist

57. Not naughty
59. Record-holder
63. Lucky break
66. The ones right here
67. Word of exclusivity
68. Balder's father
69. Lowered, as pressure
70. Remunerates
71. Dim-light sensors

Down

1. "Be on the lookout messages," briefly
2. "If I Didn't ___" (The Ink Spots)
3. "All By Myself" singer Carmen
4. A woofer is part of one
5. Bone in a column
6. Suffix with correct
7. Part of Maverick's attire
8. Made a larger pot?
9. Product's freshness period
10. Old seaman
11. *West Side Story* character
12. Overly sentimental
13. Contesting teams
18. Oligarchical group
19. Emotional request
24. Spring events

26. It's overhead
27. It's a lock when pinned
28. Member of the first family
29. Molten spew
31. Burglar-alarm warning
34. Drawn-out
35. Kindled again
37. Word with "study" or "bomb"
38. Swamp thing
39. Holmenkollen overlooks it
41. Plus others, briefly
42. Fills with happiness
47. Singer plus two, for example
49. A man of the cloth
50. Cut counterpart
51. See ya in Hawaii?
52. "Blue" singer
53. Reporter's goal
55. Toreador's trophy
58. Buchanan or Ferber
60. Accolade
61. Camelot character
62. Teller's stack
64. Chin attachment?
65. Succeed, as a proposal

Puzzle 122: Lend Me Your Year
Treacherous

Across

1. *Belling the Cat* author
6. Ones of a kind?
10. Brief attempt
14. Pasta source
15. Use a lot?
16. Cabbage family member
17. Heroic 1920s sled dog
18. 1953 Pulitzer playwright William
19. Otherwise
20. Commitment minus one year?
23. Of majestic proportions
24. Con's dream
25. Monroe film minus one year?
30. First letter of "census," for example
31. From point ___ point B
32. Caterwaul
36. Middle Eastern org. founded in 1964
37. Shaded, like some '50s cars
41. John, to Ringo?
42. Muralist Jose Maria
44. Bean counter, for short
45. ML pitchers that hit
47. Time for some to vote, minus one year?
51. Nobel laureate Sakharov

54. Group standard
55. Certain work force, minus one year?
60. Vesuvius relative
61. First in a string of popes
62. Opposite of waxed
64. Pine nut, for example
65. Aykroyd and Fogelberg
66. More than like
67. ___ buco (veal dish)
68. Editorial notation
69. Acquiescent responses

Down

1. Andrews or Edwards, briefly
2. Ardor
3. Catch of the day, perhaps
4. Where many American pioneers settled
5. Potential client
6. Per person
7. Six-pack units
8. "Cogito, ___ sum"
9. Type of key
10. Like some details
11. A costar of Sylvester
12. Columnist brothers Joseph and Stewart
13. Designer Geoffrey
21. Randall's *6 Rms ___ Vu*

22. George Lucas attended it
25. Cough syrup amts.
26. Moth's legacy
27. Get an ___ effort
28. Birth-related
29. "What was ___ think?"
33. Dairy case spread
34. Like bald tires
35. Bottom-line bummer
38. Star of *The Bank Dick*
39. "O Henry, ___ thine eyes!" (Shakespeare)
40. Door, for example
43. Destructive funnel
46. Citrus drink
48. Word with "well" or "force"
49. Join up
50. Whisper one's affection
51. "You ___ Beautiful"
52. Lecture souvenirs
53. Desert features
56. Ravioli filling, perhaps
57. Corn cake
58. Baseball's Slaughter
59. In desperate need of water
63. Goethe's *Die Leiden ___ jungen Werthers*

Puzzle 123: 64-Across
Treacherous

Across

1. ___ *Set* (Tracy/Hepburn film)
5. Like Rambo
10. Wanders (about)
14. Bar on a car
15. Garment for a cook
16. Etcher's purchase, perhaps
17. Biggest portion
19. Bonnie one
20. Familiar octagon
21. Mary Lincoln's maiden name
22. Mel who scored 1,859 runs
23. Warren Beatty flick
24. Like a Seoul man
26. Full of dandelions, say
28. Peculiar to a locale
29. Edible root
30. Colorful, flowering shrub
33. Electronic-music pioneer Brian
34. Golden-brown quartz stone
37. The highest degree
40. Toyota model
41. Insect life stage
45. Mexican-American
47. Where Alice worked
48. Outcome
49. Queen of the Nile, informally
52. PC display device
53. *Laura* director Preminger
54. Cuisine served in 24-Across?
56. Captain Picard's counselor
57. Is obviously successful
59. Wolf head?
60. Middle of some plays
61. Team attachment?
62. Vanderbilt and Tan
63. Parenthetical script comment
64. Refrain from Dorothy and hint to the theme

Down

1. ___ segno (from the repeat sign, in music)
2. Had a life
3. Having narrow grooves
4. Kin of bingo
5. En ___ (in one group)
6. Ladybug snack
7. Rugged rocks
8. Unicorn feature
9. A wee hour
10. Aplenty
11. University environment
12. Scorn
13. '60s radical sit-in org.
18. Like Granny on *The Beverly Hillbillies*
21. Yesterday's tomorrow
22. "...I ___, so off to work I go"
24. Prepare to present a proposal?
25. Sgt., for example
27. "I" piece?
28. "Will there be anything ___?"
30. Paid go-between
31. Abysmal test score
32. Bow-shaped line
35. *Cosmicomics* author Calvino
36. Prefix with center or dermis
37. Point-of-purchase equip. giant
38. Pythagorean proposition
39. It's all in the past
42. Crude
43. Daily allowance

44. "Jealous mistress," to Emerson

46. Adorable ones

47. Tip, as a hat

49. Raccoon relative

50. Gruesome, as some details

51. Trademarked cow

54. Parts of mins.

55. Approximately

56. U.S. airline, once

57. Rambouillet remark

58. Give it a go

Puzzle 124: Rotten Luck
Treacherous

Across

1. Becomes worthy of
6. Golden Horde member
11. "A clue!"
14. Bad business partner
15. Plus end, for example
16. Response to "When do we want it?"
17. It's almost lucky?
19. Application before feathers
20. Aspirin has several
21. Aristotle's H
22. Supermarket section
24. Having pauses in conversation
27. Squirming baby, sometimes
31. Reporter's need
35. No longer together
36. Richard Branson, for example
38. Ankle bones
39. It's almost lucky?
42. Commercial suffix with "Star" and "Sun"
43. "___ honor . . ." (oath)
44. Apt to stay put
45. Big building
47. Dodges
48. In a harmonious manner
51. Penetrating cold
54. Formal requirement
55. Astronomer's sighting, perhaps
59. Center of activity
60. It's almost lucky?
64. Steak partner
65. Low pair
66. Word with "main" or "blessed"
67. Push to the limit
68. Set out suddenly
69. Serves beer after beer, for example

Down

1. Lamp shade shade
2. Armenia's chief river
3. It goes on after a bath
4. British bigwigs
5. "___ Utah!" (license plate phrase)
6. Discernment
7. Pavlova and Karenina
8. "___ Much" (Presley chart-topper of '57)
9. Sun spots in Baltimore?
10. Make further corrections
11. Certainly not pro
12. Cold coating
13. All wrong
18. Certain duck
23. A source of chloroform
24. "Don't get ___ with me!"
25. Bring together
26. West Point alternative
27. Applesauce-topped treat
28. Agricultural pest
29. Zoroastrian
30. In a troubled state
32. Asphalt worker
33. "Heads up!," for example
34. Agronomist's samples
36. *John Brown's Body* author
37. Paul McCartney album of 1971
40. Graph points
41. *History of Rome* author
46. Coastal coves
47. Not aweather
49. Type of alcohol
50. Scatterbrained
51. Many people now do it online
52. Sinuous dance
53. Alpine goat
55. Field of granular snow
56. Child's appliance?
57. Sell by machine
58. Woodpecker's prey
61. *A Kiss Before Dying* novelist Levin
62. It sticks to your hair
63. Net judge's call

Puzzle 125: Construction Crew
Treacherous

Across

1. '90s Philippines president
6. It's on the staff
10. Drops off
14. Correct the camber
15. Dwarf's refrain words
16. Race pace, sometimes
17. An upright citizen, for example
20. Parting phrase
21. Bark component
22. *The Spanish Tragedy* playwright
23. Create a stir
24. Well-to-do gents
28. Genesis paradise
29. Marketplace near the Acropolis, perhaps
30. Where most people are
31. Has a bawl
35. A strong person, emotionally
38. It takes two to make eleven
39. Some Korean imports
40. Passerine bird
41. Larson of *The Far Side*
42. Hinge
43. Benchwarmer
47. Make public

48. Desdemona's faithful servant
49. Temporary inactivity
54. Part of a balancing act?
56. Toward the mouth
57. *Chicago* star
58. Wall tapestry
59. Wall St. landmark
60. Meaning of wavy lines, in the comics
61. Mythical weeper

Down

1. Absorbed
2. "Et" or "inter" follower
3. Beverage for Wally and the Beaver
4. Act like a wolf
5. Munchie locale
6. A musician may strike it
7. Limb partner
8. Expressions of confusion
9. Hiking boots, for example
10. Tour of duty
11. Where some sports teams play
12. Catch phrase?
13. "Funny Girl" composer
18. Beta and gamma

19. 28-Across exile
23. Mine entrances
24. Brussels-based org.
25. Dramatic conflict
26. Former heavyweight champ Riddick
27. Borax and bauxite, for example
28. Swift work
30. Blazing
31. Short cut?
32. Grimm creature
33. Bingo call, perhaps
34. Wearing 9-Down
36. Botswana river
37. Your average Joe
41. Dispiriting
42. "Mon ___!"
43. Military scouting mission, briefly
44. Atlanta university
45. ___ *Marner*
46. Slip past
47. Dogpatch denizen
49. Big, round do
50. Rock shelter
51. Roman ruler
52. Fiddler on the reef?
53. In ___ (existing)
55. Noted Brit lexicon

1
2
3
4
5
6
7
8
9
10
11
12
13
14
15
16
17
18
19
20
21
22
23
24
25
26
27
28
29
30
31
32
33
34
35
36
37
38
39
40
41
42
43
44
45
46
47
48
49
50
51
52
53
54
55
56
57
58
59
60
61

Puzzle 126: Making Progress
Treacherous

Across

1. ". . . against ___ of troubles" (Shakespeare)
5. Gardeners' repositories
10. *Dungeons and Dragons* beasts
14. Bellyache
15. Like much of Poe's work
16. Fish with an uphill battle
17. Tom, Dick, and Harry
18. One place to get slapped
19. Adam's oldest
20. Dwelling type
23. Sympathetic attention
24. Symphony or sonata
25. Woo musically
30. Gaucho's lariat
34. Japanese leader Hirobumi
35. Airplane boarding site
37. Little bits
38. Certain insurance claim
42. Diciembre–febrero link
43. Actress Thompson of *Family*
44. West of old films
45. Determine whether it's gold
46. Most insolent
49. They break in the morning
52. 10th anniversary material
53. Kentucky Derby, for one
61. Shiva's spouse in Hinduism
62. Caribbean island whose capital is Oranjestad
63. Type of historian
64. Bypass
65. Company clerk of classic TV
66. G permits them all
67. Lovers' quarrel
68. Save alternative
69. Successful crossword solver's cry

Down

1. *Macbeth* quintet
2. Bombay garb
3. "___ go bragh!"
4. Highest point in an orbit
5. It's wasteful to Ed Norton
6. "Three cheers" recipient
7. Word maven Partridge
8. Music associated with the '70s
9. Play matchmaker
10. Wedding or birthday, for example
11. Chestnut red horse
12. Dressed by Armani
13. Panasonic competitor
21. Interlinked computing abbr.
22. Jewish festival
25. Musician's better half?
26. Some stiff collars
27. Men on the make
28. Lectern platform
29. Old lab equipment
31. Classic TV sitcom, *One Day at ___*
32. Suffolk send-offs
33. Till now
36. Scandinavian myth
39. He had a part in *Thelma & Louise*
40. Like a friend in need
41. From Colorado to Kansas
47. Wasting food, says Mom
48. Encroachment
50. Millennium makeup
51. Throw out
53. Boxing decisions
54. Motorcycle daredevil's apparatus
55. Mother of Romulus and Remus
56. Uncivil
57. Scottish seaport
58. Jason's command
59. D-Day city target
60. Word in a conditional statement

1	2	3	4	■	5	6	7	8	9	■	10	11	12	13
14				■	15					■	16			
17				■	18					■	19			
20				21					■	22				
■	■	■	23			■	24				■	■	■	■
25	26	27			■	28	29	■	■	30		31	32	33
34			■	■	35			36	■	37				
38			39	40					41					
42				■	43				■	■	44			
45				■	■	46			47	48				
■	■	■	49		50	51	■	■	52			■	■	■
53	54	55				■	56	57			■	58	59	60
61				■	62				■	63				
64				■	65				■	66				
67				■	68				■	69				

Puzzle 127: At Last!
Treacherous

Across

1. Bargain basement sign
5. What clematis plants do
10. Token punishment
14. Adjective for Death Valley
15. Wireless apparatus
16. Heap
17. "Charlie Hustle" Rose
18. Alamogordo event
19. Ore deposit
20. Emphatic last words
23. New York Giants pitcher Maglie
25. Mr. ___ (old mystery game)
26. Not just damp
27. Analyzes chemically
29. *Major Barbara* author
31. Foot in the forest
34. Bio-Bio locale
35. *A Prayer for ___ Meany*
36. First name in wit
37. Pilot's last words
40. Osprey's cousin
41. Swimmer's practice
42. Vantage point
43. Plaines preceder
44. Young, female swine
45. Rude one
46. Decline in value
47. Loss leader?

48. They're not from around here
49. Last words in animation?
55. Get to one's feet
56. Violin bow application
57. Presque ___, Maine
60. New Balance competitor
61. "The Rural Muse" poet
62. Dramatist Simon
63. Type of performer
64. Is unable to stand
65. Catch sight of

Down

1. Aphid's sustenance
2. "Who ___ you kidding?"
3. A doctor may check them
4. *East of ___*
5. Some hold peaches
6. Motorized shop tool
7. Concept
8. Rain forest feature
9. The former Bechuanaland
10. Bowler's bane
11. Zodiac creature
12. Swit colleague
13. Slip hazard
21. Washroom appliance, often

22. "Chosen" quantity
23. Like some vows
24. Walking the beach, for example
28. Avoiding the draft?
29. Did a household chore
30. One of a matching pair?
31. Advances steadily
32. Protective charm
33. Tends to the plants, in a way
35. Elliptical
36. Bart's educator
38. Member of a small governing faction
39. Pertaining to birth
44. Beetles go nowhere without it?
45. Rollers in a saw
46. It may be served rarely?
47. Like a house ___
49. Green flanker
50. Bee flat?
51. Mt. Everest locale
52. Kinks classic
53. Wannabe attorney's hurdle
54. Cattle, archaically
58. Type of service
59. A TV Tarzan

1	2	3	4		5	6	7	8	9		10	11	12	13
14					15						16			
17					18						19			
		20		21					22					
23	24			25				26						
27			28			29	30				31	32	33
34					35					36			
37				38				39					
40				41				42					
43				44				45					
		46				47				48			
49	50	51			52	53				54			
55				56					57		58	59	
60				61					62				
63				64					65				

Puzzle 128: One for All
Treacherous

Across

1. Dreadlocks sporter, for short
6. Certain Arabian garments
10. Agt.'s cuts
14. *A Lesson From* ___
15. The Andrews Sisters, for example
16. What little things mean?
17. Common currency
19. Sly tactic
20. A Vanna turnover
21. Island explored by Magellan
22. Find abhorrent
24. Certain military force
26. Western mount?
27. Talk in the '60s?
28. Some shop machines
32. Warm and pleasant
35. Alley-___ (basketball maneuver)
36. Damascus is its capital
37. Keystone State port
38. Dig up dirt?
39. "___ In the Clowns"
40. Some freshwater fishes
42. Cross or crow finale
43. Tent post
44. From a poor plan

46. It could start 17- and 58-Across and 10- and 25-Down
47. Give it ___ (make an attempt)
48. Nail and tooth coverings
52. 1972 Jack Lemmon film
55. "Take ___ from me" (follow advice)
56. Zhou En-___
57. Like this crossword puzzle
58. It may hold your reading glasses
61. Oppositionist
62. Befuddled
63. It takes two to do it
64. Paragon of redness
65. "Afterward . . ."
66. City near Great Salt Lake

Down

1. *M*A*S*H* character
2. In bad company, to Ambrose Bierce
3. Neither liquid nor gaseous
4. ___ Aviv-Jaffa
5. American botanist
6. Cornered, as a hunted animal

7. Part of some hats
8. Feel malaise
9. Convinced of
10. Governmental form in Britain
11. Game with a candlestick
12. Turn partner
13. Editor's override
18. Hindquarters
23. Partner of odds
25. Highwayman with a weapon
26. News follower
28. Display displeasure to a performer, in a way
29. Floor measure
30. Playful signal
31. Marquis de ___
32. Earth bank
33. Wild African sheep
34. They're blown in anger
35. Expression of delight
41. Rectangular paving stone
43. Gets the ball in the hands of the quarterback
45. Show pleasure toward
46. "Don't bet ___!"
48. Wharton's Frome

49. Fawn-colored antelope

50. *Tootsie* Oscar winner

51. Ancient Phoenician city

52. White-whale pursuer

53. Wind direction indicator

54. "Verrry interesting" Johnson

55. 1958 Pulitzer winner James

59. Relative of "-esque"

60. License plate

Puzzle 129: Mystery Solved
Treacherous

Across

1. Firewood, finally
4. *Beau Geste* author
8. Irrigation aid
13. Commando's mission
15. Piece of correspondence
16. Climb up on the soapbox
17. Start of a mystery-solving quip
20. Avoid ignorance
21. Birth-related
22. Pro-___ (certain tournaments)
23. *Love ___ Many-Splendored Thing*
25. Weaver's apparatus
27. Start of a mystery-solving quip (Part 2)
35. That gentleman's
36. Hairy Himalayan mystery
37. Tuck of legend
38. Suffix denoting residents of
40. Underwater detection system
43. Taj Mahal's town
44. Twisted fastener
46. Blueprint item
48. "If I ___ a Hammer"
49. Start of a mystery-solving quip (Part 3)
53. Mock fanfare
54. Bauxite, for example
55. Farming tool
58. Slowly, in music
61. Tokyo's entertainment district
65. End of a mystery-solving quip
68. Absolutely astound
69. Construction piece
70. Fit to be tried
71. Examinations
72. Presses for payment
73. Many of Joe Louis's wins

Down

1. Nutmeg cover
2. Umpire's call, sometimes
3. Casual greeting
4. Boise-to-Portland dir.
5. Book manufacturer's leather
6. Italian volcano
7. Vex
8. Simmer down
9. Old Testament craft
10. *Peter Pan* dog
11. Small matter
12. Ayres and Wallace
14. Greek order of architecture
18. Far from bashful
19. Art colony in New Mexico
24. They may be split in casinos
26. Sorvino with an Oscar
27. Early form of bridge
28. Sudden snag
29. River to the Rhone
30. Palindromic Platte River people
31. Capital of Belarus
32. Political wing?
33. Isaac's mother
34. What they do on Wall Street
39. Chip off the old flock?
41. Rue Morgue killer
42. Gambling mecca
45. Pequod crew
47. Welsh barker
50. "What's the big ___?"
51. Like Funt's camera
52. They hold their horses
55. Weight

56. Leer lasciviously
57. They may be boosted or fragile
59. Forbidden cologne?
60. "Do not take ___ empty stomach"
62. Mont. neighbor
63. Founder of Stoicism
64. Tomahawks, for example
66. Decay
67. Many, many mos.

Puzzle 130: Solid
Treacherous

Across

1. Certain Arabian
6. "Open, Sesame!" speaker
10. *A Farewell to ___*
14. De Niro film
15. Bruised or inflated items
16. Crotchety one
17. ___ first (diamond call)
18. Hard to believe, as a story
19. Grayish yellow
20. Weasel-like animal
23. Understanding
24. About 22 degrees
25. "From ___ shining . . ."
27. Frowned-on, fire-resistant material
32. It may be gross
35. Leader of the Long March
36. Spine-tingling
38. *A Bell for ___*
39. Border on
41. Dustin in *Midnight Cowboy*
43. Lenin's police org.
44. Like many bathroom floors
46. "___ pray" (pulpit petition)
48. Pt. of EEC
49. "Positively!"
51. They know the drill

53. Ano Nuevo time
55. Something to chew
56. General address?
58. One place to golf
64. Likelihood ratio
66. Flying prefix
67. Hindu gentleman
68. "How peachy keen!"
69. This answer contains a lot of letters
70. Andes fleece provider
71. Like venison
72. *A Light in the Attic* author Silverstein
73. Elizabeth I's ill-fated favorite

Down

1. B'way hit signs
2. Summer month in France
3. ". . . ___ dust shalt thou return"
4. *Hannah and Her Sisters* Oscar-winner Wiest
5. Like extreme emotions
6. Type of blocker
7. Culture contents
8. Frankenstein monster features
9. Fast follower?
10. Maven
11. Solid old hymn?
12. Greater quantity

13. Bowl over
21. Olympic measure
22. Japan's first capital
26. Words with "well"
27. Valuable violin
28. Polio vaccine developer
29. It was renamed for Herbert Hoover
30. Type of history
31. Situated
33. Contributed suggestions
34. Travels with the band
37. Punta del ___ (Uruguay resort)
40. Ump chaser?
42. Gold measure
45. Profound
47. Five o'clock shadow
50. Sleep images
52. Models of excellence
54. African witchcraft
56. ___ and dance
57. You might bounce it off someone
59. Cheese enjoyed with Chardonnay
60. Hang in the hammock, for example
61. Bedouin robes
62. "Rain" or "shine" preceder
63. Fraudulence
65. It's fit for a pig

Puzzle 131: Remote Target
Treacherous

Across

1. 1979 Roman Polanski film
5. Mil. training class
9. "A likely story!"
12. Eye nerve
14. Geometry calculations
16. Matter of self-interest?
17. Delaying strategy
19. Set aflame
20. One supporting a habit?
21. Company that bought Time Warner
22. Goes ballistic
24. Big game?
26. Leather cleaner
29. Assaults olfactorily
31. It comes before a dropped name
32. Lincoln, for one
33. It may whiz past one's knees
35. Chaplin prop
38. Vietnamese holiday
39. Archivist's material
42. Lively dance
45. Sought damages from
46. Begs
50. Guthrie Center founder
52. ___ Moines, Iowa

54. Polio fighter Albert
55. Gracious winners, for example
59. Elvis's daughter
60. Open, in a way
61. It gradually increases in depth from mouth to head
63. One way to make a bough break
64. They may be ripped or crunched
65. Virginia shipbuilding center
69. *Norma* ___ (Sally Field film)
70. Challenged
71. Assistant who handles letters
72. Many AARP members
73. Use an IBM Selectric, for example
74. Vanquish

Down

1. Word in the title of a Steve Martin/Goldie Hawn film
2. Shoulder adornment
3. Bugs Bunny, according to Bugs Bunny
4. Kennel order

5. Sweater style
6. End of some e-mail addresses
7. Japanese ceremonial drink
8. Bedouin transporter
9. Lend a hand
10. Stir up
11. Popular nightclub
13. KGB counterpart
15. Waterless
18. Discouraging words
23. It's in the heart of Jerusalem?
25. Read quickly
27. Reader of secret messages
28. Unhearing
30. Winter transports
34. Old gold coin
36. Bit of brandy
37. Wings on buildings
40. Overhaul
41. Sit-down occasion
42. Jacksonville team
43. Jail cell feature
44. Women's lip applications
47. Site of the Eisenhower Library
48. Renounces

49. Responds harshly to

51. Horace work, for example

53. Walked

56. Hourglass filler

57. Fabric fold

58. Business letter addressee, perhaps

62. Off-road rambler, for short

66. Like some humor

67. Zing

68. Collar

Puzzle 132: Classic!
Treacherous

Across

1. Mayberry's Otis, for example
4. It has a point
9. Ambergris source
14. ___ for the books
15. Suggestion box fill
16. A status symbol
17. Asimov book that became a sci-fi classic
20. Arena parts
21. Pulitzer-winning columnist Herb
22. Setting for many jokes
23. "A" or "an"
26. Pot-bellied pet
27. PC key
28. De Niro classic
31. Smash into
34. Jack Benny's 39
35. Abominable snowmen
38. Commiserator's word
40. Floor models
43. Relinquish
44. One of Zeppo's brothers
46. Tiny Tim's instrument, briefly
47. Caviar, for example
48. 1964 Best Picture
53. Fifth sign
55. Chinchilla's coat
56. Alarm clock, for example
60. Tabloid aviators, briefly
61. Bass or treble, for example
63. Sound beginning?
64. Film about a Little League team
68. Noted billionaire
69. Virus carrier, sometimes
70. Coxcomb
71. Surprise attack
72. Annie's pooch
73. Spider's parlor invitee

Down

1. Feature of the word "car" but not "cake"
2. Broadcasting
3. Basic principle
4. Total disaster
5. Pitched messages
6. Track record?
7. Worldly rather than spiritual
8. Con's preoccupation
9. Bad way to be convicted
10. Today, in Madrid
11. Statue material, perhaps
12. Word with "tender" or "aid"
13. Exercise, as influence
18. "What's your sine?" subj.
19. One of seven, to Salome
24. Washday unit
25. Part of a blade
29. Biggest human bone
30. Former nuclear agcy.
31. Bit of a cheer
32. ___ mode
33. Long-tailed South American monkeys
36. Wedding promise
37. Come to understand
39. Operative
41. Sooners' st.
42. Seal in the juices
45. Thrown aside
49. "___ Lang Syne"
50. Papas and Castle
51. Twofold or a way to be sure
52. Type of log
53. Fire, euphemistically
54. ___ Frome
57. Type of car or nurse
58. Filmdom's Flynn
59. Unpleasantly grating
62. Disaster relief org.
65. It may sting a little
66. Obi-___ Kenobi
67. Caesar's first name

Puzzle 133: Before and After?
Treacherous

Across

1. Break a certain commandment
6. Mess maker
10. David, for one
14. Verdi forte
15. Poi party
16. Atlas datum
17. Like Mozart's flute
18. Entomologist's specimens, perhaps
19. *The Alienist* author
20. Vader's psionic weapon?
23. Bass attachment
24. New issue on the NYSE
25. Temporary, as a position
29. Annapolis initials
31. Escape clause
34. Word with "brain" or "blind"
35. Partner of "aid"
36. Hybrid fruit
37. Where votes for best films are counted?
40. Fit to ___
41. Noted international marketplace
42. Oliver Mellors, to Lady Chatterley
43. "Why, certainly!"
44. Tang anagram
45. Cutting beams
46. Sailor, slangily
47. Place to hang your hat
48. Kermit making a significant change?
57. Reverse, on a PC
58. James of *The Godfather*
59. Greek salad morsel
60. Bullet point
61. Firing chamber
62. Like beasts of burden
63. Region
64. Do in, as a dragon
65. Put forth

Down

1. Search thoroughly
2. Gem for some Libras
3. Lyra star
4. Colonizer of Greenland
5. Supplement, as a bill
6. "Hast thou ___ the Jabberwock?"
7. Air chamber
8. Invective
9. Raid, perhaps
10. Chocolate source
11. Certain Middle Easterner
12. Insignificant
13. Henry VIII's last wife
21. Cabin component
22. Curative waters
25. In check
26. Bucket of bolts
27. Western bulrushes
28. Avalon, for one
29. Lusitania sinker
30. Like the Beatles' Sadie
31. Pointed architectural arch
32. Worrier's health risk
33. La Scala features
35. Self-titled 1975 pop album
36. Tabloid subjects
38. Two "Lincolns"
39. Attachment to government buildings
44. Understood
45. Poet's pasture
46. Folklore dwarf
47. Small amount of change
48. Quickie exam
49. "Do ___ others . . ."
50. Middle Eastern gulf
51. Correspondence
52. Land for the looney?
53. Linen fiber source
54. Aptly named astronaut
55. "Your turn," in radiospeak
56. Chap

1	2	3	4	5		6	7	8	9		10	11	12	13
14						15					16			
17						18					19			
20				21					22					
			23					24						
25	26	27	28				29	30				31	32	33
34					35					36				
37				38					39					
40				41					42					
43			44					45						
		46					47							
48	49	50			51	52				53	54	55	56	
57				58					59					
60				61					62					
63				64					65					

Puzzle 134: Busy, Busy, Busy
Treacherous

Across

1. "Let's not forget . . ."
5. Urban oasis
9. Swahili boss
14. Carson's Carnac, for example
15. Fencing gear
16. Lent a hand
17. Finish superficially
20. Similar
21. Supplement (with "out")
22. Moved about energetically
26. Come to grips
30. Disentangled
31. Smudge on Santa
32. Audio receiver
33. Christie's *The Seven ___ Mystery*
34. Pseudonym of H.H. Munro
35. Garage compartments
36. Get right down to business
39. Oodles
40. Beam
41. Whistles when the police are spotted
43. Roman candle path
44. Chuck wagon fare
45. Slim and trim

46. Have through a gene
48. Ms. Clinton
49. Kettle and Barker
50. Bed end
51. Waste no time with
59. Adds one to three, for example
60. Gala event
61. Classic opera
62. Dave Thomas's kid
63. Cold feet
64. Contrary current

Down

1. Ember, in the end
2. Orchid necklace
3. Harden
4. Bit for the dog bowl
5. Cheated at hide-and-seek
6. Pest for a rose
7. Restraining influence
8. Powder container
9. Hoop dunk
10. Diaper bag items
11. Shakespearean fuss
12. Where many surf
13. Commercial blurbs
18. Most robust
19. Awe-inspiring
22. Potato eye

23. Horned creature
24. Steadfast
25. Fights with lances
26. Snatched from dreamland
27. Old World prickly plants
28. Baby shower gift, perhaps
29. Sounds of hesitation
31. Hindu's sir
34. Walk like a chanticleer
35. Genesis tower
37. Like a giant of fairy tales
38. Must
39. ___ chi (martial art)
42. Coral, for one
44. Flush with fescue
45. April event
47. Improve text
48. Terra ___
50. Complimentary
51. Kittenish call
52. Hail to Caesar
53. He's a real doll
54. Wide of the mark
55. Actress ___ Dawn Chong
56. *The Karate ___* (1984)
57. Roulette play
58. Wray in *King Kong*

Puzzle 135: Not Quite Sure
Treacherous

Across

1. Curly Howard's replacement
6. Russian pancake
11. Spicy
14. "Mangia!"
15. Angry, and then some
16. Vladimir Nabokov novel
17. Conjecture
19. Spare part
20. Type of coach (Abbr.)
21. Cinco minus cuatro
22. Rise and shine!
24. Brownish-red chalcedony
26. Tight situation
27. State positively
30. Name in a Harold Robbins title
31. Conjecture (with 44-Across)
33. Persuade
37. Reproductive cells
38. Solid ground
41. Lead-in for Branco or Bravo
42. Dispense
44. See 31-Across
46. Vegetates
49. Slip away, as time
50. Publisher's payment

53. Cosby TV series
54. Tristan's secret love
55. It does a bang-up job
56. Man of Steel's accessory
60. Put down
61. Attempt
64. It may need massaging
65. From the East
66. Joe Louis, for one
67. Referendum choice
68. Aussie tennis star Fraser
69. Tropical nut or palm

Down

1. Big name in home video games
2. Herr's home
3. Summers on the Seine
4. Words with "TV" in an old NBC slogan
5. Second letter addendum
6. Hunter's hiding place
7. Wheels for wheels
8. ___ Toguri (Tokyo Rose)
9. Dummy
10. Standards of perfection
11. Concubine center
12. Ill will
13. St. Pete neighbor

18. Chelonian reptile
23. Low islands
25. Graceful steed
26. Stop on a line
27. Molecular component
28. Create interest?
29. Game with 32 cards
30. Livestock abodes
32. Uplift morally
34. Finish a take
35. A show of vanity
36. Couple for a brace
39. Coffers
40. Seaweed
43. Airline to Tel Aviv
45. Modern workplace perk
47. River of song
48. Private instruction?
50. NBA coach Pat
51. Inedible orange
52. Toys that go around the world
53. Absurd
55. Pond-dwelling duck
57. Watch for the cops, maybe
58. Glazier's cutting
59. Inclusive abbr.
62. Hyundai competitor
63. Check for drinks

1	2	3	4	5	■	6	7	8	9	10	■	11	12	13
14					■	15					■	16		
17					18						■	19		
20				■	21			■	22		23			
■	■	■	24	25			■	26						
27	28	29				■	30					■	■	■
31					32			■			33	34	35	36
37			■	38					39	40	■	41		
42			43	■		44					45			
■	■	■	46	47	48			■	49					
50	51	52					■	53				■	■	■
54						■	55			■	56	57	58	59
60			■	61		62				63				
64			■	65				■	66					
67			■	68				■	69					

Puzzle 136: Stopping Points
Treacherous

Across

1. Toast comparative
5. Dust busters?
10. Sellers' market?
14. Fancy needle case
15. Brains, for sure
16. Jiggs' daughter
17. Deutschland divider, once
19. Type of wire
20. Castrogiovanni, today
21. Chemical salts
23. Moroccan's capital
26. Turkey mo. in the U.S.
28. Oka River city
29. Words to the wise
31. Be a pain
33. Bull foe
34. Exasperates
35. Blue
38. Has it wrong
39. "___ porridge hot . . ."
41. "___ added expense"
42. Variety of whale
43. Kind of film
44. Put in the pen
46. Go by
48. Reduce to rag condition
49. Hammer's target, sometimes
50. Real attachment
52. They come a courting?
53. Storied invader
55. Nora's terrier
57. "Makes sense!"
58. Boundary one can cross
63. Some disinformation
64. Wipe the slate clean
65. Cut of veal
66. It's absolutely not right!
67. Tear repairer
68. Ho-ho-ho time

Down

1. Part of a baseball mitt
2. Filled the bill?
3. Capek's notable play
4. Expense account factors
5. Thomas who wrote *The Magic Mountain*
6. Nile-regulating dam
7. "It ___ far, far better thing . . ."
8. Comes through
9. Manche dept. capital
10. Plenary
11. Texas or Vermont, for example
12. Tempestuous spirit?
13. Hound sounds
18. Act or play start
22. Pointillist's points
23. Motel posting
24. Be wild about
25. Offshore coral ridge
27. Painkillers
30. Use a sponge or biscuit
32. Shooting sport
36. The Hulk's catalyst
37. Type A types
40. Chez Hamlet
41. In fact
43. Muslim judge
45. Far from nice
47. Gossip (with "the")
49. Count on the 88s
51. Parson's place
53. Paper producer
54. Good opening pair
56. Hoop ending
59. Car makers' grp.
60. Debtor's paper
61. Zippo
62. Chemical suffix

Puzzle 137: Thirsty?
Treacherous

Across

1. Backless footgear
5. Word after 17-, 38-, and 59-Across, and 11- and 34-Down
10. Coal carrier
14. Play to ___ (deadlock)
15. Vacuous
16. "Now then, where ___?"
17. Form of liquor smuggling
19. October birthstone
20. Distinguishing feature
21. "Clue" piece
23. Clothes lines?
26. Take ___ off (sit down)
27. Conceal from danger
29. Special talents
32. Jocularity
35. Meadowland
36. Transmitting
37. Infant fare
38. Naval veteran
40. Dull daily routing
41. Show with clarity
43. File suit against
44. Teachers' favorites
45. *The Balcony* playwright
46. You, at this very moment
48. Informed

50. Go awry
54. Steakhouse order
57. Per ___ (yearly)
58. Prefix meaning "bone"
59. Wintertime affliction
62. Letters on some planes
63. Dobie Gillis's buddy
64. Ultimatum's ultimate word, usually
65. Retained
66. Biblical matriarch
67. Penn with an Oscar

Down

1. Cuban patriot José
2. Auto maneuver
3. Succotash, in part
4. Least explainable
5. Best the rest
6. ___ Arbor, Michigan
7. Follow furtively
8. Group of nine
9. Majestic
10. Poker holding, perhaps
11. In quick succession
12. Letters of haste
13. Eight furlongs
18. Zion National Park location
22. Give less than 100 percent

24. Choreographer Agnes de ___
25. Tournament ranking
28. Cowboy's apparatus
30. Fastening item
31. Pepper and Preston (Abbr.)
32. Computer image file format
33. Roof overhang
34. Band in a 1984 film parody
36. Pain relief brand
38. Group of eight
39. New Year's word
42. 1960s political movement
44. Charles, William, and Harry
46. Spanish woman's title
47. *The Blackboard Jungle* novelist Hunter
49. Neil Diamond's "Love on the ___"
51. Iguanalike critter
52. Oklahoma city
53. German port city
54. Queeg's creator
55. To be, to Brutus
56. *ER* part
60. Wharton deg.
61. City in Kyrgyzstan

Puzzle 138: Game Time
Treacherous

Across

1. Thermometer's terminus
5. Island handouts
9. Arab cloaks
13. "Not ___" ("Think nothing of it")
15. Straddling
16. Upholstered piece
17. Country with a red, white, and blue flag
18. Term used in hockey
20. Algonquian speaker
22. It's not returnable, in tennis
23. This year's grads
24. Florida citrus center
26. Retained
28. Strongbox
31. Term used in darts
35. Sternward
36. Officer Malloy of *Adam 12*
37. Kind of curtain
38. Sleep stage abbr.
39. Airport components
40. Wells or Lupino
41. Myanmar locale
43. Tiresome routines
44. French impressionist painter Claude
46. Term used in squash
48. Destroy or injure severely
49. Kitten's plaything
50. "Nothing ___!"
52. "___, drink, and be merry"
54. Tack on
56. North Pole twosome
60. Term used in rugby
63. Without worldly sophistication
64. Ballpark level
65. Word after "rest" or "staging"
66. Shakespearean forest
67. Earthly paradise
68. ". . . ___ and not heard"
69. Bang-up result?

Down

1. "Nozze di Figaro" part for Dr. Bartolo
2. 45th state
3. Dalai ___ (chief Tibetan monk)
4. Fail to attend, as a party
5. Jacket part
6. D.D.E.'s WWII command
7. 29th state
8. Trout features
9. Nile creature
10. Supporting
11. Many miles away
12. What Simon does
14. Sharp surgical instrument
19. Projectionist's unit
21. "In one ___ and out the other"
25. Assisted in crime
27. Abbreviation on tires in Greece?
28. Jeweler's weight
29. Needing to take off?
30. Genealogist's map
32. Salt Lake City students
33. Sing Swiss-style
34. Mother's relative
36. Epistle apostle
39. Family matriarchs
42. King intro?
44. Tomorrow, in a Peggy Lee song
45. Alert
47. Monorail unit
48. Wire measure
51. Great expanse
52. Powerful Italian family
53. Word with "rock," "rain," or "test"
55. Venture
57. Rectangle or triangle part
58. Uniform
59. Dispatched
61. Final resting place, for some
62. Word from Beaver Cleaver

Puzzle 139: Passing Grade
Treacherous

Across

1. Brand bought by Wile E. Coyote
5. Acts as lookout, for example
10. Pt. of IRA
14. Attempt to persuade
15. Camp David accords participant
16. Ayatollah's predecessor
17. ". . . or ___ me?"
18. Poppycock
19. Fillable bread
20. 1978 Best Picture (with *The*)
22. The "dismal science," for short
23. Where some jams are made
24. Noise from the farm
26. Vivacious actress West
27. Barbecue rod
29. Bowlike curve
32. ___ d'art
35. Rosary items
36. Arrived lifeless, briefly
37. Plain of Jars locale
38. Loads the hook
39. ___ *Window*
40. Tough wood
41. It may be grand
42. Watering hole items
43. Boggy area
44. Dover specialty
45. X-ray unit
46. Raw information
48. Dunce
52. "Bullets" in poker
54. Period of suspended activity
57. Needle apertures
58. Sing the praises of
59. In ___ (bored with things)
60. One in a million
61. Wheel brace
62. Like some circumstances
63. Addition column
64. Chromatic nuances
65. Divination practitioner

Down

1. Acetic and nitric
2. Mathematical grouping
3. Gold medalist skier Hermann
4. They're polar
5. On the ball
6. Sights in the country
7. Prepare for publication
8. Word with "deck" or "measure"
9. Banned NFL substances
10. Forest quaker
11. Word in a W.C. Fields film title
12. "The Elder" of history
13. "Better you ___ me!"
21. Kind of wave
25. Part of TGIF
27. Take by force
28. Fancy chopped liver
30. Laugh heartily
31. What some plants produce
32. Patron saint of Norway
33. Bag of diamonds?
34. Plow pioneer
35. What some people jump
38. With the most breadth
39. Lucille Ball and many others
41. Western time
42. Roseanne, before Tom
45. Searches through
47. Hinny and ninny, for example
48. Pig in ___
49. Ghastly strange
50. Color of a clear sky
51. Dissuade
52. Aviation prefix
53. Primary color in photography
55. Public art show or former Montreal athlete
56. British school

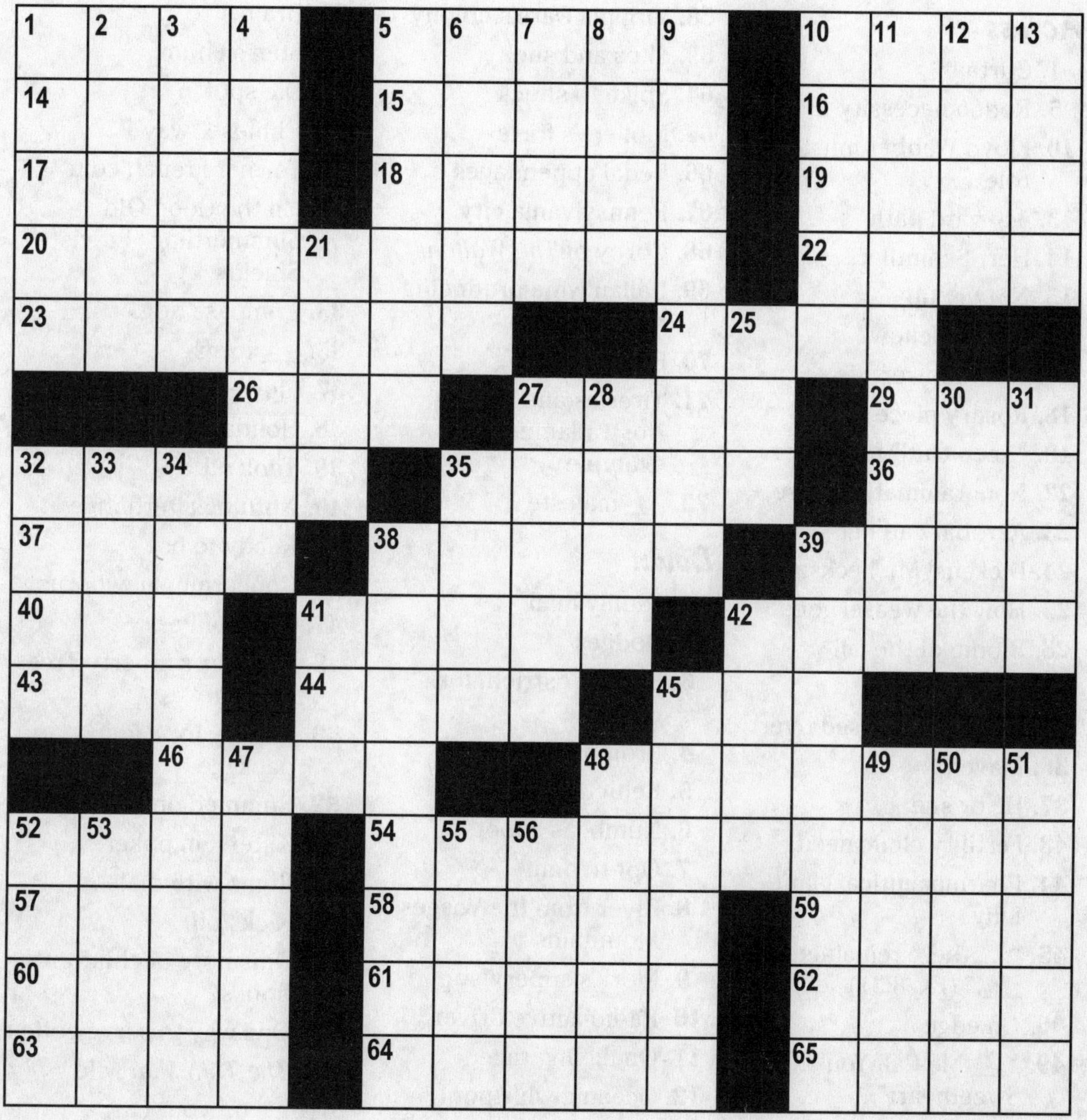

Puzzle 140: Secret Solving
Treacherous

Across

1. Curtail
5. Rodeo necessity
10. Lloyd Webber musical role
13. 440-yard path
14. Herr Schindler
15. Not yet up
16. Sneaky fellow?
17. Aka follower
18. Rosary piece
19. "Keep Out!" follower
22. Nongrammatical case
23. Acrobat catcher
24. Dickens' Mr. Pecksniff
25. How the weasel goes
28. Bloom of the fall
32. Unit of time
34. It may be glossed over
36. Maven
37. He or she
43. Fertility clinic needs
44. Pharmaceutical giant Lilly
45. ". . . there remained not ___." (Ex. 8:31)
46. On edge
49. "___ Me Call You Sweetheart"
51. Male turkeys
54. Trains on high

56. Virginia Dare's colony
59. Slips and such
64. Spike to shuck
65. Moliere's forte
66. Pedal appendages
67. Pennsylvania city
68. Corby of *The Waltons*
69. Italian wine-producing region
70. Block
71. Tiresias and Nostradamus, for example
72. ___ majeste

Down

1. Family man
2. Dodges
3. Emu or ostrich, for example
4. Promotes
5. Reluctant
6. Numb, as a foot
7. Opt to omit
8. River from the Vosges Mountains
9. Mork's supervisor
10. Radio-active driver
11. Qualifying race
12. Oceanic whirlpool
15. Aids in dirty deeds
20. Cause for a blessing

21. Brain size
26. Stan's chum
27. Die spot
29. Chinese "way"
30. Former French coin
31. "In the Good Old Summertime" lyricist Shields
33. Compass hdg.
35. ___ forma
37. Flower holder
38. Holiday precursor
39. Took off
40. Nothing alternative
41. Ready to use
42. Concerning newborns
47. River of Paris
48. America's Liberty Tree was one
50. Inquiry for a lost package
52. Bummed out
53. Kilters, in poker
55. Items with dials
57. Kicks off
58. Dinsmore of children's books
59. One way to serve coffee
60. *The Thin Man* wife
61. It's on your car
62. Fisherman's offering?
63. Perry's creator

1	2	3	4	■	5	6	7	8	9	■	■	10	11	12
13				■	14					■	15			
16				■	17					■	18			
19				20					21					
22						■		23				■	■	■
■	24				■	25	26	27	■	28		29	30	31
■	■		32		33	■	34		35	■		36		
37	38	39				40				41	42			
43			■		44			■	45			■	■	■
46			47	48	■	49		50	■	51		52	53	■
■	■	■	54		55	■	■	56	57				■	58
59	60	61				62	63							
64				■	65				■	66				
67				■	68				■	69				
70			■	■	71				■	72				

Puzzle 141: Off to the Shrink
Treacherous

Across

1. Economical Halloween costume
6. Gin flavoring
10. ". . . sting like ___"
14. Beauty queen adornment
15. The Piltdown man, for example
16. "Agreed!"
17. Suffering from nyctophobia
20. Zero, in soccer
21. Heist haul
22. Maltreat
23. Helvetica, for one
24. Equipped
25. Brings down
28. Bird of Old Rome
29. CBS show set in Las Vegas
32. Not moving
33. Without ___ (daringly)
34. Hemoglobin component
35. Xenophobia
38. Object of desire?
39. Settles with certainty
40. Send to seventh heaven
41. School of tomorrow?
42. Dolt

43. Examine
44. Shed, snake-style
45. Pro ___ (free)
46. One way to be washed
49. Spring bloom
50. Ceiling figure
53. Suffering from zoophobia
56. Home of ancient Irish kings
57. Triumphant cry
58. Pathogens
59. Follow the code
60. Meshworks
61. Explosive trial

Down

1. "___ the Man" Musial
2. CD player ancestor
3. Sandwich man?
4. Slice of history
5. Adapt for
6. "Go ahead and ask"
7. Studio site, sometimes
8. Bit in a horse's mouth?
9. Initial bit of evidence
10. Discombobulate
11. Gal's sweetheart
12. They usually listen well
13. Sommer of films

18. Gangland bigwigs
19. Pipe bends
23. Take to the bank?
24. Says with no uncertainty
25. Permanent pen pal?
26. Bridge bid, briefly
27. Intertwine
28. Paid to play
29. Floorboard sound
30. To some degree
31. Map feature
33. Knotted neckwear
34. Home of *Nanook of the North*
36. Worked as a sub
37. Advertising lure
42. Heart
43. Cut of meat
44. Coral reef denizen, perhaps
45. Grain husks
46. Concerning
47. Striker's anathema
48. Fabled napper
49. "___ ain't broke . . ."
50. Supervision
51. Poor box donations
52. "Hey, over here!"
54. Have bills
55. Bumped into

1 2 3 4 5 6 7 8 9 10 11 12 13
14 15 16
17 18 19
20 21 22
23 24
25 26 27 28 29 30 31
32 33 34
35 36 37
38 39 40
41 42 43
44 45
46 47 48 49 50 51 52
53 54 55
56 57 58
59 60 61

Puzzle 142: Cover Your Rear
Treacherous

Across

1. "Couldn't have said it better myself"
5. There's no accounting for it
10. Turkish topper
13. Amount spent
14. Greek alphabet starters
16. George's musical brother
17. Nature personified
19. Con's sheet
20. Zeta-theta connection
21. Courage
22. Cheer for the matador
24. Assemble
26. Owing on one's payments
30. Negligent
32. Clinging part of a climbing plant
33. Start to dominate?
34. Cartridge holder
35. Mortar rounds
36. Bygone
39. Weasely critters
42. One way to follow a pattern
43. ___ mater (brain membrane)
45. Long, long time
46. Type of reaction

48. Pizza sauce enhancer
50. Respectable
53. Shuffle
55. Has down pat
57. Butting bighorn
58. Molded, frozen dessert
60. By way of
61. Slugging stat
63. A bit too serious
66. Valdez cargo
67. 40th president of the U.S.
68. Player's stake
69. Tarzan film character
70. Improve, as a text
71. Angler's prize

Down

1. Heights of perfection
2. More debatable
3. Elvis' Graceland, for example
4. Unspecific degree
5. Poi source
6. French historian de Tocqueville
7. New World colonizer
8. Imperil
9. Gormandize
10. Combat supplies
11. Historical time
12. Laser gun sound effect

15. Like many a sheep
18. Napoleon's realm
23. "___ and the Swan" (Yeats)
25. Guy who cries foul
27. Back out
28. Frost
29. Give me a brake?
31. Star close to Venus?
34. Word with "fraternity" or "hair"
36. Olfactory perception
37. Tackle box item
38. Without much cheer
40. Night light
41. Chump
44. Indian tourist site
47. Comaneci accomplishment
49. Museum suit
50. Abase
51. Repeated Catholic prayer
52. Ironic turns
54. Eat more than one's fill
56. Eats more than one's fill
59. Group marching, perhaps
61. Scottish hero Roy
62. Short life story?
64. Rock singer Bobby
65. Capture a crook

The grid below is an empty crossword puzzle grid.

1	2	3	4	■	5	6	7	8	9	■	10	11	12
13				■	14				15	■	16		
17			18							■	19		
20			■	21				■	22	23		■	
24			25		■	26		27				28	29
■	30				31		■	32					
■		33			■	34			■	35			
36	37	38	■	39		40			41	■	42		
43			44	■	45			■	46		47	■	
48				49			■	50				51	52
53						54		■	55				56
■		57			■	58		59			■	60	
61	62		■	63	64					■	65		
66			■	67					■	68			
69			■	70				■	71				

Puzzle 143: One Vowel Off
Treacherous

Across

1. Band of seven
7. First of billions
11. 16.5 feet
14. *Rocky* villain
15. Andean city
16. Wax trapper
17. Antic
18. Yankee in the news, informally
19. Four-stringed instrument, for short
20. Doc wannabes
23. Tadpole cousins
27. Hobby-store buys
28. Pumas' pads
29. Balsamic, cider, or white
31. Seat for two or more
32. Gain access
33. Nullify
36. Always, in verse
37. Perfectly away from either bank
40. Test starter?
43. Polyphonic song
44. Old photo tint
48. Go back
50. Thoroughly
52. Rousseau novel
53. Draped dress

55. Little one
56. Garb for the jet set
59. "___ Gotta Be Me"
60. Walk with weariness
61. Make-believe food
66. Fractional monetary unit of Japan
67. Water drainer
68. *Foreign Affairs* Pulitzer winner Lurie
69. Time of the 75th meridian
70. Cultivated grasses
71. Identifying

Down

1. *The Wild Bunch* director Peckinpah
2. 1972 DDT banner
3. Container of peas
4. ICU specialty
5. *Big Bad John* actor Jack
6. Brown v. Board of Education city
7. "With ___ of thousands!"
8. Pub competition
9. Baseball brothers' surname
10. Area near the Mediterranean
11. Get exes to become ex-exes
12. Yellow ribbon bearer

13. Armoire kin
21. Most urgent
22. Snack or nosh
23. Time before anything important
24. *Jaws* sighting
25. It does blowups
26. Appear to be
30. Scythe-bearing visitor
31. 180 degrees from NNW
34. 66, for one (Abbr.)
35. Conductor Toscanini
38. URL punctuator
39. Satisfy, as demands
40. Assumption
41. Subtracts
42. Clearly visible
45. Snoop
46. Kind
47. Supporter's response
49. Folklore being
51. Jack Haley role
53. What push comes to
54. Executive's staff
57. Leave helpless with laughter
58. Toni Morrison novel
62. Not very bright, really
63. Chi–Omega connection
64. Accord ender?
65. Chang's bosom buddy?

1
2
3
4
5
6
7
8
9
10
11
12
13
14
15
16
17
18
19
20
21
22
23
24
25
26
27
28
29
30
31
32
33
34
35
36
37
38
39
40
41
42
43
44
45
46
47
48
49
50
51
52
53
54
55
56
57
58
59
60
61
62
63
64
65
66
67
68
69
70
71

Puzzle 144: It R Squared
Treacherous

Across

1. Like user-friendly notebook paper
6. Federal organization that may inspect your workplace
10. Super-deluxe
14. Esteem to the extreme
15. Continuous-play tape
16. First words in the title of Mae West's "angelic" film
17. Captain Hook's "Jolly Roger"
19. Road to Damascus figure, later
20. Greek island that is part of the Cyclades
21. "Switch" or "buck" attachment
22. The "E" in Einstein's formula
24. Greg, to Carol Brady
26. He eulogized Julius
27. Word screamed with joy before "a boy" or "a girl"
28. Orlando's love in *As You Like It*
32. Visually-challenged excavators
35. Greg Louganis's specialty
36. "I saw ___ kissing Kate" (tongue twister)
37. Eurasian range
38. Like wartime messages
39. Eyes a bull's-eye
40. It's gassy and exists to get your attention
41. Breaks new ground
42. When it comes to the atlas, it's not the big picture
43. Questionable patent medicines
45. Snoopy, when wearing his scarf
46. Red-___ (franks)
47. Hammer and anvil mate
51. Lyricist with Richard Rogers, Hart
54. Dagwood's creator
55. Get some good out of
56. Son of Zeus and Hera
57. Feature of a gas stove, but not an electric one
60. Mild partner?
61. River associated closely with Shakespeare
62. Glowing, smoldering coal
63. Good wine quality
64. Half of an infamous dual personality
65. *Heidi* author Johanna

Down

1. Displays astonishment, with the mouth
2. Dostoevsky's ding-a-ling
3. It can be found in runes
4. Cenozoic, for one
5. Hates with a passion
6. "Maximus to Gloucester" poet Charles
7. Trendy Manhattan area
8. ___ polloi
9. Mollified
10. Flexible tufted wire for meerschaum users
11. Noted tent tycoon
12. Comfortable and cozy
13. Sacrosanct
18. February 14 figure
23. Org. that sticks to its guns?
25. Half-baked utopia?
26. They're recorded in chess columns
28. Fair offers?
29. Cow-headed goddess of fertility
30. Although you have a first and last, your last is often used
31. Composition of some very dirty clouds
32. *Buddenbrooks* novelist Thomas
33. Little pat on your buns?
34. Vientiane is its capital
35. Destines to a tragic fate
38. Yiddish audacity
42. Eaves droppers?

44. He's right up there with Mick

45. Words with "while you're" or "take a crack"

47. Glittered

48. British sport that resembles American football

49. One who'll help you get with the program?

50. Microorganism-growing dish

51. It's younger than ewe?

52. Cookie sold in a White Fudge version in winter

53. *From Here to Eternity* Oscar winner, Donna

54. Clump of earth

58. It's creepy, but they love it at Wrigley's Field

59. Mischievous little rascal

Puzzle 145: Ear to the Ground
Treacherous

Across

1. Motivation to keep a doctor's appointment
5. Rhymester
9. Trumped-up
14. Let fall, as tears
15. Restless yearning
16. Bermuda border
17. Indication of detachment
20. Change in a major way
21. Place to walk
22. "Chances ___" (Johnny Mathis hit)
23. *The Cask of Amontillado* author
25. Sidekicks
29. Aping avian
31. Drove up the wall
33. Genetic material
34. Chain of mountains
36. In the offing
38. Cornered
42. Arabian coffee
43. Prepared a pineapple
44. Boat propeller?
45. One who'll put you in your place
47. Bit of a tiff
51. Commandment
54. Showy dance maneuver
56. Letter from Greece?
57. WWII predator

59. Like some escapes
61. How the sensible stand
65. Commence
66. Viscount's superior
67. Pre-Soviet royalty
68. Humor with a twist
69. Something to do to the music
70. Slippery and slimy

Down

1. Getaway with a guru
2. Chipper
3. Realm for St. Peter
4. Work attributed to Snorri Sturluson
5. Zero in on
6. Mel with 511 home runs
7. Twice-heard sound
8. From that place
9. System of numbering pages
10. One struck Chicken Little
11. Romanian money
12. Down in the dumps
13. Printer's measures
18. Little rascal
19. It may be drawn by hand?
24. Hence
26. Figure in a pagoda, perhaps

27. Organic compound
28. Wasn't off one's rocker?
30. Sole's curve
32. Sailing ship
35. Wanted-poster abbreviation, perhaps
36. Reverent wonder
37. Passing fancies
38. *Lord of the Flies* creature
39. "God's Little ___"
40. Did groundbreaking work
41. In a mistaken manner
42. Implement in a bucket
45. Abreast of
46. Union members
48. Examine with attention to detail
49. Lacking a musical key
50. Cheap and shoddy
52. Interrupt, as a news broadcast
53. Dark black hardwood
55. Big deal for a duffer
58. Springtime occurrence
60. Education by memorization
61. Edgar J. Hoover's org.
62. Auction end
63. Braggart's problem
64. Historical segment

1	2	3	4	■	5	6	7	8	■	9	10	11	12	13
14				■	15				■	16				
17				18					19					
20					■	21						■	■	■
22			■	23		24	■	25				26	27	28
29			30	■	31		32			■	33			
■	■	■	34	35				■	■	36	37			
■	38	39					40	41						■
42				■	■	43					■	■	■	■
44			■	■	45	46				■	47	48	49	50
51			52	53			■	54		55	■	56		
■	■	57				58	■	59		60				
61	62	63				64								
65				■	66			■	67					
68				■	69			■	70					

Puzzle 146: Vanishing Ink
Treacherous

Across

1. Long, long time
5. Defense grp. that includes the U.S.
9. Inflict a heavy blow on
14. Foul
15. Gossip topic
16. Office copier need
17. "I knew ___ instant . . ."
18. Horror film feature
19. Management course subject?
20. Night application, for some
23. Be decisive
24. Suspect's demand (Abbr.)
25. Exhausting, hectic routines
30. Betty or Barney, of cartoons
34. A quarter of four
35. Involuntarily let go
37. Respiratory noises
38. Illusionist's feat
42. Kate's sitcom partner
43. Used a firehouse pole
44. Feminine subject
45. Close by
47. Woodworker's worry
50. Work as a barker
52. One-time queen of Spain
53. Auction-ending statement
60. "Lemon Tree" singer Lopez
61. Ultimatum conclusion
62. Queue after R
63. Daniel follower, in the Bible
64. Deadly septet
65. "___ boy!"
66. Washstand containers
67. Small children
68. Stone's throw, for example

Down

1. Tel ___, Israel
2. Actress Lollobrigida
3. Brio
4. Year on campus
5. Romantic evening extender
6. Yours, to the French
7. Gull relative
8. The ___ Man (Heston film)
9. Bravura performance
10. Wells Fargo pickup
11. Swenson of Benson
12. Rain, but good
13. Behave humanly?
21. Masseuse employer
22. Basketball pos.
25. 1956 movie monster
26. Old-womanish
27. Electrical pioneer Nikola
28. They're no longer together
29. Navy elite
31. Criticize in no uncertain terms
32. Cafe con ___ (coffee with milk)
33. Acid–alcohol compound
36. Icicle starter
39. People can get quite high on it
40. Funnel-shaped flowers
41. Inaction
46. URL ending, sometimes
48. Gerund finale
49. Pesters
51. Cast off from the body
53. Mushroom
54. Seine feeder
55. Hodgepodge
56. Does not exist
57. Sergeant Snorkel's dog
58. Cashews or filberts
59. Gabor and Peron
60. Not just any

Puzzle 147: Elbow Room
Treacherous

Across

1. ___ *Flanders*
5. Home in Havana
9. Surrounded by
13. Lacking human warmth
15. Trashy trait?
16. Arhus native
17. Space to maneuver
19. It may be compact
20. Any French king
21. Hardly ordinary
22. Kitchen appliance
24. Kind of alert
26. Place for hands
27. Blackjack card with two values
28. Show with a prince and fairies
32. Mobile site
33. Sturgeon yield
34. Always, poetically
35. White, brown, or basmati
36. Choose
38. British Revolutionary War commander
42. Judge Judy's org.
45. Japanese ceremonial drink
47. Modern auction site
48. Business that doesn't want to keep the books
53. Vancouver-to-Calgary dir.
54. Trade org. since 1960
55. Tear violently
56. Letter opener, sometimes
58. Architect I.M.
59. Center of activity
62. ". . . marching ___ war"
63. Investment choice
66. TV crime show
67. Anagram of lies
68. Potato, for one
69. Spacious type of bag
70. Fifth Ave. crime fighters
71. Main point

Down

1. Bryn ___ (Pennsylvania college)
2. Vaudeville shtick
3. Related to the handling of details
4. Birling unit
5. Appliance attachment
6. Fuss
7. Appease
8. Wardrobe relative
9. Comments further
10. Drink with rum and lime
11. Air-breathing arthropod
12. Edict
14. Amaze
18. Mystery Writers of America award
23. Altar area
25. Flockhart role
26. Doubting Thomas
28. Maker of checkout devices
29. Tell's home canton
30. Business VIP or dove call
31. Root for
37. Gymnast's dream score
39. Capital of the United Arab Emirates
40. You may step on it or burn it
41. Pupil's place
43. Short personal profiles
44. Medicine cabinet staple
46. Achieve harmony
48. Intellectual showoff
49. Promoter of intl. cooperation
50. "Get outta here!"
51. Opinion opposed to usual belief
52. It should set off alarms
57. Floral gift
58. Answered a charge
60. All-purpose trucks
61. Parks of Atlantic City?
64. Jungfrau, for example
65. Indication of a fish on a line

1	2	3	4			5	6	7	8		9	10	11	12
13				14		15					16			
17					18						19			
20				21				22		23				
		24	25				26					27		
28	29					30					31			
32					33				34					
35						36		37			38	39	40	41
			42	43	44		45		46		47			
48	49	50				51				52				
53				54				55						
56			57				58				59	60	61	
62					63		64			65				
66					67				68					
69					70					71				

Puzzle 148: Fighting Words
Treacherous

Across

1. High dudgeon
6. Go well together
10. "Fernando" singers
14. *Green Acres* character
15. Mixed bag
16. Layer of ore
17. Mixed it up
20. Grant opponent
21. "Mockingbird" singer Foxx
22. Nymphs of Greek myth
23. Made waves?
25. Price fixer
27. From the top
29. Packing material
33. Mixed it up
37. ___ Beta Kappa
38. Gathering dust
39. Infamous Ugandan Amin
40. Big name
41. One of The Three Stooges
42. Mixed it up
46. Affirm
48. "En garde" weapon
49. Silent screen's Harold
51. Impact noise
55. Swamp
58. Monetary exchange premium

60. China "way"
61. Mixed it up
64. First name in diarists
65. Popular cookie since 1912
66. Goddess of home and family
67. Stages of a journey
68. Handful of straw
69. "Abandon hope, all ye who ___ here"

Down

1. Impudent youngster
2. Hindu noblewoman
3. It makes you hot
4. 4:00 refreshment, perhaps
5. Sanitary measures
6. Ways and means
7. *My Fair Lady* lady
8. Commandment violation
9. Sinatra's hometown
10. In the wake of
11. Old videotape format
12. Tread-bare
13. City on the Skunk River
18. Put the kibosh on
19. Parts of a house
24. Mass-produce
26. New soft drink of 1961

28. Element of Dr. Seuss's work
30. Capable of
31. Grow genial
32. They're dubbed
33. Flaccid
34. Polecat's trademark
35. Marc Antony's love, familiarly
36. Dedicatory verse
40. 1977 Triple Crown champion Seattle ___
42. Rostropovich's instrument
43. Henceforth
44. Some nerve you've got
45. Be incumbent on
47. Lucky breaks
50. Secluded valleys
52. "This is only ___!" (radio message)
53. ___ blanche
54. '80s–'90s quarterback Bernie
55. Inclusive abbr.
56. Love points
57. Saucer-shaped instrument
59. Baby food, more or less
62. *Exodus* hero
63. ". . . all ___ are created equal"

Puzzle 149: Table Setting
Treacherous

Across

1. Word in Einstein's equation
5. Ye ___ shoppe
9. Screenwriter Chayefsky
14. "Gymnopedies" composer Satie
15. Lowing places
16. Leave out
17. *Let Us Now Praise Famous Men* author James
18. Crazed
19. Eskimos' kissers?
20. "Do You Believe in Magic" band
23. Gregg specialist, for short
24. Blunt sword
25. Be decisive
28. Bowery bums
31. Draws out
33. Campgrounds residue
36. Jude or James
39. Ms. Teasdale
40. 1962 Polanski film
44. Reckless
45. Land and sea meeting place
46. Curvy letter
47. Skater Baiul
50. Program command
52. Marshal of Waterloo
53. There are 54 in a game, usually
56. Okra soup
60. Decision spot
64. Gambler's loss, figuratively
66. Spaghetti sauce brand
67. Kind of van or bus
68. Cockney's challenge
69. Emerald Isle
70. Commodious crafts
71. Steep-walled land formations
72. Adept
73. Hatchling's home

Down

1. Square trio
2. In-group lingo
3. Colander kin
4. Coils of yarn
5. Automotive pioneer
6. Spring
7. Actor Willem
8. Prohibit legally
9. Like some fattened livestock
10. Felipe, Jesus, or Matty of baseball
11. Disjoint
12. H.S.T. successor
13. Conciliatory response
21. Lariat's end
22. Born
26. Shimon of Israel
27. Pre-Revolution leaders
29. Mai ___
30. Confessor's revelations
32. Superpower's letters
33. Ohio city
34. Grass inhabitant?
35. Whiny temper tantrums
37. Highest degree
38. Archaic pronoun
41. Agcy. for homeowners
42. East or West ending
43. Golf club
48. Some bridge positions
49. Shore bird
51. Start of a James Coburn film title
54. Out of gas
55. Drum type
57. Watery-patterned cloth
58. Safe places?
59. Keats or Milton, notably
61. Killer whale
62. End of the workweek letters
63. Peck partner
64. Uncle of 32-Down
65. Hurry

Puzzle 150: Color Wheel
Treacherous

Across

1. Basil or sage
5. Legwear of yore
10. Some Morse symbols
14. Middle Eastern potentate
15. Take one's sweet time
16. With a clean slate
17. Wheels for wheels
18. Peculiar speech form
19. Vehicle at an auction, perhaps
20. Whipped along
21. It's colorful in your head
23. Norton Sound city
25. Reverberated
26. Rapeseed oil
29. Small speck
31. Not under one's breath
32. Parcheesi, for example
37. Yard holder
38. Irritable
39. Very funny one
40. Canned fruit
42. It may be cast out
43. They're caught on the beach
44. Daily ritual, below the border
45. Joint injury
49. Trumpeting bird
50. Bechamel, for example
53. Ballet finale, for example
57. Freedom from hardship
58. Pondered
59. Mountains of Russia
60. Befuddled
61. "Goodnight" girl of song
62. Water source
63. Glossary entry
64. Some pastries
65. Fawning females?

Down

1. First of two parts
2. First name in Olympic long distance running
3. Frosty covering
4. Power company problems
5. Mark of infamy
6. Military chaplain
7. Verdi's "Caro nome," for example
8. Helen's destination
9. Feature of crossword grids
10. Villainous Vader
11. ___ a customer
12. Wickiup relative
13. Scimitar, for example
22. Scored perfectly
24. Word with "Glory" or "Testament"
26. Summer getaway
27. Winglike
28. Narrow victory margin
29. Painting Grandma
30. Horse feed
32. Group of quails
33. Foreigner's work permit
34. Aspires
35. Subject to debate
36. Peak seen from the Ionian Sea
38. Pass on, as a genetic trait
41. Canal with a mule named Sal
42. Day in Durango
44. Nobel and others
45. Blood–tears link
46. Full moon or first quarter, for example
47. Stair part
48. Col. Hannibal Smith and friends
49. Olfactory sensation
51. Surrounding glow
52. Manipulative person
54. Spicy stew
55. Hill partner
56. Is green without envy?

Part III
Checking the Solutions

The 5th Wave   By Rich Tennant

©RICHTENNANT

"I'm going to conduct a little word association exam with you. Just tell me what 7-letter word pops into your head when I say, 'metallurgical waste product.'"

In this part . . .

This part serves two very important functions. First, it offers you a nice pat on the back if you've solved an entire puzzle and just want to check your accuracy. (You don't really *need* to check your accuracy if you're confident about your answers and the grid is complete, but the validation sure does feel nice, doesn't it?) Second, it offers the answers to those oh-so-frustrating clues that threaten to keep you awake at night. Just promise me you won't peek at a solution until you've given your puzzle of choice a run for the money!

Chapter 4

Checking the Solutions

· ·

*H*opefully you know better than to read through this chapter before you have a chance to work on the puzzles in Chapter 3! However, there is one answer I can show you right now, which is the answer to the puzzle example in Chapter 2:

Sample Puzzle: How Grueling!

P	E	K	E		B	E	R	M		S	I	C	E	M
U	V	E	A		A	L	A	I		E	N	A	M	I
T	I	E	C	L	A	S	P	S		A	S	P	O	T
A	L	P	H	A	B	I	T	S		S	A	N	T	E
			N	A	E		P	R	A	N	C	E	R	
M	A	S	A	D	A		D	I	A	L	E	R		
E	L	M	O	S		P	A	G	E	T		U	M	P
O	V	A	L		L	O	N	G	S		R	N	A	S
W	A	R		D	O	P	E	Y		L	I	C	K	S
	T	H	E	S	I	S		R	E	D	H	O	T	
I	T	S	O	P	E	N		A	A	A				
N	A	T	A	L		J	U	S	T	R	I	G	H	T
A	C	A	R	E		A	L	I	E	N	R	A	C	E
W	O	R	S	T		Y	E	A	R		A	R	F	S
E	S	T	E	E		S	E	N	S		S	P	A	T

Answers to the remaining puzzles in this book begin on the next page!

Puzzle 1: A Pinpoint Solution

```
A B B A   O H A R E   A D D S
R O E S   P A L M S   V I I I
A R R I V E D O N T H E D O T
B E T   E R N E   E R O D E
      B L A T   G L A S S E S
L I L A C S   B L A D E
O N A I R   D E E M   W H O
V I C T O R I A N P E R I O D
E T E   E A R N   N O L L E
    S T I R S   S C A L D S
C O T T O N Y   S T A R
A V I A N   M A I M   L A S
J U M P I N G O F F P O I N T
U L E E   Y O D E L   L A N A
N E S S   S T E R E   D R A B
```

Puzzle 2: Turn-Ons

```
C H A T   T B O N E   O H N O
R I C H   H E L I X   M O O N
U P T O   A R E N T   A L D A
S P I N N I N G J E N N Y
T O N G A     A N T   G A B
    V I V A   D H A R M A
  I M B E C I L E   L A I T
W H I R L I N G D E R V I S H
H A N A   O A T M E A L S
A V I D L Y   E V I L
T E A   E O S   E B S E N
  T W I R L I N G T E A M S
B L U R   K A R O L   F L A Y
M Y R A   E V A D E   I S I N
W E E P   R E N E E   T A L C
```

Puzzle 3: Shoot!

```
G R A S P   A P S E   C A M P
O N A I R   C O A L   O H I O
B A R R E L R O L L   G E L S
    F U E L     I N A N E
S T R E A K   T I R A D E S
C H A M B E R M U S I C
R E B U S   E A R L S   B A M
U R I S   B A R R E   B A L E
B E D   B U L G E   P E S O S
    B U L L E T T R A I N S
S H O R T L Y   O A K L E Y
T A C I T   S E M I
O P E D   H A M M E R H E A D
O P A L   A L U M   I M A G E
D Y N E   G A G A   E S T E S
```

Puzzle 4: Stop Bugging Me!

```
S E M I   S R I S   D E C A F
A X E D   M O N K   A N E R A
I T S Y B I T S Y S P I D E R
T R A L A L A   O H D E A R
H A S   L E T D O W N
    F L Y O N T H E W A L L
A T R I A   R A T A   I L I E
H A I R D O   T U S S L E
A L P S   R I F F   S P O T S
B E E T L E B A I L E Y
  A G E N D A S   A U K
D O S I D O   G R U M B L E
A N T S I N O N E S P A N T S
S T O L E   T O T O   S E R E
H O P E S   B R Y N   T R A Y
```

Puzzle 5: From the Crow's Nest

```
L O K I ■ B O G I E ■ R E E F
A S I N ■ A C O R N ■ A R C O
I L L S ■ A C A S T ■ D I R E
C O L U M B U S ■ A B A C U S
■ ■ ■ L I A R ■ S N O R T ■ ■
H A V A N A ■ S A G A ■ H E W
A R E T E ■ P A U L S ■ E R A
S I R E ■ C A S T E ■ F R A T
T A R ■ H O R S E ■ G E E S E
E S A ■ I N K Y ■ L E A D E R
■ ■ Z E L D A ■ H E R R ■ ■ ■
D A Z Z L E ■ M A G E L L A N
O M A R ■ N A I V E ■ E A S E
L E N A ■ S I R E N ■ S K I S
E N O S ■ E M E N D ■ S E A T
```

Puzzle 6: Hut, Two, Three, Four

```
T O T E M ■ E F T S ■ S L O G
O K A P I ■ G R I P ■ E X P O
M A X I M ■ G A P E ■ L I A R
■ ■ ■ C O M P U T E R F I L E
S P A ■ S O L ■ O D E ■ ■ ■ ■
H I T P A R A D E ■ N O S E S
O G E E ■ G N U ■ S T O P U P
R O A N ■ A T R I A ■ M I R A
T U S C A N ■ E M U ■ P R E Y
S T E E D ■ P R I C E H I K E
■ ■ ■ A M I ■ T E X ■ T A D
F R E D R I C M A R C H ■ ■ ■
L O D E ■ S K I T ■ E A S E L
A L G A ■ E L L E ■ S W E D E
K E E N ■ R E D S ■ S K A T E
```

Puzzle 7: Get It Together

```
B O S S ■ A T A L E ■ S E N T
O L I O ■ G E T O N ■ A D U E
S E A M ■ E T A T S ■ M A D E
C O M B I N E D I N C O M E ■
■ ■ ■ R E D S ■ A H A ■ ■ ■
S C L E R A ■ L U R E ■ S R A
W E A R ■ B E S E E C H E S ■
A S S O C I A T E D P R E S S
B A S S I N E T S ■ O D E A
S R O ■ V A L S ■ F O S S E Y
■ ■ ■ R E S ■ D A I S ■ ■ ■
■ U N I T E D A I R L I N E S
B R A T ■ N A L D I ■ N O N E
E A S E ■ S T A I N ■ G L O W
A L A S ■ E A R N A ■ S A S S
```

Puzzle 8: It's In the Mail

```
R A C E ■ F L O A T ■ E C O L
A L E C ■ L O T T A ■ S A B E
B I L L M U R R A Y ■ P R O S
B E L I E ■ N A T L ■ O D E S
I N S P I R E S ■ O P U S ■ ■
■ ■ ■ S R O ■ C R U S H E D
S A L E ■ T H O U ■ L E A V E
O R E ■ C H E C K U P ■ R E F
P I T C H ■ S T E P ■ S P R Y
H A T R E D S ■ O A T ■ ■ ■
■ ■ E U R O ■ S U N L A M P S
F A R M ■ I R A S ■ T R A S H
L U M P ■ N O T E W O R T H Y
O R A L ■ G L A R E ■ E T A L
P A N E ■ S E N S E ■ D E W Y
```

Puzzle 9: Now's the Time

Puzzle 10: Hair Today, Gone Tomorrow

Puzzle 11: To the Rear

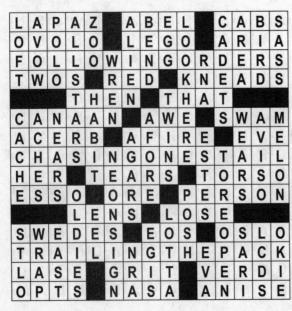

Puzzle 12: Money, Honey

Puzzle 13: Back Me Up

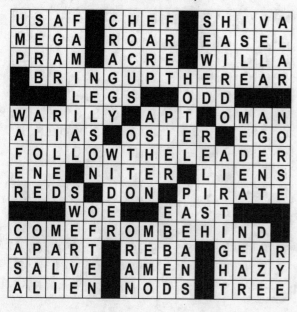

Puzzle 14: Fool Me Once

Puzzle 15: Nice House!

Puzzle 16: Fire!

Puzzle 17: Mr. Fix-it

L	A	I	C		L	A	S	T			S	T	R	A	Y
I	S	N	O		A	R	E	A			H	E	A	V	E
B	R	O	K	E	D	O	W	N			O	R	G	A	N
R	E	P	E	A	L	S		K	N	E	E				
A	D	E		R	E	E	F		A	S	S	I	S	T	
		R	U	M	S		I	D	O		A	N	N	E	
S	N	A	F	U		P	R	I	M	E		D	O	E	
O	U	T	O	F	C	O	M	M	I	S	S	I	O	N	
U	R	I		F	A	L	S	E		T	E	S	T	S	
R	S	V	P		F	L	U		S	O	A	R			
S	E	E	T	H	E		P	A	I	N		E	T	A	
		B	A	S	S		C	R	I	S	P	E	R		
J	A	S	O	N		C	A	M	E	A	P	A	R	T	
I	L	I	A	D		A	D	E	N		A	I	R	S	
G	E	N	T	S		M	O	S	S		T	R	A	Y	

Puzzle 18: Top Performance

M	E	A	L		O	M	E	G	A		G	R	A	B
A	X	L	E		R	O	M	A	N		R	O	P	E
C	A	S	T	S	D	O	U	B	T		A	L	E	E
S	M	O	T	H	E	R	S		E	S	T	E	R	S
			E	Y	R	E		C	L	A	I	M		
	A	C	R	E	S		B	L	O	S	S	O	M	S
O	T	H	E	R		T	R	A	P	S		D	E	E
R	A	I	D		G	R	I	M	E		C	E	N	T
E	L	L		C	L	A	N	S		M	A	L	L	S
M	E	D	D	L	I	N	G		L	A	S	S	O	
	S	E	E	M	S		R	O	N	A				
L	A	P	T	O	P		S	O	N	I	N	L	A	W
E	R	L	E		S	T	A	G	E	C	O	A	C	H
T	E	A	R		E	A	G	E	R		V	I	N	E
S	A	Y	S		S	T	A	R	S		A	N	E	W

Puzzle 19: Bye!

T	W	I	S	T		P	A	S	T		R	U	E	D
E	A	R	T	H		E	L	H	I		U	N	T	O
A	R	M	O	R		L	O	O	M		N	I	T	E
L	E	A	V	E	I	T	T	O	B	E	A	V	E	R
		E	A	R		K	E	R	R					
M	C	M		T	A	C	O		R	I	O	T	E	D
I	R	I	S		T	O	A	D		C	U	O	M	O
R	E	C	K	L	E	S	S	A	B	A	N	D	O	N
E	E	R	I	E		T	I	N	Y		D	A	T	A
S	P	O	N	G	E		S	E	R	F		Y	E	S
		T	I	D	E		O	A	S					
S	P	L	I	T	I	N	F	I	N	I	T	I	V	E
T	R	I	G		T	O	R	N		S	O	N	A	R
E	A	C	H		O	L	E	G		A	N	T	I	S
N	Y	E	T		R	A	T	E		L	E	O	N	E

Puzzle 20: New Shoes

S	L	O	T		B	O	P	P	E	R		S	I	T
H	O	B	O		O	R	I	O	L	E		C	O	N
A	N	T	I		R	E	E	K	E	D		H	U	T
D	E	A	L	I	N	G	D	E	V	I	C	E		
E	L	I		N	E	O		E	N	A	M	E	L
S	Y	N	O	D		N	S	A		K	N	I	F	E
			T	I	S		I	L	E		I	N	F	O
	B	R	A	K	E	L	I	N	I	N	G			
R	H	E	A		Y	A	K		E	W	E			
A	M	E	N	D		T	S	P		A	S	T	O	R
M	O	R	T	A	R		I	N	N		A	D	E	
	M	O	N	O	P	O	L	Y	T	O	K	E	N	
G	N	U		G	U	R	G	L	E		F	E	S	T
A	U	G		L	E	E	R	A	T		F	U	S	E
P	T	S		E	N	T	E	R	S		S	P	A	R

Puzzle 21: Lit Up

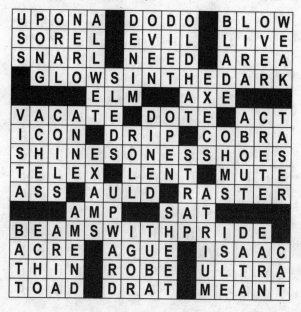

Puzzle 22: Getting Around

Puzzle 23: Kingdoms

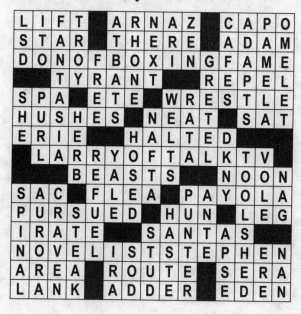

Puzzle 24: Connected

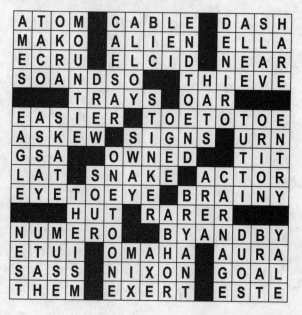

Puzzle 25: Visiting the Zoo

Puzzle 26: What Did You Say?

Puzzle 27: Two of a Kind

Puzzle 28: Physically Fit

Puzzle 29: Opposites Attract

T	S	K	E	D		D	A	T	A			I	T	C	H
O	K	A	P	I		A	M	E	N		M	U	L	E	
O	U	T	I	N	F	R	O	N	T		P	R	O	M	
K	A	O	S		I	R	K		F	I	E	N	D	S	
			O	S	L	O		P	A	N	D	A			
	O	L	D	N	E	W	Y	O	R	K	E	R	S		
K	N	E	E	L		A	R	M	Y		O	I	L		
Y	E	A	S		D	O	S	E	S		H	U	L	A	
D	A	D		S	E	M	I			P	I	N	K	Y	
	L	A	S	T	F	I	R	S	T	L	A	D	Y		
		S	T	I	L	T		M	E	O	W				
S	A	T	I	R	E		B	U	C		A	I	D	A	
T	U	R	F		C	O	L	D	H	O	T	D	O	G	
A	R	A	L		T	H	U	G		P	H	O	N	E	
G	A	Y	E		S	M	E	E		T	A	L	E	S	

Puzzle 30: Careful!

A	D	L	I	B		B	O	L	D		G	R	I	D
B	O	O	N	E		A	S	I	A		R	O	D	E
B	L	I	N	D	A	L	L	E	Y		A	V	O	N
E	E	N		T	R	I	O		L	O	V	E	L	Y
		C	I	A	O		S	I	R	E				
	S	T	U	M	B	L	I	N	G	B	L	O	C	K
C	H	O	R	E		R	A	H	S		P	A	N	
U	R	N	S		C	R	E	P	T		M	A	N	E
J	U	G		R	U	I	N		B	E	L	O	W	
O	B	S	T	A	C	L	E	C	O	U	R	S	E	
			A	G	U	E		U	R	G	E			
T	R	U	I	S	M		E	T	A	L		P	A	S
H	A	L	L		B	O	T	T	L	E	N	E	C	K
A	R	N	O		E	R	N	E		R	I	A	T	A
W	E	A	R		R	E	A	R		S	P	R	I	T

Puzzle 31: A Little Seasoning

S	H	A	F	T		R	A	S	P	S		S	A	T
H	E	A	R	A		A	V	E	R	T		U	R	I
S	P	R	I	N	G	F	E	V	E	R		M	U	D
			S	K	I		E	W	E		M	B	A	
M	A	W	K	I	S	H		R	A	W	D	E	A	L
A	L	I			N	E	A	P		R	E	A	R	
Y	O	N		G	L	U	E	S		D	I	S	C	S
O	N	T	O		E	N	T	E	R		S	T	O	P
R	E	E	L	S		T	A	T	E	R		O	U	R
		R	E	N	E		L	U	C	E		C	P	A
U	N	S	O	U	N	D		P	A	S	S	K	E	Y
N	E	T		F	R	I		L	E	I				
I	P	O		F	A	L	L	C	L	A	S	S	I	C
T	A	R		I	G	L	O	O		L	A	U	R	A
E	L	M		T	E	S	T	Y		S	L	E	E	T

Puzzle 32: Table Setting

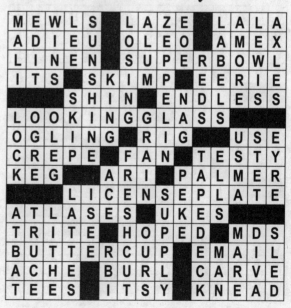

M	E	W	L	S		L	A	Z	E		L	A	L	A
A	D	I	E	U		O	L	E	O		A	M	E	X
L	I	N	E	N		S	U	P	E	R	B	O	W	L
I	T	S		S	K	I	M	P		E	E	R	I	E
			S	H	I	N		E	N	D	L	E	S	S
L	O	O	K	I	N	G	G	L	A	S	S			
O	G	L	I	N	G		R	I	G			U	S	E
C	R	E	P	E		F	A	N		T	E	S	T	Y
K	E	G			A	R	I		P	A	L	M	E	R
		L	I	C	E	N	S	E	P	L	A	T	E	
A	T	L	A	S	E	S		U	K	E	S			
T	R	I	T	E		H	O	P	E	D		M	D	S
B	U	T	T	E	R	C	U	P		E	M	A	I	L
A	C	H	E		B	U	R	L		C	A	R	V	E
T	E	E	S		I	T	S	Y		K	N	E	A	D

Puzzle 33: Brushing Up

A	L	T	A	R		V	I	N	O		S	T	A	T
T	E	R	N	E		E	V	E	N		H	I	V	E
R	A	I	N	F	O	R	E	S	T		A	G	E	E
A	R	G	U	E	R	S		T	A	M	P	E	R	S
		A	R	E	A	S		R	U	E	R			
A	M	B	L	E	S		T	O	G	S		W	O	E
B	O	U	L	E		E	L	S	E	S		O	U	S
R	O	S	Y		F	A	U	L	T		P	O	T	S
A	S	H		D	I	S	C	O		H	O	D	G	E
M	E	L		O	N	E	I		L	E	S	S	O	N
	E	H	U	D		A	E	O	N	S				
I	N	A	T	R	A	P		A	L	R	I	G	H	T
C	A	G	E		J	U	N	G	L	E	B	O	O	K
B	T	U	S		O	R	A	L		I	L	O	S	T
M	E	E	T		B	E	B	E		D	Y	N	E	S

Puzzle 34: Off to the Races

A	S	P		U	S	P	S		D	O	F	F	S
N	I	L		S	P	L	I	T		O	C	A	L	A
E	K	E		I	R	A	G	E	R	S	H	W	I	N
W	H	A	T	N	O	T		R	E	S	E	N	T	S
		A	G	O		O	N	A	I	R				
M	A	R	K	E	T	P	L	A	C	E		E	R	A
O	B	I	E		S	O	D		T	R	A	C	E	R
L	I	P	I	D		D	N	A		S	C	O	P	E
A	D	O	N	I	S		E	V	A		E	L	E	A
R	E	N		S	H	O	W	A	N	D	T	E	L	L
		H	O	R	N	S		T	E	A				
A	P	P	A	R	E	L		S	H	A	L	L	O	W
F	I	E	L	D	W	O	R	K	E	R		A	L	E
R	E	E	V	E		A	D	A	M	S		V	I	P
O	S	L	E	R		N	A	T	S			A	N	T

Puzzle 35: Heard Through the Beanstalk?

S	C	A	M	P		S	T	A	G		P	A	L	E
A	L	I	B	I		T	E	T	E		I	V	A	N
C	A	R	A	T		O	N	T	O		F	A	D	E
S	P	Y		F	E	A	T	U	R	E	F	I	L	M
			S	A	L	T	S		G	A	L	L	E	Y
A	N	G	E	L	A		R	I	S	E				
F	I	N	A	L	N	O	T	I	C	E		S	M	U
A	L	A	N		A	I	L		S	E	A	S		
R	E	T		F	O	R	M	L	E	T	T	E	R	S
		T	A	N	S		M	E	A	N	E	R		
A	S	S	A	I	L		A	S	I	A	N			
F	U	M	B	L	E	D	B	A	L	L		I	T	S
O	R	E	O		A	R	A	B		E	I	G	H	T
R	E	A	R		V	A	S	E		A	D	O	R	E
E	R	R	S		E	W	E	R		F	O	R	U	M

Puzzle 36: Eyes Right

D	R	U	M	S		M	I	D	I		A	G	R	A
R	A	N	U	P		A	M	O	S		B	R	I	E
A	N	I	T	A		L	A	I	R		L	E	S	S
G	I	V	E	T	H	E	G	L	A	D	E	Y	E	
			D	E	A		O	Y	E	R				
S	R	S		S	R	O		L	E	A	R	N	S	
N	E	A	L		I	N	A	P	I	G	S	E	Y	E
A	T	T	A	R		C	P	A		S	P	L	A	T
P	R	I	V	A	T	E	E	Y	E		S	I	L	O
S	O	N	A	T	A		S	V	U		C	A	N	
			E	L	M	O		A	N	O				
	A	P	P	L	E	O	F	O	N	E	S	E	Y	E
A	N	I	L		N	I	T	A		A	C	R	E	S
B	E	T	A		T	R	E	S		S	A	G	A	S
S	W	A	N		S	E	N	T		E	R	O	S	E

Puzzle 37: Opposite Attraction

Puzzle 38: On the Surface

Puzzle 39: What's On?

Puzzle 40: Waist Management

Puzzle 41: Pantry Raid

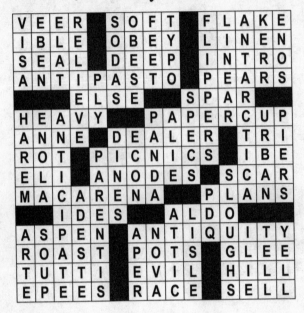

V	E	E	R	■	S	O	F	T	■	F	L	A	K	E
I	B	L	E	■	O	B	E	Y	■	L	I	N	E	N
S	E	A	L	■	D	E	E	P	■	I	N	T	R	O
A	N	T	I	P	A	S	T	O	■	P	E	A	R	S
■	■	■	E	L	S	E	■	S	P	A	R	■	■	■
H	E	A	V	Y	■	■	P	A	P	E	R	C	U	P
A	N	N	E	■	D	E	A	L	E	R	■	T	R	I
R	O	T	■	P	I	C	N	I	C	S	■	I	B	E
E	L	I	■	A	N	O	D	E	S	■	S	C	A	R
M	A	C	A	R	E	N	A	■	P	L	A	N	S	■
■	■	I	D	E	S	■	■	A	L	D	O	■	■	■
A	S	P	E	N	■	A	N	T	I	Q	U	I	T	Y
R	O	A	S	T	■	P	O	T	S	■	G	L	E	E
T	U	T	T	I	■	E	V	I	L	■	H	I	L	L
E	P	E	E	S	■	R	A	C	E	■	S	E	L	L

Puzzle 42: Road Rules

G	A	S	P	■	C	O	R	E	■	P	A	T	T	I
A	G	A	R	■	A	M	E	N	■	A	P	H	I	D
R	A	R	E	■	L	E	N	T	■	G	E	R	M	S
B	I	G	Y	E	L	L	O	W	T	A	X	I	■	■
O	N	E	■	M	A	E	■	I	O	N	■	L	A	D
■	■	M	U	S	T	A	N	G	S	A	L	L	Y	■
S	A	R	I	S	■	■	L	E	A	■	T	E	E	N
L	E	A	N	■	A	M	I	S	S	■	T	R	U	E
I	R	I	S	■	D	A	B	■	■	M	I	S	T	S
P	I	N	K	C	A	D	I	L	L	A	C	■	■	■
S	E	C	■	A	I	M	■	I	A	N	■	H	A	S
■	■	H	O	T	R	O	D	L	I	N	C	O	L	N
A	D	E	P	T	■	N	O	I	R	■	I	O	T	A
L	O	C	A	L	■	E	G	A	D	■	T	H	A	I
A	N	K	L	E	■	Y	E	N	S	■	E	A	R	L

Puzzle 43: Parental Control

M	M	L	I	■	S	L	O	S	H	■	E	M	M	A
G	O	O	N	■	H	O	O	K	Y	■	L	O	I	N
M	O	T	H	E	R	S	H	I	P	■	A	M	M	O
T	R	I	A	G	E	■	S	P	E	C	I	M	E	N
■	■	L	O	D	E	■	■	S	O	N	Y	■	■	■
C	A	S	E	S	■	N	B	C	■	T	E	T	R	A
H	O	U	R	■	R	A	R	E	S	T	■	R	O	T
E	R	G	■	F	A	M	I	L	I	A	■	A	G	O
A	T	A	■	E	J	E	C	T	S	■	S	C	U	M
P	A	R	E	R	■	L	E	I	■	D	U	K	E	S
■	■	■	D	I	A	S	■	■	C	R	U	Z	■	■
S	H	A	L	L	O	T	S	■	E	M	E	R	G	E
W	A	D	E	■	C	I	T	Y	F	A	T	H	E	R
A	I	D	E	■	K	N	E	E	L	■	T	E	A	R
B	R	Y	N	■	S	A	P	P	Y	■	E	A	R	S

Puzzle 44: 2K Race

S	T	Y	E	S	■	C	A	N	E	■	K	E	G	S
A	R	E	S	O	■	R	I	O	S	■	I	R	A	N
K	U	N	T	A	K	I	N	T	E	■	T	A	M	E
I	E	S	■	P	O	E	T	S	■	I	T	S	M	E
■	■	■	K	I	N	D	■	O	L	D	Y	E	A	R
F	I	G	L	E	A	F	S	■	A	O	K	■	■	■
U	L	N	A	R	■	O	U	S	T	■	E	L	H	I
E	S	A	U	■	O	U	N	C	E	■	L	E	A	D
L	A	W	S	■	A	L	I	A	■	S	L	I	M	E
■	■	■	K	I	T	■	N	F	L	T	E	A	M	S
G	O	W	I	T	H	S	■	F	U	R	Y	■	■	■
A	L	A	N	A	■	P	O	O	N	A	■	T	E	A
M	E	S	S	■	K	U	B	L	A	I	K	H	A	N
B	A	N	K	■	A	M	I	D	■	N	O	I	S	E
A	N	T	I	■	T	E	E	S	■	S	I	N	E	W

Puzzle 45: Finishing Up

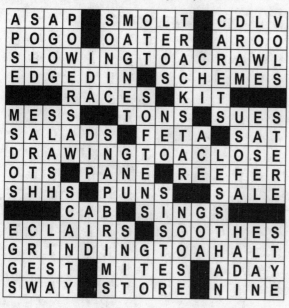

Puzzle 46: Guy Talk

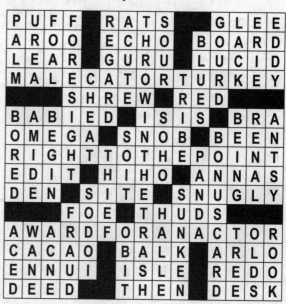

Puzzle 47: Capital Idea!

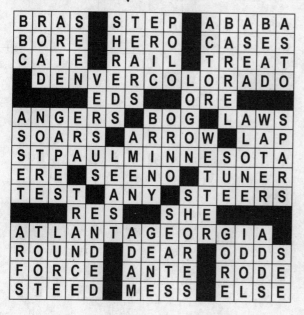

Puzzle 48: Blink, Blink

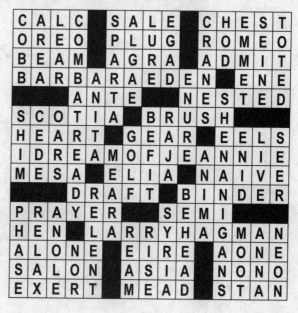

Puzzle 49: Bird Watching

```
T O T A L █ S T E P █ R I F E
U T I C A █ P E E L █ O V U M
N I L E S C R A N E █ B A N E
E S T █ T E E M █ T W I N G E
█ █ P A L E █ T H I N A I R █
A S P I C S █ P R O N G █ █ █
S W E P T █ M U I R █ I L I E
E A S E █ C O R E A █ V E N D
A M O R █ U N E S █ C E A S E
█ █ L A T E R █ B A N K O N █
M E G A H I T █ T A R S █ █ █
I L L U S E █ S E R A █ G A P
L I A R █ P E T E R F I N C H
L O D I █ I R A N █ E L A N D
A T E E █ E E G S █ S O R E S
```

Puzzle 50: Buckle Up

```
A R C H █ █ S H O D █ █ S C A B
C O L A █ S A U T E █ L O R E
M O O D █ T I E B R E A K E R
E M U █ L A D D █ R A V I N E
█ D E I G N █ A I R █ E A T █
C O N V E Y O R B E L T █ █ █
A L I E N █ H E R █ U C L A
P E N N █ D I O D E █ L A O S
E O E S █ R O D █ M A N E T
█ O B I W A N K E N O B I █
A S H █ O V A █ O A T E N █
S N O O Z E █ N O S E █ I O N
W I N D O W S A S H █ E Z R A
A P E D █ A T S E A █ L E A P
N E S S █ Y E A S █ █ I D L E
```

Puzzle 51: I Want It All

```
B A U D █ F E E D S █ B A S H
T U N E █ A T T I C █ A S T A
U N D E R L O C K A N D K E Y
█ T O P E S █ E T A G E R E
█ █ V E S T █ █ M E D E S
T A M P A █ C O L D E R █ █
I D I O M █ A W A Y █ █ M A E
M A N I P U L A T E S T O C K
E M T █ M A R E █ T O R R E
█ █ S H A R D S █ A N N E S
O M A H A █ S T A T █ █ █
R E C I T A L █ P E O N S
B A R R E L O F M O N K E Y S
E R I K █ D R E A R █ R E N O
D A D S █ A N E N T █ A D E N
```

Puzzle 52: Suits Me Fine

```
C R A G █ D A T U M █ O M A R
B O N O █ E L U D E █ V A N E
S E T O F C A R D S █ A K I N
█ █ F A R █ N E S S █ E S T
S T L U K E S █ R E L A C E S
T H E P I P E R █ S O S O
R I G █ R I D E R █ T E N L B
I N A N █ T U N I S █ A T E E
A G L O W █ M A G I C █ E V A
█ A S I F █ L I L A B N E R
B O C E L L I █ D E N O T E D
A R T █ L O N I █ N O W █ █
L A I R █ O F F I C E W E A R
E T O N █ D R I V E █ O K R A
D E N S █ S A T Y R █ W E E P
```

Puzzle 53: School Days

Puzzle 54: Breaking Bread

Puzzle 55: Ladies, Ladies, Ladies

Puzzle 56: Puzzle for Two

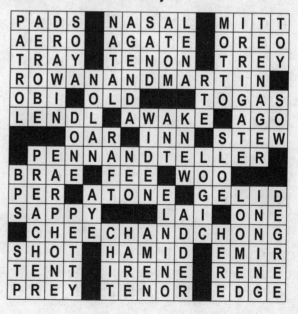

Puzzle 57: Shark Attack

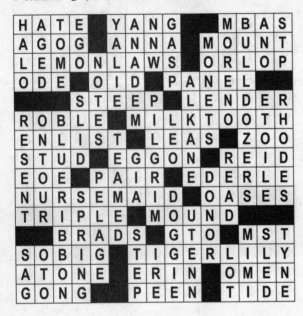

Puzzle 58: Verbs on the Run

Puzzle 59: Spy Game

Puzzle 60: Light Dining

Puzzle 61: To the Letter

Puzzle 62: Eat!

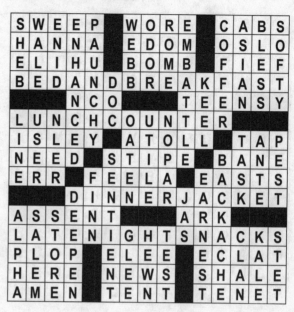

Puzzle 63: Comet Watching

Puzzle 64: You Bet!

B	A	B	E		C	H	A	R		S	P	U	D	S
E	C	R	U		H	I	R	E		L	A	P	I	N
S	C	A	R		E	P	I	C		A	S	T	R	O
T	R	Y	O	N	E	S	L	U	C	K		H	E	W
S	A	S	S	E	S			T	H	E	S	E		
			A	E	R	O		E	S	T	A	T	E	
I	N	F	E	R		A	G	E	S		E	N	I	D
T	O	L	L		C	U	R	L	S		E	T	O	N
E	L	I	A		A	L	E	S		A	R	E	N	A
R	A	P	T	O	R		S	E	A	S				
	A	E	S	O	P			T	H	R	I	C	E	
M	A	C		P	L	A	Y	T	H	E	O	D	D	S
A	M	O	U	R		P	O	R	E		O	A	R	S
A	M	I	L	E		A	K	I	N		S	H	O	E
M	O	N	T	Y		L	E	O	S		T	O	M	S

Puzzle 65: Look Up

Puzzle 66: Feeling Lucky?

Puzzle 67: On Tap?

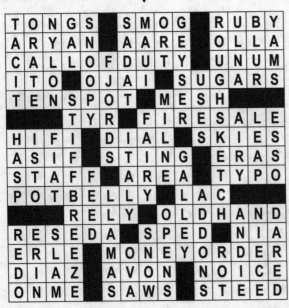

Puzzle 68: Tricky Situation

Puzzle 69: Clean Up

Puzzle 70: A Shrilling Puzzle

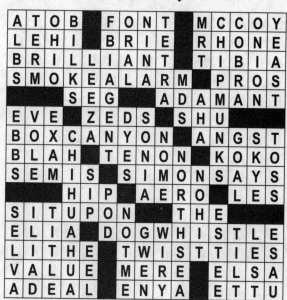

Puzzle 71: Community Puzzle

Puzzle 72: Hi, Chum!

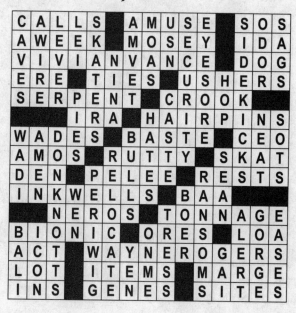

Puzzle 73: To the Letter

S	W	A	Y		M	E	T	A		S	T	E	A	K
T	Y	P	E		I	R	O	N		T	I	T	L	E
A	L	P	S		N	E	O	N		E	T	U	D	E
P	I	E		E	X	C	L	A	M	A	T	I	O	N
H	E	A	D	S	E	T		I	L	L				
		R	O	S	S		S	P	A		E	S	T	E
C	L	A	R	A		A	N	I	M	A		W	A	F
H	O	N	E	Y	O	F	A	N	I	N	S	E	C	T
A	R	C		S	T	A	K	E		O	L	E	O	S
T	E	E	S		T	R	Y		D	I	E	T		
			I	R	E		M	A	N	D	E	L	A	
S	U	M	M	E	R	S	H	I	R	T		N	O	R
A	L	O	O	F		H	O	N	K		B	E	A	R
I	N	A	N	E		O	N	C	E		O	R	C	A
L	A	T	E	R		P	E	E	R		A	S	H	Y

Puzzle 74: Get a Job

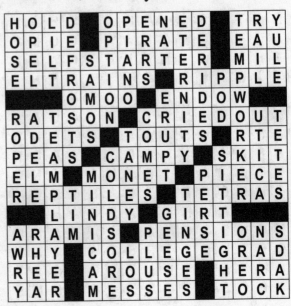

H	O	L	D		O	P	E	N	E	D		T	R	Y
O	P	I	E		P	I	R	A	T	E		E	A	U
S	E	L	F	S	T	A	R	T	E	R		M	I	L
E	L	T	R	A	I	N	S		R	I	P	P	L	E
			O	M	O	O		E	N	D	O	W		
R	A	T	S	O	N		C	R	I	E	D	O	U	T
O	D	E	T	S		T	O	U	T	S		R	T	E
P	E	A	S		C	A	M	P	Y		S	K	I	T
E	L	M		M	O	N	E	T		P	I	E	C	E
R	E	P	T	I	L	E	S		T	E	T	R	A	S
		L	I	N	D	Y		G	I	R	T			
A	R	A	M	I	S		P	E	N	S	I	O	N	S
W	H	Y		C	O	L	L	E	G	E	G	R	A	D
R	E	E		A	R	O	U	S	E		H	E	R	A
Y	A	R		M	E	S	S	E	S		T	O	C	K

Puzzle 75: Shake!

C	E	D	E	S		C	A	L	F		C	L	A	M
A	X	I	A	L		A	L	O	E		A	U	R	A
V	I	S	T	A		S	I	G	N	A	P	A	C	T
E	T	C		C	H	I	T		S	O	U	S	E	
		O	A	K	E	N		E	M	I	T			
H	A	M	M	E	R	O	U	T	A	D	E	A	L	
E	L	F	I	N		I	N	G	E		V	A	T	
L	I	O	N		S	I	N	A	I		L	A	N	A
P	A	R		C	A	R	T		P	O	L	A	R	
	S	T	R	I	K	E	A	B	A	R	G	A	I	N
		O	V	I	D		A	L	I	E	N			
S	W	E	D	E		E	L	A	N		C	A	L	
M	A	K	E	T	E	R	M	S		T	A	H	O	E
O	V	E	N		L	I	M	A		E	V	E	N	T
G	E	S	T		L	O	A	M		R	E	S	E	T

Puzzle 76: Look Here!

T	A	P	E	D		C	A	L		S	C	O	T	T
O	S	A	K	A		L	I	E		L	O	R	R	E
W	A	T	E	R	P	O	L	O		U	N	I	O	N
E	R	E		T	I	S		R	E	F	O	L	D	
L	U	L	L		P	E	C	C	A	D	I	L	L	O
E	L	L	I	S		T	R	A	P		T	E	E	N
D	E	A	R	I	E		E	S	T	E		S	R	S
			A	N	D	B	E	H	O	L	D			
C	S	T		S	K	I	P		R	A	I	S	E	S
A	H	A	S		O	G	E	E		N	O	T	M	E
M	O	N	T	E	C	A	R	L	O		R	E	A	R
P	O	T	A	S	H		F	R	A		A	I	M	
E	T	A	T	S		A	R	M	A	D	I	L	L	O
R	A	R	E	E		T	O	A		A	L	I	E	N
S	T	A	N	S		M	E	N		M	E	N	D	S

Puzzle 77: Oh Baby

Puzzle 78: It's About Time

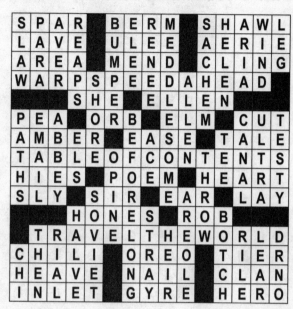

Puzzle 79: Join In

Puzzle 80: Having Fun

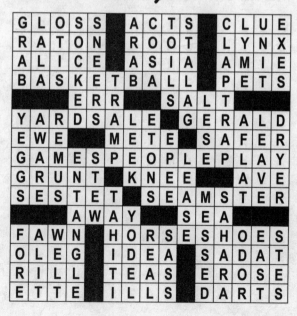

Puzzle 81: Facing Bills

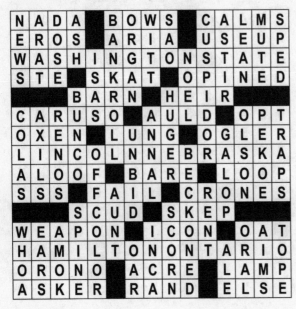

N	A	D	A		B	O	W	S		C	A	L	M	S
E	R	O	S		A	R	I	A		U	S	E	U	P
W	A	S	H	I	N	G	T	O	N	S	T	A	T	E
S	T	E		S	K	A	T		O	P	I	N	E	D
		B	A	R	N		H	E	I	R				
C	A	R	U	S	O		A	U	L	D		O	P	T
O	X	E	N		L	U	N	G		O	G	L	E	R
L	I	N	C	O	L	N	N	E	B	R	A	S	K	A
A	L	O	O	F		B	A	R	E		L	O	O	P
S	S	S		F	A	I	L		C	R	O	N	E	S
			S	C	U	D		S	K	E	P			
W	E	A	P	O	N		I	C	O	N		O	A	T
H	A	M	I	L	T	O	N	O	N	T	A	R	I	O
O	R	O	N	O		A	C	R	E		L	A	M	P
A	S	K	E	R		R	A	N	D		E	L	S	E

Puzzle 82: Write On!

B	A	N	E		A	B	O	D	E		S	H	O	P
A	L	E	E		L	E	V	E	L		P	U	R	L
B	A	W	L	O	F	F	I	R	E		O	L	E	O
A	S	S		A	R	I	D		P	H	I	L	L	Y
			S	T	E	T		P	H	I	L	O		
R	A	F	T	E	D		G	L	A	S	S	F	U	L
O	C	E	A	N		B	R	A	N	S		F	R	O
A	H	A	B		T	R	E	N	T		M	A	G	I
C	O	T		A	R	I	E	S		T	I	M	E	R
H	O	O	D	W	I	N	K		C	H	E	E	S	E
		F	R	O	C	K		S	H	I	N			
S	I	C	I	L	Y		A	L	O	E		F	O	E
P	O	L	L		C	O	T	E	O	F	A	R	M	S
E	T	A	L		L	A	N	D	S		B	E	E	T
W	A	Y	S		E	R	O	S	E		E	T	N	A

Puzzle 83: Or What?

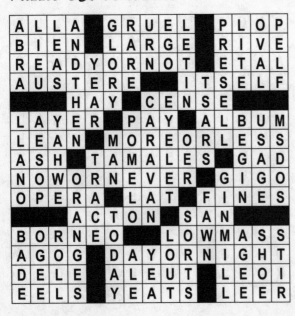

A	L	L	A		G	R	U	E	L		P	L	O	P
B	I	E	N		L	A	R	G	E		R	I	V	E
R	E	A	D	Y	O	R	N	O	T		E	T	A	L
A	U	S	T	E	R	E		I	T	S	E	L	F	
		H	A	Y		C	E	N	S	E				
L	A	Y	E	R		P	A	Y		A	L	B	U	M
L	E	A	N		M	O	R	E	O	R	L	E	S	S
A	S	H		T	A	M	A	L	E	S		G	A	D
N	O	W	O	R	N	E	V	E	R		G	I	G	O
O	P	E	R	A		L	A	T		F	I	N	E	S
			A	C	T	O	N		S	A	N			
B	O	R	N	E	O			L	O	W	M	A	S	S
A	G	O	G		D	A	Y	O	R	N	I	G	H	T
D	E	L	E		A	L	E	U	T		L	E	O	I
E	E	L	S		Y	E	A	T	S		L	E	E	R

Puzzle 84: Open Wide

A	P	S	E		U	S	U	A	L		E	G	G	S
S	A	K	S		N	E	G	R	O		R	O	L	E
S	L	I	P	O	F	T	H	E	T	O	N	G	U	E
T	E	N		W	A	T	S		H	U	S	H	E	S
			C	L	I	O		P	A	S	T			
I	M	P	A	I	R		S	O	R	T		S	A	O
N	O	E	L	S		K	I	R	I		H	E	N	S
F	R	O	M	H	A	N	D	T	O	M	O	U	T	H
E	O	N	S		T	E	E	S		A	T	S	E	A
R	N	S		P	L	E	D		G	R	A	S	S	Y
			A	L	A	S		A	R	K	S			
D	A	E	M	O	N		I	S	E	E		N	I	T
A	R	M	E	D	T	O	T	H	E	T	E	E	T	H
R	E	I	N		I	V	I	E	D		R	I	C	A
T	A	R	S		C	A	N	N	Y		E	L	H	I

Puzzle 85: A Trio of Trios

Puzzle 86: In the Waiting Room

Puzzle 87: Smooth Landing

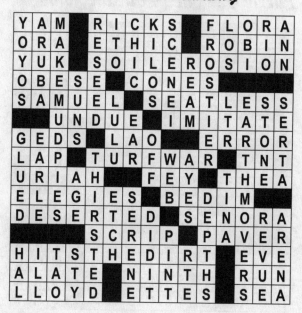

Puzzle 88: Temperature Rising

Puzzle 89: Rules are Rules

Puzzle 90: Water Ways

Puzzle 91: Who's Trying Now?

Puzzle 92: Check Out the Joint

Puzzle 93: Bye Bye!

Puzzle 94: Gardening 101

Puzzle 95: Try It On

Puzzle 96: New Approach

Puzzle 97: Masterpiece!

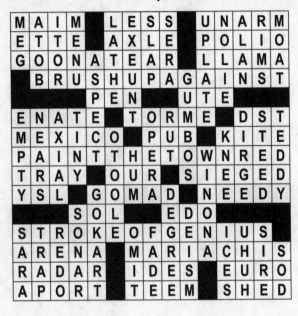

M	A	I	M		L	E	S	S		U	N	A	R	M
E	T	T	E		A	X	L	E		P	O	L	I	O
G	O	O	N	A	T	E	A	R		L	L	A	M	A
	B	R	U	S	H	U	P	A	G	A	I	N	S	T
			P	E	N			U	T	E				
E	N	A	T	E		T	O	R	M	E		D	S	T
M	E	X	I	C	O		P	U	B		K	I	T	E
P	A	I	N	T	T	H	E	T	O	W	N	R	E	D
T	R	A	Y		O	U	R		S	I	E	G	E	D
Y	S	L		G	O	M	A	D		N	E	E	D	Y
			S	O	L			E	D	O				
S	T	R	O	K	E	O	F	G	E	N	I	U	S	
A	R	E	N	A		M	A	R	I	A	C	H	I	S
R	A	D	A	R		I	D	E	S		E	U	R	O
A	P	O	R	T		T	E	E	M		S	H	E	D

Puzzle 98: Just Be U

B	A	N	G		A	D	E	P	T		L	O	V	E
A	F	O	R		R	O	G	E	R		A	R	E	A
T	A	R	A		G	R	I	P	E		M	E	A	T
U	R	A	N	I	U	M	S	S	Y	M	B	O	L	
			D	O	E			S	A	D				
A	T	R	A	S		S	A	L		C	A	R	E	D
S	W	A	M		E	C	L	A	I	R		I	D	O
P	E	R	S	O	N	A	L	P	R	O	N	O	U	N
C	E	E		R	E	P	O	S	E		E	T	C	H
A	D	R	A	G		E	Y	E		P	A	S	E	O
			G	A	S			A	I	R				
	B	A	R	N	Y	A	R	D	F	E	M	A	L	E
J	O	K	E		S	Q	U	A	T		I	N	O	N
E	R	I	E		O	U	N	C	E		S	K	I	D
T	E	N	S		P	A	G	E	R		S	A	S	S

Puzzle 99: And the Band Played On

S	O	W		S	C	A	L	A		B	E	L	L	E
N	U	I		T	O	M	E	S		A	G	A	I	N
A	T	L		O	V	E	N	S		C	O	W	E	D
F	I	D	D	L	E	S	T	I	C	K	S			
U	N	S	E	E	N		O	S	U		R	I	D	
			S	N	A	P		T	E	M	P	U	R	A
H	O	O	P		N	A	B		A	A	R	O	N	
O	R	G	A	N	T	R	A	N	S	P	L	A	N	T
R	A	D	I	O		G	I	T		E	L	S	E	
S	T	E	R	N	E	R		P	A	S	T			
E	E	N		R	U	M		M	U	T	U	A	L	
		H	O	R	N	O	F	P	L	E	N	T	Y	
A	E	S	O	P		S	T	E	E	L		F	A	R
P	R	O	S	E		T	I	L	D	E		I	R	E
E	A	T	E	N		O	F	T	E	N		T	I	S

Puzzle 100: Ringing in the Ears

P	A	S	E	O		S	H	U	S	H		S	S	S
O	U	T	D	O		T	O	S	C	A		C	A	T
S	N	O	O	Z	E	A	L	A	R	M		R	I	O
E	T	A		E	R	L	E		O	S	W	E	G	O
		P	O	R	K		H	O	T	H	E	A	D	
C	Y	P	R	U	S		P	I	G	E	O	N		
R	E	L	E	T		H	A	L	E	R		D	E	N
A	A	A	S		B	E	L	L	S		T	O	R	E
W	R	Y		T	A	M	E	S		S	H	O	T	S
	E	R	A	S	E	S		S	T	A	R	E	S	
A	B	D	O	M	E	N		H	A	U	T			
M	Y	D	E	A	R		T	E	R	M		A	S	H
I	C	U		L	A	D	Y	L	I	B	E	R	T	Y
G	A	M		E	T	A	P	E		L	E	G	U	P
O	R	B		S	E	V	E	N		E	R	O	D	E

Puzzle 101: Keep Trying

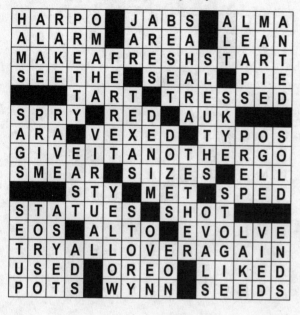

Puzzle 102: Parts of the Body

Puzzle 103: PC

Puzzle 104: Take Off

Puzzle 105: What's Your Rank?

Puzzle 106: Finding Felines

Puzzle 107: Problems, Problems

Puzzle 108: Glad Inside

Puzzle 109: Material World

Puzzle 110: On the Sea

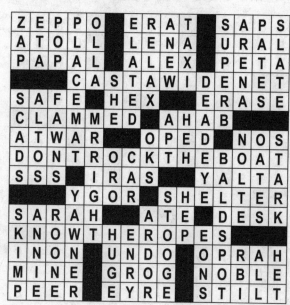

Puzzle 111: Mother of Invention?

Puzzle 112: Sea to Shining Sea

Puzzle 113: The Works

Puzzle 114: B Hive

Puzzle 115: Toasty

Puzzle 116: B Exterminator

Puzzle 117: Nice Arrangement

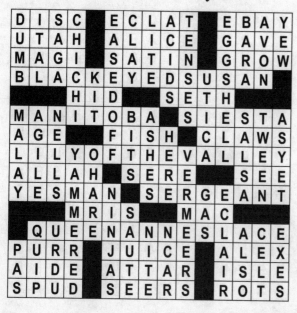

Puzzle 118: Off the Market

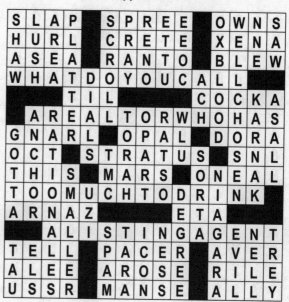

Puzzle 119: Moving Crew

Puzzle 120: In the Pocket

Puzzle 121: Give Me a Break

A	C	E	S		V	I	V	A		S	T	A	G	S
P	A	R	T		E	V	E	N		H	A	N	O	I
B	R	I	E	F	R	E	S	T	P	E	R	I	O	D
S	E	C	R	E	T		T	E	L	L		T	E	E
			E	W	E	R		D	E	F	R	A	Y	S
H	A	L	O		B	A	D		A	L	E			
A	B	A		P	R	I	E	R		I	N	T	R	O
S	E	V	E	R	A	N	C	E	O	F	T	I	E	S
P	L	A	T	O		S	A	L	V	E		M	E	L
		A	L	T		L	I	E		R	E	D	O	
P	A	R	L	O	R	S		T	R	E	E			
A	L	I		N	I	C	E		J	A	C	K	E	T
S	O	M	E	G	O	O	D	F	O	R	T	U	N	E
T	H	E	S	E		O	N	L	Y		O	D	I	N
E	A	S	E	D		P	A	Y	S		R	O	D	S

Puzzle 122: Lend Me Your Year

A	E	S	O	P		A	C	E	S		S	T	A	B
F	L	O	U	R		P	A	R	K		K	A	L	E
B	A	L	T	O		I	N	G	E		E	L	S	E
	N	E	W	S	R	E	S	O	L	U	T	I	O	N
		E	P	I	C			E	S	C	A	P	E	
T	H	E	S	E	V	E	N	I	T	C	H			
S	O	F	T	C		A	T	O		Y	O	W	L	
P	L	O		T	W	O	T	O	N	E		L	O	O
S	E	R	T		C	P	A			N	L	E	R	S
	O	F	F	E	L	E	C	T	I	O	N	S		
A	N	D	R	E	I		N	O	R	M				
R	O	U	N	D	E	M	P	L	O	Y	E	E	S	
E	T	N	A		L	E	O	I		W	A	N	E	D
S	E	E	D		D	A	N	S		A	D	O	R	E
O	S	S	O		S	T	E	T		Y	E	S	E	S

Puzzle 123: 64-Across

D	E	S	K		M	A	C	H	O		G	A	D	S
A	X	L	E		A	P	R	O	N		A	C	I	D
L	I	O	N	S	S	H	A	R	E		L	A	S	S
	S	T	O	P	S	I	G	N		T	O	D	D	
O	T	T		R	E	D	S		K	O	R	E	A	N
W	E	E	D	Y		E	N	D	E	M	I	C		
E	D	D	O		A	Z	A	L	E	A		E	N	O
		T	I	G	E	R	S	E	Y	E				
N	T	H		T	E	R	C	E	L		P	U	P	A
C	H	I	C	A	N	O			D	I	N	E	R	
R	E	S	U	L	T		C	L	E	O		C	R	T
	O	T	T	O		S	O	U	L	F	O	O	D	
T	R	O	I		B	E	A	R	S	F	R	U	I	T
W	E	R	E		A	C	T	I	I		S	T	E	R
A	M	Y	S		A	S	I	D	E		O	H	M	Y

Puzzle 124: Rotten Luck

E	A	R	N	S		T	A	T	A	R		A	H	A
C	R	O	O	K		A	N	O	D	E		N	O	W
R	A	B	B	I	T	S	N	O	S	E		T	A	R
U	S	E	S		E	T	A			D	A	I	R	Y
			C	A	E	S	U	R	I	C				
L	A	P	F	U	L			N	O	T	E	P	A	D
A	P	A	R	T		B	R	I	T		T	A	L	I
T	H	R	E	E	L	E	A	F	C	L	O	V	E	R
K	I	S	T		O	N	M	Y		I	N	E	R	T
E	D	I	F	I	C	E			A	V	E	R	T	S
	U	N	I	T	E	D	L	Y						
C	H	I	L	L		T	I	E		N	O	V	A	
H	U	B		E	I	G	H	T	E	L	E	V	E	N
A	L	E		T	R	E	Y	S		E	V	E	N	T
T	A	X		S	A	L	L	Y		T	E	N	D	S

Puzzle 125: Construction Crew

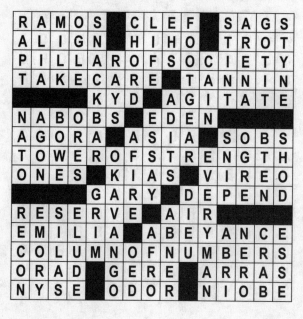

R	A	M	O	S		C	L	E	F		S	A	G	S
A	L	I	G	N		H	I	H	O		T	R	O	T
P	I	L	L	A	R	O	F	S	O	C	I	E	T	Y
T	A	K	E	C	A	R	E		T	A	N	N	I	N
			K	Y	D		A	G	I	T	A	T	E	
N	A	B	O	B	S		E	D	E	N				
A	G	O	R	A		A	S	I	A		S	O	B	S
T	O	W	E	R	O	F	S	T	R	E	N	G	T	H
O	N	E	S		K	I	A	S		V	I	R	E	O
			G	A	R	Y		D	E	P	E	N	D	
R	E	S	E	R	V	E		A	I	R				
E	M	I	L	I	A		A	B	E	Y	A	N	C	E
C	O	L	U	M	N	O	F	N	U	M	B	E	R	S
O	R	A	D		G	E	R	E		A	R	R	A	S
N	Y	S	E		O	D	O	R		N	I	O	B	E

Puzzle 126: Making Progress

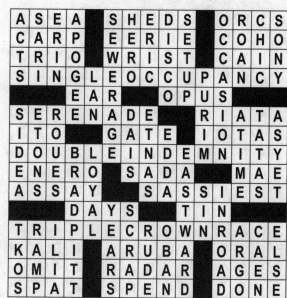

A	S	E	A		S	H	E	D	S		O	R	C	S
C	A	R	P		E	E	R	I	E		C	O	H	O
T	R	I	O		W	R	I	S	T		C	A	I	N
S	I	N	G	L	E	O	C	C	U	P	A	N	C	Y
			E	A	R			O	P	U	S			
S	E	R	E	N	A	D	E			R	I	A	T	A
I	T	O			G	A	T	E		I	O	T	A	S
D	O	U	B	L	E	I	N	D	E	M	N	I	T	Y
E	N	E	R	O		S	A	D	A			M	A	E
A	S	S	A	Y			S	A	S	S	I	E	S	T
			D	A	Y	S			T	I	N			
T	R	I	P	L	E	C	R	O	W	N	R	A	C	E
K	A	L	I		A	R	U	B	A		O	R	A	L
O	M	I	T		R	A	D	A	R		A	G	E	S
S	P	A	T		S	P	E	N	D		D	O	N	E

Puzzle 127: At Last!

S	A	V	E		C	L	I	M	B		S	L	A	P
A	R	I	D		R	A	D	I	O		P	I	L	E
P	E	T	E		A	T	E	S	T		L	O	D	E
		A	N	D	T	H	A	T	S	F	I	N	A	L
S	A	L		R	E	E			W	E	T			
A	S	S	A	Y	S		S	H	A	W		P	A	W
C	H	I	L	E		O	W	E	N		E	R	M	A
R	O	G	E	R	O	V	E	R	A	N	D	O	U	T
E	R	N	E		L	A	P	S		A	N	G	L	E
D	E	S		G	I	L	T		S	T	A	R	E	R
			S	A	G		A	T	A		E	T	S	
T	H	A	T	S	A	L	L	F	O	L	K	S		
R	I	S	E		R	O	S	I	N		I	S	L	E
A	V	I	A		C	L	A	R	E		N	E	I	L
P	E	A	K		H	A	T	E	S		E	S	P	Y

Puzzle 128: One for All

R	A	S	T	A		A	B	A	S		P	C	T	S
A	L	O	E	S		T	R	I	O		A	L	O	T
D	O	L	L	A	R	B	I	L	L		R	U	S	E
A	N	I		G	U	A	M		D	E	T	E	S	T
R	E	D	A	R	M	Y		P	O	N	Y			
			R	A	P		B	A	N	D	S	A	W	S
B	A	L	M	Y		O	O	P		S	Y	R	I	A
E	R	I	E			H	O	E				S	E	N	D
R	U	D	D	S		B	A	R		S	T	A	K	E
M	I	S	B	E	G	O	T		O	N	E			
			A	T	R	Y		E	N	A	M	E	L	S
A	V	A	N	T	I		A	T	I	P		L	A	I
H	A	R	D		N	I	G	H	T	S	T	A	N	D
A	N	T	I		A	S	E	A		T	A	N	G	O
B	E	E	T		T	H	E	N		O	G	D	E	N

Puzzle 129: Mystery Solved

Puzzle 130: Solid

Puzzle 131: Remote Target

Puzzle 132: Classic!

Puzzle 133: Before and After?

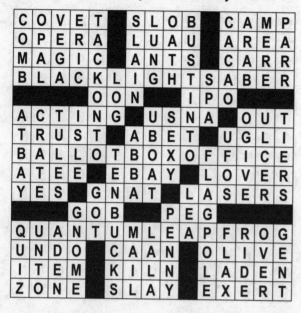

Puzzle 134: Busy, Busy, Busy

Puzzle 135: Not Quite Sure

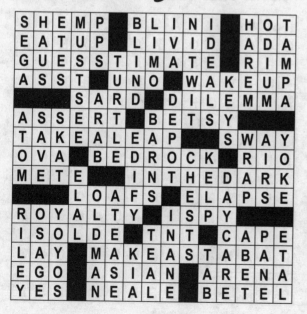

Puzzle 136: Stopping Points

W	A	R	M		M	A	I	D	S			E	B	A	Y
E	T	U	I			A	S	S	E	T		N	O	R	A
B	E	R	L	I	N	W	A	L	L			T	R	I	P
			E	N	N	A			I	O	D	I	D	E	S
R	A	B	A	T			N	O	V		O	R	E	L	
A	D	A	G	E	S		P	E	S	T	E	R			
T	O	R	E	R	O		I	R	K	S		S	A	D	
E	R	R	S		P	E	A	S	E		A	T	N	O	
S	E	I		C	U	L	T		E	N	C	A	G	E	
		E	L	A	P	S	E		T	A	T	T	E	R	
	B	R	A	D		I	S	M		S	U	E	R	S	
M	A	R	T	I	A	N		A	S	T	A				
I	S	E	E		C	O	U	N	T	Y	L	I	N	E	
L	I	E	S		E	R	A	S	E			L	O	I	N
L	E	F	T		S	E	W	E	R		Y	U	L	E	

Puzzle 137: Thirsty?

M	U	L	E		W	A	T	E	R		T	R	A	M
A	T	I	E		I	N	A	N	E		W	A	S	I
R	U	M	R	U	N	N	I	N	G		O	P	A	L
T	R	A	I	T			L	E	A	D	P	I	P	E
I	N	S	E	A	M	S		A	L	O	A	D		
			S	H	I	E	L	D		G	I	F	T	S
J	E	S	T		L	E	A		A	I	R	I	N	G
P	A	P		O	L	D	S	A	L	T		R	U	T
E	V	I	N	C	E		S	U	E		P	E	T	S
G	E	N	E	T		S	O	L	V	E	R			
	A	W	A	R	E		D	E	V	I	A	T	E	
W	E	L	L	D	O	N	E			A	N	N	U	M
O	S	T	E		C	O	M	M	O	N	C	O	L	D
U	S	A	F		K	R	E	B	S		E	L	S	E
K	E	P	T		S	A	R	A	H		S	E	A	N

Puzzle 138: Game Time

B	U	L	B			L	E	I	S		A	B	A	S
A	T	A	L	L		A	T	O	P		S	O	F	A
S	A	M	O	A		P	O	W	E	R	P	L	A	Y
S	H	A	W	N	E	E		A	C	E		S	R	S
			O	C	A	L	A		K	E	P	T		
C	O	F	F	E	R		B	U	L	L	S	E	Y	E
A	B	A	F	T		P	E	T	E		I	R	O	N
R	E	M		G	A	T	E	S		I	D	A		
A	S	I	A		R	U	T	S		M	O	N	E	T
T	E	L	L	T	A	L	E		M	A	N	G	L	E
	Y	A	R	N		D	O	I	N	G				
E	A	T		A	D	D		C	L	A	U	S	E	S
S	C	R	U	M	M	A	G	E		N	A	I	V	E
T	I	E	R		A	R	E	A		A	R	D	E	N
E	D	E	N		S	E	E	N			D	E	N	T

Puzzle 139: Passing Grade

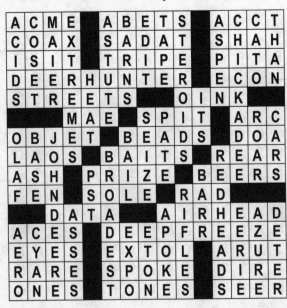

A	C	M	E		A	B	E	T	S		A	C	C	T
C	O	A	X		S	A	D	A	T		S	H	A	H
I	S	I	T		T	R	I	P	E		P	I	T	A
D	E	E	R	H	U	N	T	E	R		E	C	O	N
S	T	R	E	E	T	S			O	I	N	K		
			M	A	E		S	P	I	T		A	R	C
O	B	J	E	T		B	E	A	D	S		D	O	A
L	A	O	S		B	A	I	T	S		R	E	A	R
A	S	H		P	R	I	Z	E		B	E	E	R	S
F	E	N		S	O	L	E		R	A	D			
		D	A	T	A		A	I	R	H	E	A	D	
A	C	E	S		D	E	E	P	F	R	E	E	Z	E
E	Y	E	S		E	X	T	O	L		A	R	U	T
R	A	R	E		S	P	O	K	E		D	I	R	E
O	N	E	S		T	O	N	E	S		S	E	E	R

Puzzle 140: Secret Solving

P	A	R	E		L	A	S	S	O			C	H	E
O	V	A	L		O	S	K	A	R		A	B	E	D
P	E	T	E		A	L	I	A	S		B	E	A	D
P	R	I	V	A	T	E	P	R	O	P	E	R	T	Y
A	T	T	A	C	H	E			N	E	T			
	S	E	T	H		P	O	P		A	S	T	E	R
		E	O	N		L	I	P			A	C	E	
P	E	R	S	O	N	A	L	P	R	O	N	O	U	N
O	V	A		E	L	I		O	N	E				
T	E	N	S	E		L	E	T		T	O	M	S	
			E	L	S		R	O	A	N	O	K	E	
I	N	T	I	M	A	T	E	A	P	P	A	R	E	L
C	O	R	N		F	A	R	C	E		T	O	E	S
E	R	I	E		E	L	L	E	N		A	S	T	I
D	A	M		S	E	E	R	S			L	E	S	E

Puzzle 141: Off to the Shrink

Puzzle 142: Cover Your Rear

Puzzle 143: One Vowel Off

Puzzle 144: It R Squared

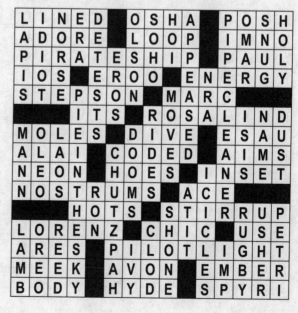

Puzzle 145: Ear to the Ground

Puzzle 146: Vanishing Ink

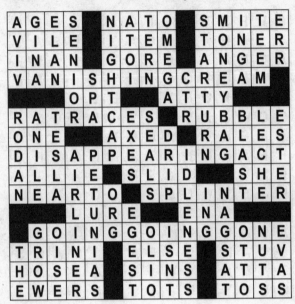

Puzzle 147: Elbow Room

Puzzle 148: Fighting Words

Puzzle 149: Table Setting

Puzzle 150: Color Wheel

Part IV
The Part of Tens

The 5th Wave   By Rich Tennant

RICHTENNANT

...stat...moor...fen...iota...nom...

Never line a parrot's cage with finished crossword puzzles.

In this part . . .

Even the best puzzlers get stuck sometimes. After all, we puzzle masters can be a tricky lot. That's why in this part I offer ten of my best tips for solving even the trickiest puzzles, as well as a list of ten great Web resources that you may want to check when solving certain types of clues. (Don't think of it as cheating — think of it as expanding your knowledge base with the assistance of some very helpful Webmasters.)

Chapter 5

Ten Tricks for Successfully Tackling the Trickiest Puzzles

This chapter offers ideas for how to set the stage to succeed at working a challenging crossword. I also offer some simple tricks for trying to push through the inevitable *solver's block:* the feeling that you're truly stuck mid-puzzle and can't find a way to move forward.

Nailing Down Your Puzzle Editor's Style

The person responsible for compiling and styling the puzzles in a certain newspaper, book, or Web site is called the *puzzle editor,* and it can help to get familiar with that person's style. As I mention in Chapter 1, the difficulty level of a crossword depends on how the clues are written. Whether the puzzle editor creates each crossword himself or edits crosswords from other puzzle constructors, his influence on the style of each puzzle is strong. For this reason, when you first start working puzzles, it can help to focus on puzzles published in the same source.

Setting the Mood

The right environment to work a crossword depends on your personal preferences, of course. For me, these things are essential:

✔ A comfortable chair

✔ Silence or soft music

✔ Good lighting

🖝 Easy access to resources (whether books or a computer)

🖝 Ample time to complete the puzzle — or at least to make a good effort!

Analyzing the Theme

Not every puzzle constructor creates themed crosswords. You'll often see crosswords that don't have titles, which means they don't have themes. But all the puzzles I edit, including the ones in this book, are themed, and the title hints at the theme.

The *theme* of a crossword is simply a central idea that the longer clues tie back to. For example, I created an Easy puzzle for this book called "Now's the Time" that contains many time- and date-related clues.

If a puzzle does have a theme, try to keep it in mind as you read each clue. Doing so may help you tap into the puzzle constructor's point of view, which may make solving clues easier.

The puzzle title doesn't always present the theme in a crystal-clear way: Sometimes you have to give the title a bit of thought (and work a few clues) before figuring out what it means. For example, the Tough puzzle in this book titled "Open Wide" could, I suppose, have been about dentistry. It's not. Instead, many of its clues relate to speech and speaking.

Focusing on Fill-in-the-Blanks

As I explain in Chapter 1, fill-in-the-blank clues are often the easiest type to solve. These clues usually involve a familiar phrase or title from which one or more words have been deleted. The puzzle constructor uses an underline to indicate where those words are missing, and you have to determine what they are.

Studying Crosswordese

I bet you didn't realize that working crosswords involves learning a new language. In truth, *crosswordese* is just a subset of English words — specifically, a group of words that you often run across in crosswords but don't often use when you talk to your friends and family. Puzzle constructors love crosswordese because it's chock full of short words (usually three to five letters long) that can get them out of jams. They try not to use too many of them in any given puzzle, but they do lean on them pretty regularly.

Let me give you just three examples of the types of words I'm talking about:

- An *epee* is a type of fencing sword.
- A *gam* is a pinup model's leg.
- Another name for margarine is *oleo*.

Getting Familiar with Common Fillers

In addition to crosswordese, puzzle constructors sometimes fall back on certain short entries to help them make a puzzle gel. Following are three types of these short entries you're likely to encounter if you work crosswords often enough:

- **Compass points:** If you come across a two- or three-letter entry whose clue asks for a direction, you know you're being asked for a compass point. A two-letter entry has only these four possible answers: NE, NW, SE, and SW. A three-letter entry has eight possible answers: NNE, NNW, SSE, SSW, ENE, ESE, WNW, and WSW.

- **Roman numerals:** If it's been a while since you've worked with Roman numerals, you may find that crosswords force you to reacquaint yourself with this numbering system. You may run across clues that even force you to do some math! Here's a simple example: The clue "Half of XXVI" requires that you first know that you're looking at the number 26. Then you divide by 2 to get 13, and finally you translate 13 into Roman numerals to arrive at your answer: XIII.

- **Latin words:** While we're doing as the Romans did, you may want to brush up on your basic Latin — especially Latin abbreviations. I explain in Chapter 1 that puzzle constructors often create entries from foreign words (and must alert you to which language they're looking for). Along with French and Spanish, Latin is a favorite, in part because it's chock full of short words (such as *circa, vox,* and *unum*) and abbreviations (such as *A.D., ibid,* and *etc.*) that can serve as the glue holding together an unwieldy section of a puzzle.

Picking Out Plurals

As I mention in Chapter 1, a simple but useful trick when you're stuck mid-puzzle is to search your list of unanswered clues to find those written in a plural form. If the clue is plural, the answer must be plural as well (assuming your puzzle constructor is doing a decent job!). Using a pencil, lightly write an S at the end of each grid entry that you know must be a plural word or phrase. You can't assume that the S will work in every case — the English language is never that easy (think about the plural forms of *mouse, dice,* or *child,* for example). But in many cases, that S will be correct. And you'll be surprised at how often a single letter may inspire you to solve an intersecting clue.

Looking at Verb Tenses

Again, if the puzzle constructor is worth his salt, the verb tense used in a clue will match the verb tense used in the answer. So if you're looking at a clue that contains a verb in the past tense, you may want to pencil in the letters ED at the end of the corresponding entry. Of course, the English language has a lot of irregular verbs that don't end in *-ed* in the past tense (consider *think, eat,* and *write*). But if you're stuck mid-puzzle and are searching for ways to break through your solver's block, this tip is definitely worth a try.

Clues that contain verbs ending in *-ing* are worth a look as well. Depending on how the clue is written, the answer could also end in ING.

Gathering Great Resources

Throughout this book, I encourage you to consider outside resources (whether books, Web sites, or friends and family members) as fair game when you're working a crossword. You may know people who think otherwise — who consider cracking open a dictionary while working a crossword the ultimate form of cheating. But I consider it a simple act of learning and a very appropriate means of becoming a better puzzler.

Taking a Breather!

If you've worked for a long time on a puzzle and still can't quite figure it out, walk away. Do something else that you enjoy — even another (perhaps easier) puzzle — and return to your challenge with fresh eyes. Working puzzles should be fun — even when it's frustrating. So if the frustration threatens to smother the fun, give yourself a break!

Chapter 6

Ten Web Resources to Try When You're Stuck

In This Chapter

▶ Looking up abbreviations, quotations, and biblical names

▶ Finding translations

▶ Using an online atlas, thesaurus, and encyclopedia

We all have our online favorites, and depending on the specific nature of the clues that are tripping you up, the resources I list here may or may not be useful. But I suspect the ten I feature here will come in handy if you work crosswords frequently.

Abbreviations

If you're stuck on a clue that contains or asks for an abbreviation, the Web site at www.abbreviations.com is a gold mine. Here's how it works: If you need to find out what an abbreviation means, type it into the search box at the top of the home page and click "Search." For example, say you need to know what "var" stands for. The page that pops up gives you a list of options, in order of the popularity of their usage. So, from most to least popular, "var" could mean *variation, variety, value at risk, variante, value added reseller,* and so on.

If you need to find the accepted abbreviation for a word or phrase, you change the setting on the home page to "word >> abbreviation." Then type your word or phrase (for example, "British pound") and click "Search." If more than one answer is available, you get a list ordered by popularity. If not, you get a single response: In this case, GBP.

Bartleby Quotations

This site (www.bartleby.com/quotations) features tens of thousands of famous quotations that you can search using the words you know. For example, say the puzzle clue is "'. . . against _____ of troubles' (Shakespeare)." On the home page, type "against of troubles" into the search box and press "Go." The list of possibilities that appears includes a quote from *Hamlet* that features the words "against a sea of troubles."

Bible Gateway

If you're stuck on a clue that contains a biblical reference, this site (www.biblegateway.com) may be able to help. On the home page, you can type in key words you know (such as a name or place) and click "Search the Bible." The list that appears lets you know which Bible books and verses contain references to that name or place, and a quick scan of the possibilities may lead you to a helpful passage.

For example, say the crossword clue asks you to identify "Mordecai's cousin." You may recall that Mordecai is a biblical name (as opposed to, say, a Shakespearean character) but not remember anything more. By typing "Mordecai" in the search box, you get a list of passages from the Book of Esther — who was, indeed, Mordecai's cousin.

English/Latin Dictionary

The Web site at www.freedict.com/onldict/lat.html translates words between Latin and English. As I mention in Chapter 5, puzzle constructors love Latin, and you may feel the love for this Web site if you get stuck on a clue that calls for a Latin translation. On the home page, you have two search boxes to choose from: "English to Latin" and "Latin to English." Type your word into the appropriate box and click "Search." Presto! (To translate between English and another language, check out www.translate.google.com, which I explain later in this chapter.)

The Internet Movie Database

The Internet Movie Database (www.imdb.com) is the place to turn for baffling clues related to movies and TV shows and their stars and directors. The search box at the top of the home page lets you type in what you know (perhaps the name of a film or an actor) and click "go." What shows up is a laundry list of info about that film, TV show, actor, or director.

For example, maybe you can't recall the name of the actress who played Louise Jefferson on the TV show *The Jeffersons*. If you type in "The Jeffersons," one of the many pieces of information that shows up is a cast list that identifies the actress as Isabel Sanford.

Infoplease World Atlas

If your world geography is rusty (and whose isn't?), this site (`www.infoplease.com/atlas`) offers an easy way to get reacquainted with countries and major cities. The home page features a world atlas. Click on a continent to get a look at its countries, and then click on a country to zoom in on its cities.

This site features lots of other handy tools as well, including lists of all the oceans and seas in the world, the world's highest mountains, and the languages spoken in each country. Even if you aren't stuck on a crossword clue, check this site out just for the fun of it!

Thesaurus

Often, a puzzle clue will ask you to figure out a synonym for a word. You can turn to the thesaurus at `www.thesaurus.com` for help in that situation. Simply type in the word that's been given in the clue, click "Search," and pore through the list of results for words that match your length requirements. For example, say the clue is "peevish." Maybe you know that the eight-letter answer must begin with CH, and you just can't figure out what word would work. From the list of possibilities on this site, you can identify two possibilities: "childish" and "churlish."

Google Translate

This Web site (`www.translate.google.com`) offers an easy way to translate from English to another language or vice versa. On the home page, you find a large box in which to type the word or phrase you need translated. Below the box, you choose which language to translate from and which language to translate to. Say you want to find out the French word for "bread," for example. Type in "bread" and set the translation from English to French. Click "Translate," and you get the word "pain."

Keep in mind that Latin is not one of the languages featured on this site. Check out www.freedict.com/onldict/lat.html (which I introduce earlier in the chapter) if you're in need of Latin translation.

Wikipedia

This online encyclopedia (www.wikipedia.org) is a handy resource for historical and bibliographical information. If you're looking at a clue that references a historical event or an important person, you're likely to find an entry on Wikipedia that offers the information you're seeking.

You can start your search at the Wikipedia home page if you like, but I find it's just as easy to type "Wikipedia" and my search term into my search engine. Doing so should lead you directly to the online article(s) that covers the topic in question.

And If You're Truly Stuck . . . Crossword Dictionary

Okay, so you're really stuck on a certain entry. It's eight letters long, and you have just three of the letters filled in. You've tried searching other resources and gotten nowhere. You can't figure out any other intersecting entries, and you don't want to turn to the puzzle solution because you want to work this puzzle through to the end. What to do?

If you've exhausted your other possibilities for solving the clue, give the Web site at www.crossword-dictionary.com a try. Type a period to indicate any letter you don't know in the word you're trying to solve. For example, with our eight-letter word example, maybe you know the first letter is P, the fifth letter is E, and the last letter is D. Type "p . . . e . . d" in the search box and click "Search." You get back a list of possible entries, including *packeted, pampered,* and *pandered.* With luck, one of them will make perfect sense to solve your clue.

About the Author

Born in 1988, John Hennessy became entranced by the
world of fantasy and sci-fi at a young age, playing video
games and reading books for many long nights/early morn-
ings. He recently graduated from Western Washington
University, and now lives in the Rose Lands of Portland,
OR, at work finishing The Road to Extinction Trilogy. Visit
his website at: http://www.johnhennessy.net